Encyclopedia
of American
Government

Encyclopedia of American Government

Volume I
Accountability in Government – Criminal Justice System

Consulting Editor
Joseph M. Bessette
Claremont McKenna College

Project Editor
R. Kent Rasmussen

SALEM PRESS, INC.
PASADENA, CALIFORNIA   ENGLEWOOD CLIFFS, NEW JERSEY

Managing Editor: Christina J. Moose
Project Editor: R. Kent Rasmussen
Research Supervisor: Jeffry Jensen
Photograph Editor: Karrie Hyatt
Production Editor: Joyce I. Buchea
Bibliographical Research: Kevin J. Bochynski

Library of Congress Cataloging-in-Publication Data
Encyclopedia of American government / consulting editor Joseph M. Bessette ; project editor R. Kent Rasmussen.
  v. <1 > ; cm.
  Complete in 4 vols.
Includes bibliographical references and index.
  1. United States—Politics and government—Encyclopedias. I. Bessette, Joseph M. II. Rasmussen, R. Kent.
JK9.E52   1998
320.473'03—dc21   98-28986
ISBN 0-89356-117-7 (set)   CIP
ISBN 0-89356-118-5 (vol. 1)

First Printing

PRINTED IN THE UNITED STATES OF AMERICA

Publisher's Note

The strength of a democratic society depends, to a large extent, on teaching its members how their government institutions work and what their rights and responsibilities as citizens are. Government plays such an important role in the lives of Americans that its study has long been central at every level of education: from elementary school social studies units through high school civics courses and beyond. A celebration of American democracy, *Encyclopedia of American Government* is designed especially to meet the needs of middle and secondary school students, many of whom will be voting as soon as the next presidential election. It will also serve the needs of many college undergraduates and members of the general public seeking clear explanations of basic government and political topics.

The *Encyclopedia* contains two hundred alphabetically arranged articles. Varying in length from 500 to 2,500 words, each article opens with a clear statement defining the subject of the essay that follows and summarizing its significance in American government. Articles address not only basic subjects covered in middle and secondary school—from the Bill of Rights through voting processes—but a wide range of contemporary issues, such as political ethics, gay rights, and gender politics. Moreover, the set devotes extensive space to justice issues, with seventeen articles on criminal procedures, law enforcement, and related topics, and another sixteen essays on law and jurisprudence. Readers will find answers to such questions as how arrests are conducted, what criminal defendants' legal rights are, how parole officers work, and what it means to be incarcerated.

Every essay is written in clear, jargon-free language, stressing essentials and defining terms as they are introduced. Boldfaced subheads help to guide readers through the essays, and cross-references to related articles are indicated within the text by small-cap lettering. Each essay contains a select and up-to-date list of additional readings, and a general Bibliography in volume four provides additional titles.

Emphasis throughout the *Encyclopedia* is on how government and politics actually work at the local, state, and national levels. Structures and functions of government institutions are carefully explained, and appropriate examples are provided. Twenty-three essays focus on governmental bodies and officers. Another nineteen essays focus on specific government functions, such as energy and resource management. Thirty-four essays deal with a wide variety of more purely political subjects, such as elections, grassroots politics, political parties, and women in politics.

Economic issues are the subjects of seventeen essays, and twenty-seven essays on civil rights and liberties cover topics ranging from affirmative action and the Bill of Rights to the right to bear arms and voting rights. Thirteen essays treat specific historical topics, such as the American Revolution, the Civil War amendments, and the Watergate scandal. Another thirteen essays examine issues of political philosophy, such as the nature of citizenship and democracy and the ideas behind separation of powers in government. Eight essays focus on local and regional government topics, and another five look at issues relating to international politics. Nine essays focus on military topics.

Core essays are supplemented by dozens of boxed mini-essays illuminating issues raised in the main essays. For example, the article on constitutional law includes a boxed essay on the Supreme Court's landmark *Marbury v. Madison* decision, which in 1803 established the principle of judicial review that lifted the courts to a coequal role in government.

More than 350 photographs add powerful illustrative material to the essays. These are complemented by numerous maps, charts, and tables. Volume four contains an extensive glossary.

Several aids help guide readers through the *Encyclopedia*. Every article contains internal cross-references to other topics. The fourth volume includes a list of essay topics arranged by category and a detailed index.

More than 130 scholars contributed to this *Encyclopedia*, and every article is signed. Kevin Bochynski provided bibliographical research for the entire set. Joseph M. Bessette, the consulting editor on this project, was also the consultant on Salem Press's *Survey of Social Science: Government and Politics* (1995) and its award-winning *American Justice* (1996).

Contributors

Roger W. Andersen
University of Toledo College of Law

William M. Apple
Independent Scholar

James A. Baer
Northern Virginia Community College

Charles Bahmueller
Center for Civic Education

Thomas E. Baker
Texas Tech University School of Law

Timothy Bakken
Trenton State College

Jonathan J. Bean
Ohio State University

Patricia A. Behlar
Pittsburgh State University

Joseph M. Bessette
Claremont McKenna College

Kevin Bochynski
Independent Scholar

Steve D. Boilard
Western Kentucky University

Anthony R. Brunello
Eckerd College

Robert D. Bryant
Georgetown College

William H. Burnside
John Brown University

David E. Camacho
Northern Arizona University

Malcolm B. Campbell
Bowling Green State University

Edmund J. Campion
University of Tennessee

Richard K. Caputo
Barry University

David Carleton
Middle Tennessee State University

Maxwell O. Chibundu
University of Maryland School of Law

James B. Christoph
Indiana University

Lawrence Clark III
Independent Scholar

Michael Kurt Corbello
Southeastern Louisiana University

David A. Crain
South Dakota State University

Frank L. Davis
Lehigh University

Richard Davis
Brigham Young University

Robert C. Davis
Pikeville College

Loring D. Emery
Independent Scholar

Santa Falcone
University of New Mexico

Daniel C. Falkowski
Canisius College

John L. Farbo
University of Idaho

John W. Fiero
University of Southwestern Louisiana

Alan M. Fisher
California State University, Dominguez Hills

Matthew Fisher
Independent Scholar

Dale L. Flesher
University of Mississippi

John C. Foltz
University of Idaho

Roger G. Gaddis
Gardner-Webb University

Michael J. Garcia
Metropolitan State College of Denver

Karen Garner
University of Texas at Austin

Nancy M. Gordon
Independent Scholar

Robert F. Gorman
Southwest Texas State University

Robert Charles Graham
Hanover College

Frank E. Hagan
Mercyhurst College

Sam R. Hakim
University of Nebraska at Omaha

Mark David Hall
East Central University

Michael S. Hamilton
University of Southern Maine

Roger D. Haney
Murray State University

Mary T. Hanna
Whitman College

Jan Carol Hardt
Gettysburg College

Allison L. Hayes
Western Carolina University

Sarah E. Heath
University of Cincinnati

Peter B. Heller
Manhattan College

Murray Henner
Hofstra University

David G. Hicks
Independent Scholar

Charles C. Jackson
Northern Kentucky University

Robert Jacobs
Central Washington University

Ronald C. Kahn
Oberlin College

Charles L. Kammer
College of Wooster

Carolyn Ann Kawecki
Hood College

W. D. Kay
Northeastern University

Christopher E. Kent
Independent Scholar

Judy Bell Krutky
Baldwin-Wallace College

Melvin A. Kulbicki
York College of Pennsylvania

Josephine M. LaPlante
University of Southern Maine

Thomas T. Lewis
Mount Senario College

R. M. Longyear
University of Kentucky

William C. Lowe
Mount St. Clare College

Richard W. Mansbach
Iowa State University

Robert Maranto
Lafayette College

Michael Margolis
University of Cincinatti

S. A. Marino
*State University of New York
Westchester Community College*

Bruce E. May
University of South Dakota

Steve J. Mazurana
University of Northern Colorado

William V. Moore
College of Charleston

Thomas J. Mortillaro
Nicholls State University

Cathal J. Nolan
University of British Columbia

David L. Paletz
Duke University

Keeok Park
University of Virginia

Darryl Paulson
University of South Florida

Steven L. Piott
Clarion University

John Patrick Piskulich
Oakland University

Elizabeth Rholetter Purdy
University of South Carolina, Aiken

John F. Racine
University of Hawaii, West Oahu

Srinivasan Ragothaman
University of South Dakota

Sudha Ratan
Georgia Southern University

Margaret A. Ray
Mary Washington College

James W. Riddlesperger, Jr.
Texas Christian University

Joseph R. Rudolph, Jr.
Towson State University

Sunil K. Sahu
DePauw University

Jerry Purvis Sanson
*Louisiana State University at
Alexandria*

Sean J. Savage
St. Mary's College, Notre Dame

Debbie Schiedel
Independent Scholar

Elizabeth Algren Shaw
Kitchen, Deery & Barnhouse

Daniel M. Shea
University of Akron

R. Baird Shuman
*University of Illinois at
Urbana-Champaign*

Michael J. Siler
*California State University,
Los Angeles*

Donald C. Simmons, Jr.
Troy State University

Sanford S. Singer
University of Dayton

Andrew C. Skinner
Brigham Young University

Christopher E. Smith
Michigan State University

Ira Smolensky
Monmouth College, Illinois

John A. Sondey
South Dakota State University

J. Christopher Soper
Pepperdine University

Ruffin G. Stirling
Independent Scholar

Vincent James Strickler
Brigham Young University

Irene Struthers
Independent Scholar

William A. Taggart
New Mexico State University

Robert D. Talbott
University of Northern Iowa

Harold D. Tallant
Georgetown College

G. Thomas Taylor
University of Maine

Susan M. Taylor
Indiana University, South Bend

Carl A. Thames
Independent Scholar

Leslie V. Tischauser
Prairie State College

Paul B. Trescott
Southern Illinois University

Stephen D. Van Beek
San Jose State University

Fred R. van Hartesveldt
Fort Valley State College

C. Danielle Vinson
Duke University

Mary E. Virginia
Independent Scholar

Harvey Wallace
Independent Scholar

Dana Ward
Pitzer College

William L. Waugh, Jr.
Georgia State University

Donald V. Weatherman
Lyon College

Shanda Wedlock
Independent Scholar

Marcia J. Weiss
Point Park College

Scott A. White
University of Wisconsin, Platteville

Richard Whitworth
Ball State University

Richard L. Wilson
University of Tennessee at Chattanooga

Michael Witkoski
Independent Scholar

Clifton K. Yearley
State University of New York at Buffalo

Philip R. Zampini
Westfield State College

Table of Contents

Encyclopedia
of American
Government

A

Accountability in Government

Accountability in government means holding public officials and agencies responsible for their actions.

Unless people are held accountable for their actions, it is widely believed, they may possibly lie, cheat, steal, loaf, or abuse their power. The principal means of ensuring accountability in government at the policy-making level is through the election of government officials. In theory, officials responsive to constituent needs will be reelected. Those who are not responsive will be forced out of office. For politically appointed officials, direct accountability is to the elected officials who appoint them, as well as to the public they serve. Clear mechanisms for holding elected officials accountable exist.

Elected and Nonelected Officials. Holding nonelected public employees accountable for their actions is more difficult. Career public employees are generally protected by civil service laws from politically motivated interference. However, they are accountable to senior officials for their job performance. Performance appraisals provide mechanisms for measuring job performance, merit-pay systems provide rewards for good performance, and disciplinary systems provide punishments for poor performance.

Public employees are also held accountable, to some extent, for the performance of their agencies. Public agencies have increasingly been held accountable for their efficiency, rather than for their effectiveness in meeting program goals. Increasingly, legislation creating programs has included "sunset laws" requiring agencies periodically to demonstrate the effectiveness of their programs or have them eliminated. Even within governments, some agencies are much more professionally run than others. In a poorly run agency, accountability is a threat.

As programs have expanded, concerns have also increased about the amount of power exercised by career public employees and the responsiveness of those employees to elected public officials and the public at large. Public employees exercise professional discretion in the application of laws and regulations, make decisions about who will receive goods and services, translate general legislation into specific programs, make administrative rules and

---

Key Terms

LEGISLATIVE OVERSIGHT: monitoring by legislative bodies of the rules and regulations formulated by administrative agencies

PERFORMANCE APPRAISAL: system of assessing and providing accountability for individual job performance

PROGRAM EVALUATION: process of measuring the efficiency and effectiveness of government programs against available resources and performance goals

SUNSET LAW: requirement that a specified government program periodically demonstrate its effectiveness or be dissolved

SUNSHINE LAW: requirement that elected officials engaged in official government business do so in public meetings to facilitate public and media oversight

WHISTLE-BLOWER: person who brings public attention to instances of corruption and maladministration in government

regulations, and recommend new laws. Bureaucratic discretion is an unavoidable and necessary part of the political process.

Public Participation. Since the 1960's public oversight of government operations has been enhanced through requirements for direct public participation in decision making. Citizens are involved through participation in public hearings, advisory committees, interest groups, and other means. Requirements for public participation in program decision making has reinforced the principle that public administration should be open to public scrutiny. Similarly, "sunshine laws" in many states require public officials to hold meetings in which policy is made in public so that media representatives, as well as other citizens, can attend and participate.

The 1966 federal Freedom of Information Act allows private individuals access to agency information. The 1974 Privacy Act gives private citizens access to records that agencies may have collected on them. Individuals can learn how the information is being used, correct errors, and act to prevent unauthorized disclosures of the information.

Whistle-Blowing. From a public employee's perspective, the problem is how to act ethically and legally when there are conflicts among the desires of elected officials, the needs of the public at large, the demands of managers, and the employee's own standards of conduct. The encouragement of public employees to "blow the whistle" on waste, fraud, and abuse reinforces the ethic of public service. However, whistle-blowers may still lose their jobs

In response to widespread complaints about abusive practices by the Internal Revenue Service (IRS), the U.S. Senate's Finance Committee opened hearings on this issue in September, 1997. Swearing in before testifying (left to right) are former IRS historian Shelley Davis and authors Robert Schriebman and David Burnham. (Reuters/Gary Cameron/Archive Photos)

When the Senate Judiciary Committee held confirmation hearings on Clarence Thomas's nomination to the Supreme Court in 1991, Anita Hill, a law professor who had worked for Thomas a decade earlier, testified that Thomas had sexually harassed her. Her testimony touched off a national debate on sexual harassment and the accountability of government officials. (AP/Wide World Photos)

and, in some cases, face prosecution for releasing information publicly.

Professionalization of the public sector also raises standards of conduct and performance. Public employees are increasingly being held accountable to their various professional organizations. For example, professional guidance is provided to city managers through the International City Management Association. Professional organizations may also regulate the minimum qualifications necessary to work in professional positions, as well as encourage ethical conduct and standards of performance.

Public employees are also held accountable to the law. When implementing or enforcing laws, local officials are protected from liability.

When exercising their own discretion, they may be held legally liable.

Pressure for greater government accountability is largely a result of growth in government programs, limited fiscal resources to support programs, increasing professionalization of the public sector, and a general societal interest in management reform, as well as partisan political opposition to large government programs. Large, complex programs are difficult to manage, and senior officials, both elected and nonelected, seek more information on the performance of programs.

Shrinking public budgets also require greater attention to cost-saving measures. However, senior public officials typically speak of reducing service levels and eliminating programs, rather than increasing productivity.

Management Reform. Another trend has been a growing interest in management reform. Strategies for reform include increasing accountability for public agencies, but also providing greater flexibility in program management so that public officials can assume greater responsibility for the operations and the outcomes of programs. Recommendations to increase administrative flexibility and responsibility for federal programs were made in the report by the National Performance Review, chaired by Vice President Al Gore, in 1993. The recommendations were for smaller, more narrowly focused, and more directly accountable programs.

On the whole, the accountability movement has met with acceptance in some areas of government and has encountered obstacles in other areas. While accountability is a central value in agencies that have historically been open to public participation, it remains difficult to implement in agencies that have historically been closed, such as national security and law enforcement agencies.

Bibliography

Frederickson, George H., ed. *Ethics and Public Administration.* Armonk, N.Y.: M. E. Sharpe, 1993.

Glazer, Myron Peretz, and Penina Migdal Glazer. *The Whistleblowers: Exposing Corruption in Government and Industry.* New York: Basic Books, 1989.

Rosen, Bernard. *Holding Government Bureaucracies Accountable.* 2d ed. New York: Praeger, 1989.

Trask, Roger R. *Defender of the Public Interest: The General Accounting Office, 1921-1966.* Washington, D.C.: U.S. Government Printing Office, 1996.

William L. Waugh, Jr.

Activist Politics

Political activism comprises all the conventional and unconventional ways in which the public participates in political systems. Activist politics is a narrower concept describing a style of political advocacy that became an important part of American political processes during the late twentieth century; it emphasizes broad public involvement, public-awareness campaigns, and confrontational tactics.

American political activism has taken many forms. Most activists rely on conventional, or commonly accepted, methods of influence: voting, campaigning for candidates, contributing money to elections or causes, direct communication with public officials, and participation in political parties or interest groups. Less conventional activities include protest, CIVIL DISOBEDIENCE, boycotts, hunger strikes, and even violence.

Historical Background. Most Americans have historically engaged in limited political activities: voting, discussions with family and friends, and occasional letter writing. The overall amount of political activity in the United States has varied greatly over time. For example, the early 1960's marked one of the highest rates of electoral participation during the twentieth century, while the 1970's marked one of the lowest. Mass demonstrations, on the other hand, increased dramatically in the 1960's and early 1970's, but declined by the late 1970's.

The label "activist politics" emerged to characterize a style of political advocacy increasingly common after the 1960's, as activist groups began promoting issues that were new to the political agenda—such as nonsmokers' rights—or that were overlooked by more established interest groups or political parties, such as term limits. The goal of such activism was as much to increase public awareness as to enact specific laws or policies. Activist politics rely heavily on confrontation and less conventional forms of participation, such as protest marches, demonstrations, teach-ins, boycotts, and civil disobedience—all mechanisms that attract media attention and build support. As groups achieve success, their political momentum builds, and they tend to turn to more conventional political techniques, such as lobbying, lawsuits, and participation in the regulatory process.

Activist political groups grew in number and influence after World War II, due, in part, to the growing role of the mass media in American politics. The tactics and successes of

the 1950's and 1960's CIVIL RIGHTS MOVEMENT were captured live on television and conveyed to all parts of the country, inspiring other political movements. Television's preference for the dramatic also encouraged activists to find new ways to appeal to potential supporters.

Activism as a Style. Activist politics is a political style, not a specific agenda or political philosophy. The New Left orientation characteristic of the 1960's anti-Vietnam War protests was replaced by more interests. Some 1990's activist groups advocated broad social changes,

Prominent U.S. Boycotts

Date	Boycott	Ideological Reason
1950's	Martin Luther King, Jr., leads boycott of Montgomery, Alabama, bus system	To protest racial discrimination
1960's-1970	The United Farm Workers (UFW) urges a boycott against table grapes	To pressure the growers into recognizing the union
1983	The UFW renews the boycott	To protest dangerous working conditions, including the use of cancer-causing chemicals in the fields
1972-1974	ACWA union boycotts Farah Manufacturing Company	To protest alleged unfair labor practices. Notable because of the support of the boycott by the Roman Catholic Church
1977-1982	Consumers boycott all Nestle products sold in the U.S.	To protest unfair practices used to market Nestle's infant formula in Third World countries
1980-1990	Citizens boycott firms doing business in South Africa. Boycott organized by the Reverend Leon Sullivan	To protest the South African government's continuing policy of apartheid
1990	PUSH, headed by Jesse Jackson, boycotts Nike Shoes	To pressure the company to promote more African Americans to management positions and to use more African American-owned banks, suppliers, and so forth
1992	Gay rights supporters boycott all businesses in the state of Colorado, especially tourism	To protest Colorado citizens' unwillingness to pass legislation protecting gays and lesbians

such as the homosexual rights movement on the political left and the "pro-life" movement on the right. Other movements sought to change political processes rather than address specific political issues; the term-limit movement is one example.

Three characteristics set activist groups apart from more traditional interest groups, such as professional associations and unions: their broad base of membership, emphasis on direct member involvement, and wide range of political targets.

In contrast to many interest groups that are organized around specific economic interests or defined social groups, activist groups tend to cut across social class or region. One type of activist group, known as public-interest groups, became especially important in the 1960's and 1970's. Such groups advocate causes that benefit the wider community, such as consumer and environmental protection; members do not expect to benefit directly from their groups' achievements.

Activist Tactics. A second characteristic of activist groups is the use of tactics that rely heavily on confrontation and grassroots action. Resource needs, political philosophy, and group dynamics influence these tactics. "People power" often serves as a means to attract other political resources, and demonstrations or actions involving large numbers capture mass media attention.

Philosophical beliefs also contribute to the grassroots approach. Many people drawn to activist politics find the goals, structure, and leadership of traditional interest groups too inflexible or the interests they represent too narrow. The 1960's marked renewed interest in "participatory democracy" and populism: the belief that "the little guy" needed to take a stand against a government and economic system that had grown distant and unrepresentative of his interests. Proponents of participatory democracy have led many activist groups.

Confrontation. A confrontational style

helps build cohesion and motivation among group members. Although sociological researchers have found that people with higher incomes and education participate more, strong identification with a group can compensate for the lower involvement associated with social class. This tends to occur when a group's ties are strong, the group believes it receives unfavorable treatment, and it attributes this treatment to the attitudes of the wider society rather than to its own behavior.

A final characteristic of activist politics is its broad range of targets: Activists seek to influence the public debate as well as government action. Some public awareness activities have no specific target. Other activities target nonpolitical as well as political actors.

Activist groups may also alternate between tactics intended to confront authorities and those that advance a specific political solution; they are adept at forming coalitions with more established groups. For example, the spotted owl controversy pitted environmental activists against northwestern logging interests.

Activist groups' loose structures, styles, and broad range of targets create political assets and liabilities. While their ability to dramatize issues and capture public attention can attract many supporters and quickly elevate issues to a governmental agenda, the slow, resource-intensive effort to draft legislation or engage in protracted lawsuits may frustrate supporters and require a more formal structure. Many activist groups experience a crisis when their political aims receive serious attention in the governmental system.

Who Governs? The question of who governs has been the subject of much twentieth century debate. Those who reply that it is the political and social elite who rule point to the fact that those who participate the most come from the most powerful social classes and that they raise issues likely to benefit their own circumstances. The growth of the mass media after World War II enabled people to learn

Since even before the American republic was founded, protests against taxes have inspired political activism. (AP/Wide World Photos)

more about social divisions in society. The successes of the Civil Rights movement gave hope to other interests. Civil rights activists, drawing on the nonviolent protest and civil disobedience techniques of Indian independence leader Mohandas Gandhi and the confrontational tactics of America's own abolition, WOMAN SUFFRAGE, and labor movements, demonstrated how powerful the politics of activism could become.

Growth of new activist groups quickly followed. Community organizers, such as Saul Alinsky, offered practical models to action. Alinsky argued that lack of participation in many communities was a logical response to successive failures, leaving communities "organized for apathy." In his view, community activism required the reactivation of a sense of political identity. By targeting specific issues and confronting persons in power, communities heightened their awareness of their own power. The schools of community organization that Alinsky and others founded went on to train hundreds of community activists.

Post-1960 Trends. As the activist style grew in frequency and success, new interests entered the political process. The 1960's saw the emergence of protests against the Vietnam War, women's and gay liberation movements, and consumer and environmental movements. The 1970's saw the beginning of a backlash in which opponents of liberal reform used activist tactics to counter New Left gains. The NEW RIGHT, pro-life movement, Moral Majority, and taxpayer revolts of the late 1970's and early 1980's are notable examples. The 1980's and 1990's saw still further growth in activism, with the emergence of the nuclear freeze campaign, AIDS activism, and human rights protests against apartheid in South Africa.

Each instance of activist politics has drawn into the political process people previously disillusioned with or excluded from government. While the tactics and confrontational style of activist politics may raise social tensions, they also help to bridge the gap in influence between the "haves" and the "have nots." In this, they help to reaffirm the pluralist tradition.

Bibliography

Gross, Michael L. *Ethics and Activism: The Theory and Practice of Political Morality.* New York: Cambridge University Press, 1997.

Hallett, Michael A. *Activism and Marginalization in the AIDS Crisis.* New York: Haworth Press, 1997.

MacEachern, Diane. *Enough Is Enough: The Hellraiser's Guide to Community Activism.* New York: Avon Books, 1994.

Rimmerman, Craig A. *The New Citizenship: Unconventional Politics, Activism, and Service.* Boulder, Colo.: Westview Press, 1997.

Seo, Danny. *Generation React: Activism for Beginners.* New York: Ballantine Books, 1997.

Carolyn Ann Kawecki

Administrative Procedures in Government

Administrative agencies have grown greatly as American government has become increasingly complex. Agencies have derivative authority, drawn from the three branches of government, and function in partly legislative, partly executive, or partly judicial capacity.

Administrative law seeks to reduce arbitrariness and unfairness in government bureaucracy. Through regulation and by defining procedures, the law seeks to control administrative power and check abuse and excesses. The growth of administrative law has been practical, designed to meet specific needs. As modern American government has become increasingly complex and specialized, the need for expertise has also increased. Because of its growing importance, the administrative sector of government is often referred to as the fourth branch of government.

The Administrative Procedure Act. Although the 1970's and 1980's saw explosive growth in government programs with ambitious objectives, American administrative law is often said to date from creation of the Interstate Commerce Commission in 1887. The era of the New Deal was also important in the growth of administrative law. During the 1930's many innovative new programs and agencies emerged, causing President Franklin D. Roosevelt to call for the creation of a committee to study administrative procedures. That committee's recommendations led to the 1946 Administrative Procedure Act (APA), which was designed to produce uniformity and regularity among administrative agencies.

The APA divides all administrative procedure into three categories: rule making, adjudication, and other functions, such as informing, inspecting, and licensing. Rule making, a major administrative procedure, has as its core elements information, participation, and ACCOUNTABILITY (judicial review). An administrative rule is the whole or a part of an agency statement of general or particular applicability and future effect designed to implement, interpret, or prescribe law or policy. Rules generally fill a vacuum left by the three major branches of government in the formulation of public policy and legal goals and objectives. They generally apply to and affect groups rather than individuals and are said to be the administrative equivalent of statutes.

Section 553 of the APA contains provisions for "notice and comment" rule making, also known as informal rule making. Informal rule making contains three procedural requirements: prior notice, generally by publication of items in the *Federal Register*; the opportunity for interested persons to participate through submission of written comments; and the issuance of final rules with a general statement of basis and purpose after consideration of public comments.

Notices of proposed rules are codified in the *Code of Federal Regulations* and organized into fifty categories, called "titles" and "chapters," which correspond to public programs, policies, or agencies. An unpublished regulation may be determined by a court to have no legal effect.

Rule-making Procedures. Formal rule making, or "rule making on the record," involves a hearing in which interested persons can testify and cross-examine adverse witnesses before a rule is issued. Whether informal or formal rule making is required depends on the relevant statute and the nature of the interest involved. A middle ground between informal and formal rule making, "hybrid rule making," emerged in the late 1960's as a result

Public hearings on controversial issues are an essential part of the legislative process in democratic societies. Here Representative John J. Moakley conducts a hearing of the House Rules Committee on the North American Free Trade Agreement (NAFTA) in late 1993. (AP/Wide World Photos)

of the dissatisfaction with APA rule-making procedures. A general grant of rule-making authority and a requirement that the rules be subject to substantial evidence review were interpreted as necessitating hybrid procedures, including evidentiary hearings on certain contested issues.

Rules issued after a formal rule-making proceeding are subjected to closer judicial review than those of informal rule making. Rules issued after informal proceedings fall within the least formal "arbitrary and capricious" standard of review. The reviewing court applying that standard will consider the available data and reasoning processes by which the administrator made a decision and determine whether the agency's factual analysis is reasonable. Regulations issued after formal rule making are measured by the "substantial evidence" test: whether the agency has produced credible evidence on the record to support its factual findings. Thus the scope of judicial review of rules and rule making is very limited.

Rule-making proceedings have become a popular method of formulating policy as a result of their efficiency and speed. The proceedings place all affected parties on notice of impending changes in regulatory policy and provide them with an opportunity to voice comments and objections prior to the finalization of an agency's position on a given subject.

Adjudication. The second major administrative function, adjudication, may also be divided into two types: informal and formal. Informal decision making has already been discussed with reference to rule making. Formal adjudications, called "evidentiary hearings," "full hearings," or "trial-type hearings," differ significantly from court trials. Although they make up a small part of decisions made by administrative agencies, the volume of administrative trial-type hearings is substantial.

Agency adjudications, which must be determined on the record after opportunity for an agency hearing, require adequate notice to the opposing party of the time and place of the hearing and the matters to be asserted. That requirement exists to satisfy the constitutional mandate of procedural due process of law. The complaint and other documents involved in administrative adjudication are less formal than those in civil litigation. Interested persons or organizations not named as parties in the case may also testify at the request of one of the named parties, requesting permission to file a brief or otherwise taking legal action known as intervention.

Judicial Review. Significant differences in scope of JUDICIAL REVIEW exist. The initial decision of the administrative law judge is tentative, reviewable by the agency heads. An appellate court normally has only limited power of judicial review of facts found by the trial court, and no additional information may be presented initially at the appellate level. Nevertheless, the reviewing body in the agency has all the powers which it would have in making the initial decision, except as it may limit the issues on notice or by rule. Therefore, a party may present additional data or arguments to the reviewing body, which may consider them and revise its findings and conclusions accordingly.

At administrative hearings, parties are represented by legal counsel. Witnesses may be cross-examined, and objections may be raised. While these aspects are similar to those of a trial, certain important distinctions also exist. Rules for introduction and presentation of evidence are less formal than in court trials, and written evidence may be substituted for direct oral testimony, especially in claims for money or benefits or license applications. Written decisions issued at the conclusion of hearings detail agency conclusions and findings of fact and enable reviewing courts to evaluate the propriety of the agencies' action.

Other Procedures. Another administrative function is licensing: to ensure conformity with certain established standards, determine violations, and impose penalties. Still another is investigation, comprising the examination of papers, records, and other data, such as those required by government agencies (for example, tax records), as well as inspection of premises. If an agency's demand for information is resisted, it may subpoena the information, provided that the agency states its purpose so that a court may determine whether it is engaged in a lawful inquiry not designed to harass or intimidate.

Access to complete and accurate information is important to ensure the fairness of the administrative process and to give interested persons opportunities to discover, present, or challenge information. Collection and disclosure also serve the public by compelling ACCOUNTABILITY from administrators and by revealing ineffectiveness and areas where reform should be considered. Clashes have arisen between statutes that authorize investigation and Fourth Amendment protections against unreasonable searches and seizures and the Fifth Amendment's guarantee against compulsory self-incrimination. Computerization of records and files containing sensitive information has caused increased fears on the part of citizens that personal data may be misused.

Administrative agencies are usually created in response to public demand or needs to redress serious social problems. In the late nineteenth century, the INTERSTATE COMMERCE COMMISSION and the FEDERAL TRADE COMMISSION were created to control monopolies and powerful corporations. Administrative agencies proliferated during the 1930's New Deal era to provide stabilization and regulation in the economy. Agencies also established and administered price controls and rationing during wartime. As new technologies developed in communications, broadcasting, and energy, the government created bureaus to supervise and control those fledgling industries. During the 1960's, when poverty and racial discrimination became issues of public concern, programs designed to redress injustices were introduced. Later, as risks to health and safety and environmental threats emerged as newsworthy subjects and public awareness increased, new agencies and programs emerged to address those matters.

Administrative agencies deal with diverse social problems. As a result of the limited scope of their responsibilities, agencies can develop expertise in a given area. Their standards of decision making are discretionary and can be tailored to fit a given situation. The inherent flexibility of agencies, however, has been criticized as permitting unchecked power and unrestrained government, leading to bureaucratic excesses. In an effort to prevent that from occurring, the body of administrative law has developed.

Bibliography

Barry, Donald D., and Howard R. Whitcomb. *The Legal Foundations of Public Administration.* 2d ed. St. Paul, Minn.: West, 1987.

Gellhorn, Ernest, and Barry B. Boyer. *Administrative Law and Process in a Nutshell.* 2d ed. St. Paul, Minn.: West, 1981.

Kerwin, Cornelius M. *Rulemaking: How Government Agencies Write Law and Make Policy.* Washington, D.C.: Congressional Quarterly Press, 1994.

Schwartz, Bernard. *Administrative Law.* 2d ed. Boston: Little, Brown, 1984.

Marcia J. Weiss

Affirmative Action

During the 1960's affirmative action became a major strategy in the attempt to eliminate institutional discrimination in the areas of employment and education by providing minorities and women with greater access to opportunity.

Affirmative action policies and programs have created tremendous controversy since their introduction in the 1960's under Presidents John F. Kennedy and Lyndon B. Johnson. Affirmative action policies have been applied to a host of situations involving discrimination in employment and education. Their underlying purpose is to increase the prospect for equality of opportunity while eliminating systemic discrimination against specific populations. Equality of opportunity has historically been the social agenda pushed by civil rights organizations.

The enforcement of affirmative action is predicated largely on Title VII of the CIVIL RIGHTS ACT of 1964 (and to a lesser degree on Executive Order 11246, a 1965 order requiring equal employment opportunity clauses in all federal contracts). The U.S. Department of Justice, the Equal Employment Opportunity Commission, the Office of Federal Contract Compliance Programs of the Department of Labor, and the federal courts have used Title VII to dismantle long-standing patterns of discrimination in employment and education.

Ideally, affirmative action is a twofold ap-

Milestones in Affirmative Action

Year	Government Action/Court Case	Impact
1965	President Lyndon Johnson signs Executive Order 11246	Required firms doing business with the federal government in excess of $50,000/year to submit timetables and goals for diversifying their workforces
1978	*Regents of the University of California v. Bakke*	Struck down a policy that established a quota for minority admissions on the grounds that it was unfair to a qualified white applicant (reverse discrimination)
1979	*United Steelworkers of America v. Weber*	Upheld an agreement between an employer and union establishing goals for minority inclusion in a training program on the grounds that any harm done to white employees was temporary and did not create an absolute barrier to advancement
1986	*Wygant v. Jackson Board of Education*	Held that right of seniority may take precedence over affirmative action plans when workforce is reduced
1991	Civil Rights Act	Modified effects of recent Supreme Court rulings that increased burden on plaintiffs
1995	Regents of University of California	Regents vote to abolish affirmative action programs in hiring and admissions
1996	California Proposition 209	Californians vote to amend state constitution to prohibit affirmative action in state contracting, employment, and education

proach. First, it is an analysis of the existing workforce to determine if the percentages of "protected groups" in a given job classification are similar to the percentages of those groups in the surrounding community. Second, if it can be substantiated that certain practices have an exclusionary effect in the selection process, affirmative measures may be required to remedy the situation. A number of steps may be taken to alter the existing selection process, including the establishment of goals and timetables for hiring, the development of recruitment programs, a redesigning of jobs and job descriptions, substantiation of the use of testing as a selection instrument, and an attempt to improve the opportunity for advancement for those in positions with limited career paths.

An affirmative action program may involve some or all of these steps. Moreover, affirmative action may be either voluntary or mandated by the courts. Court orders or consent decrees may force offending enterprises to make restitution and to develop plans showing how they will compensate those they have discriminated against and how they will provide future promotion opportunities. Such plans may also include provisions on how the enterprises will restructure their recruitment and hiring practices.

Court-ordered goals and timetables provide indicators for employers. They are different from quotas, which reserve certain numbers of positions for members of minorities. Quotas typically do not allow for flexibility above or below the stated numbers.

Distributive and Compensatory Justice. Since the late 1970's, the debate on affirmative action has been framed within interpretations of Title VII of the Civil Rights Act of 1964, Executive Order 11246, and U.S. Supreme Court decisions. The Court's decisions have shifted between limiting and expanding affirmative action. Two major questions have been considered in its decisions: whether af-

firmative action is permissible and appropriate under the law, and whether it should be limited to victims of discrimination or should include distributive remedies.

Affirmative action has rested on two basic principles: distributive and compensatory justice. Distributive justice is concerned with the distribution of the benefits, rights, and burdens shared by members of society. These benefits and rights can be distributed in several ways. They may be based on equality of opportunity, for example, or based on need, effort, and utility. No one way best achieves distributive justice.

Compensatory justice is essentially concerned with compensation (or reparation) for past injustices against individuals or groups by the government: A victim is entitled to fair compensation or entitled to be returned to a situation comparable to that which existed prior to the injustice.

Controversy over Affirmative Action. Critics of affirmative action argue that it gives special privilege to entire categories of people whose individual members may or may not have experienced discrimination. Moreover, they maintain that affirmative action policies establish rigid quotas and may therefore extend opportunities to individuals who are otherwise unqualified. The resulting argument is that affirmative action programs create "reverse discrimination" against white males. Proponents, on the other hand, argue that race-conscious and gender-conscious measures are needed because race and gender have long been bases for discrimination. Race and gender, they say, still limit opportunities for minorities and women in certain areas of society. Consequently, minorities and women will be able to achieve equal opportunity only through the use of race- and gender-conscious strategies.

Affirmative action and equality of opportunity have been inextricably linked in the minds of some Americans. However, over the years

The underlying purpose of affirmative action programs is to overcome a long tradition of relegating members of minorities to low-paying, unskilled jobs because of the color of their skin or their gender. (Library of Congress)

that minority populations and women have experienced widespread discrimination in the past. Many, however, disagree that they continue to experience discrimination. One reason has to do with the perception that there is already widespread application of affirmative action programs in both the public and private sectors.

"Reverse Discrimination." Some opponents of affirmative action insist that such policies and programs amount to social engineering and violate the Constitution: They virtually sanction discrimination against white males, thereby simply reversing the object of discrimination. The reverse discrimination argument maintains that women and members of minority groups receive preferential treatment in employment and in admission to institutions of higher education, particularly where a past history of discrimination can be documented. In such situations white males who may demonstrate greater academic skill, may have accrued more seniority on the job, or may have scored higher on an entrance examination may be passed over so that the institution can increase the numbers of an underrepresented population. Consequently, and controversially, such decisions are not based on merit.

affirmative action has become associated with concepts that have served to bias many others against it. For example, terms such as "preferential treatment," "minority set-asides," "quotas," "managing diversity," and "reverse discrimination" have caused many whites to become hostile to the concept of affirmative action. Few Americans would dispute the fact

The Supreme Court's 1978 *Regents of the University of California v. Bakke* case was brought by a white medical school applicant who had been denied admission, although he had scored higher on the entrance examination than some members of minorities who had been admitted. He charged that the university's policy of reserving fifteen spaces for minority applicants was discriminatory. After the Court ruled in his favor, great controversy ensued. Although affirmative action policies are attempts to rectify past and present discriminatory practices, they do undeniably have a negative impact on the opportunities of some white males.

Opponents of affirmative action argue that all that can be hoped to be achieved legally is the eradication of discrimination. Nothing else, constitutionally, can be done. Any attempt to compensate victims of discrimination—especially if they are given preferential consideration in hiring, promotion, or admission to an institution of higher education—simply results in another form of discrimination. Compensation, if it were to be considered, should be offered only to the actual victims of discrimination, not to individuals simply because they belong to a particular group. Departing from its previous rulings on affirmative action, the Supreme Court gave support to this view in 1995 in its decision in *Adarand Constructors v. Peña*.

The Success of Affirmative Action. It has been argued that affirmative action programs have experienced only limited success, despite the fact that they have been an accepted strategy for many years. One reason has been poor communication between policymakers and those responsible for implementing the policies. If policies are not clearly delineated they cannot be effectively administered. Second, a lack of adequate resources may prohibit

Students at the University of California in Berkeley expressed their displeasure with the university's decision to abandon its affirmative action policies in hiring and student admissions in late 1995. (AP/Wide World Photos)

successful implementation. Third, those responsible for implementation may be antagonistic to affirmative action and may operate opposite to their directives. Fourth, poor organization structure may preclude the effective implementation of policies. Fifth, political leadership (especially at the national level) may sour the social climate for the acceptance of affirmative action. Presidents Ronald Reagan and George Bush, for example, consistently referred to affirmative action policies as "reverse discrimination" and "quota legislation."

President Reagan was a particularly outspoken critic of affirmative action policies and programs. He believed that they were unfair because they led to rigid quotas, and he appointed men and women during his administration who shared his views. Both Reagan and Bush appointed to posts in their administrations and in federal agencies minority individuals who opposed affirmative action. Reagan completely restructured the U.S. Commission on Civil Rights and selected Clarence Pendleton, Jr., an African American, to be chairman of the commission. Pendleton proved to be so extreme in his opposition to affirmative action that he was rejected by much of the African American community and rebuffed by black Republicans.

When future Supreme Court justice Clarence Thomas was chairman of the Equal Employment Opportunity Commission (EEOC), he interpreted Title VII more strictly than his predecessors had. He decided that the EEOC would pursue only individual claims of discrimination that could be explicitly proved. Therefore, neither statistical data nor the underrepresentation of certain populations in the workforce would be sufficient to demonstrate systemic discrimination. The individual complainant had to provide undeniable proof of discrimination. This policy virtually eliminated the conception of "pattern and practice" discrimination for filing suit.

During the 1980's amendments were introduced in Congress to eliminate affirmative action. During this same period, the federal courts, particularly the Supreme Court, vacillated on the applicability of affirmative action policies. A number of decisions by the Court in the 1980's and 1990's called into question the use of broad affirmative action programs.

Meanwhile, changing public opinion on this issue began to express itself. In November, 1996, for example, Californians voted to end a variety of the state's affirmative action programs in an INITIATIVE known as Proposition 209.

Bibliography

Beckwith, Francis J., and Todd E. Jones. *Affirmative Action: Social Justice or Reverse Discrimination?* Amherst, N.Y.: Prometheus Books, 1997.

Curry, George E., and Cornel West, eds. *The Affirmative Action Debate.* Reading, Mass.: Addison-Wesley, 1996.

Edley, Christopher F. *Not All Black and White: Affirmative Action, Race, and American Values.* New York: Hill & Wang, 1996.

Lawrence, Charles R., III, and Mari J. Matsuda. *We Won't Go Back: Making the Case for Affirmative Action.* Boston: Houghton Mifflin, 1997.

Charles C. Jackson

African American Politics

Long excluded from mainstream electoral politics and subjected to discriminatory treatment in the United States—particularly in the South—African Americans have a tradition of using alternative means of achieving their political goals. Such techniques as direct action, lobbying, and litigation have historically played important roles in African American politics.

By the mid-1990's, the national political scene throughout the United States had been transformed as thousands of African Americans occupied positions of political power. These ranged from cabinet positions in presidential administrations and positions on the U.S. Supreme Court to elective offices in city councils and state governors' offices.

Exercising Political Power. Voting is a key component of political power, but it is only one of the ways in which African Americans have exerted political influence. Indeed, prior to the 1960's, most black Americans were routinely kept from the ballot box and relied on other means to advance their political agendas. Litigation, LOBBYING, and direct action were essential tools in the struggle of African Americans to secure their political rights, including the right to vote.

At the time the United States won its independence from Great Britain in 1783, most African Americans were slaves legally considered to be property, not persons. As such, they were not given political rights under the new Constitution. The original Constitution tacitly preserved the institution of slavery and counted slaves as three-fifths of a person for purposes of determining congressional representation in southern states. It was not until 1865, after the Civil War ended, that Congress abolished slavery and attempted to extend political rights to blacks.

The Civil War Amendments. The passage of the Thirteenth, Fourteenth, and Fifteenth Amendments to the Constitution was particu-

Attainment of equal voting rights was an early and central goal of African Americans after the abolition of slavery. (Library of Congress)

larly important. The Thirteenth Amendment (1865) formally abolished slavery. The Fourteenth Amendment (1868) was designed to provide African Americans with "the equal protection of the laws." In other words, there would not be one set of laws for white Americans and another set of laws for everyone else. Finally, the Fifteenth Amendment (1870) said that the right to vote could not be "denied or abridged . . . on account of race, color, or previous condition of servitude."

It is important to note that the Fifteenth Amendment did not explicitly give African Americans the vote. It said only that one could not be denied the right to vote because of race. The distinction is important because it allowed southern states—in which 90 percent of the black population then lived—to eliminate black voters by the adoption of other nonracial devices.

Disfranchisement. Fearing black political domination, white southerners pushed their state legislatures to adopt a variety of laws to disfranchise black voters. Residency requirements as long as two years in some states were adopted. Poll taxes, requiring voters to pay one or two dollars per year, were instituted. The most significant barrier to black voting was the literacy test. To vote, all voters had to demonstrate their knowledge about the political systems. The problem for blacks was that white officials had the sole discretion of deciding who had passed the tests, and few blacks were given passing marks—even as late as the 1960's.

Residency requirements, poll taxes, and literacy tests appeared to be race-neutral because they ostensibly applied equally to both blacks and whites. In reality, all three devices were designed to discriminate against potential black voters. Lacking property, blacks tended to move about more frequently than whites and were thus less likely to meet the residency requirements. Black incomes lagged far behind those of whites, so they were much less likely to be able to afford the poll tax. The fact that most blacks were denied education made literacy tests a potent tool for the elimination of the black voter. In many southern states one final voting requirement virtually guaranteed that African Americans could not vote—the notorious "grandfather clauses," which required aspiring voters to show that their grandfathers had voted. It was a requirement that no former slave could satisfy.

Redress in the Courts. Shut out of the electoral process, African Americans had to turn to other ways to exercise political influence. Several black organizations, especially the National Association for the Advancement of Colored People (NAACP), turned to the courts for political protection. The advantage of litigation as a political approach is that it allowed an organization such as the NAACP to capitalize on its large pool of talented lawyers. Thurgood Marshall headed the African American Legal Defense and Education Fund. He argued thirty-two cases before the Supreme Court and was victorious twenty-nine times. His greatest victory came in *Brown v. Board of Education* (1954), the landmark decision that declared segregation in public schools to be unconstitutional. In 1967 President Lyndon B. Johnson appointed Marshall to the Supreme Court.

The disadvantages of litigation are time, money, and "paper victories." It can take years for a case to work its way through the court system. Of the small number of cases that reach the Supreme Court, an even smaller percentage are actually heard. Utilizing the courts is expensive, and even if the courts rule favorably, they cannot implement their decisions. African Americans frequently found themselves victorious before the courts, only to see nothing really changed. In 1963 Martin Luther King, Jr., the nation's leading civil rights advocate, wrote that "the failure of the nation, over a decade, to implement the majestic implications of these decisions led to the slow ebb of the Negro's faith in litigation as the dominant method to achieve his freedom."

Lobbying. A second political approach that blacks utilized was lobbying. The NAACP again excelled in this approach, particularly when it lobbied against the nomination of certain individuals to government positions. The NAACP also lobbied vigorously for the passage of various civil rights and VOTING RIGHTS laws. A clear advantage of lobbying is that it is a constitutionally protected right. In addition, lobbying does not require large expenditures to be effective. The problem with this approach was that there were few blacks in Congress until the 1970's, so there were not many sympathetic ears.

Direct Action. A third political approach used by African Americans to advance their political agenda has been nonviolent direct action. Martin Luther King, Jr., combined his religious views with the techniques of Mohandas Gandhi, the leader of India's national independence movement, to develop his nonviolent direct action approach. King believed that unjust laws, such as those supporting segregation, must be directly challenged.

The advantage of nonviolent direct action was that it allowed individuals such as King to transform a local issue, such as segregation, into a national issue of human and civil rights. In addition, it provided the opportunity for African Americans of all social classes to take to the streets to pressure political leaders to change the status quo. A weakness of the direct action approach was that it was difficult to sustain over long periods of time.

Civil Rights Legislation. With the passage of the federal CIVIL RIGHTS ACT of 1964, fundamental political rights were finally restored to African Americans, particularly the right to vote. After the passage of this legislation, the number of black elected officials began rising by almost 20 percent per

year. Black mayors have been elected in major American cities including New York, Chicago, Los Angeles, Detroit, Atlanta, Cleveland, Seattle, New Orleans, Philadelphia, and Washington, D.C.

The passage of voting rights legislation shifted African Americans from "protests to politics." Electoral politics, however, is not without its limitations. Various voting laws

Martin Luther King, Jr., at the Lincoln Memorial in August, 1963, when he delivered his "I Have a Dream" speech. (National Archives)

have limited the effectiveness of minority votes. Schemes "diluting" votes have included at-large elections, run-off elections, and racial gerrymandering. Also, it is often difficult to translate votes into public policy. Laws can be passed, but unless there is the financial and political commitment to implement them, nothing may actually change.

Because African Americans constitute only about 12 percent of the United States population, they must often form coalitions with other groups to obtain their goals. Crossover appeal and deracialization are two strategies that have been used by the black community. Crossover appeal is the ability of black candi-

dates to attract white voters. For example, Los Angeles mayor Thomas Bradley and Virginia governor Douglas Wilder were elected because of their crossover appeal. Crossover appeal also applies to the ability of white candidates to attract black voters.

Deracialization is the process of putting issues in race-neutral terms and appealing to universal values. Instead of pushing for expanded health care to benefit those unable to provide adequate protection for themselves and their families—a group that might disproportionately include African Americans—organizations push for universal health care. Selling the program as race-neutral rather

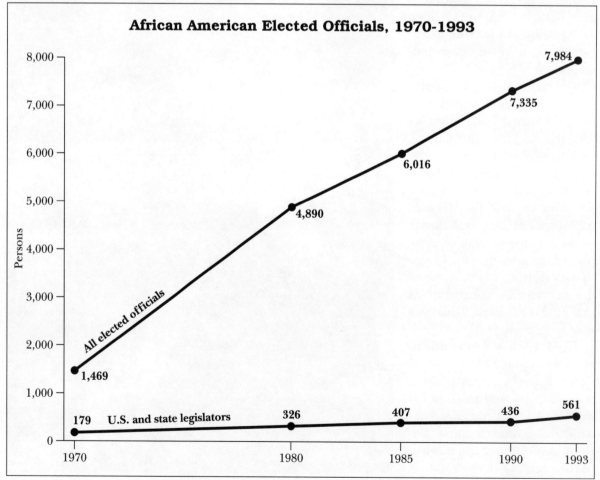

Source: U.S. Bureau of the Census, *Statistical Abstract of the United States: 1997.* 117th ed. Washington, D.C.: U.S. Government Printing Office, 1997.

Carol Moseley-Braun, the first African American woman elected to the U.S. Senate, speaks at an Illinois Democratic rally in April, 1997. (AP/Wide World Photos)

than race-specific might enhance the prospects of victory.

Bibliography

Franklin, John Hope, and Alfred A. Moss, Jr. *From Slavery to Freedom.* 6th ed. New York: Alfred A. Knopf, 1988.

Lusane, Clarence. *No Easy Victories: Black Americans and the Vote.* New York: Franklin Watts, 1996.

Rowan, Carl T. *The Coming Race War in America: A Wake-up Call.* Boston: Little, Brown, 1996.

Swain, Carol M. *Black Faces, Black Interests: The Representation of African Americans in Politics.* Cambridge, Mass.: Harvard University Press, 1993.

Walton, Hanes. *African-American Power and Politics: The Political Context Variable.* New York: Columbia University Press, 1997.

Williams, Michael W., ed. *The African American Encyclopedia.* 8 vols. New York: Marshall Cavendish, 1993.

Darryl Paulson

Agricultural Management

The production of food is so important to human survival that governments find many reasons for involving themselves in agriculture to ensure the adequate nutrition and health of their citizens. Most governments have programs to increase agricultural production, to protect farmers from foreign competition, and to assist farmers when natural disasters occur.

In many countries around the world, agriculture is an industry that has significant governmental involvement. Ensuring adequate food supplies is commonly called "food security." Typically, a country wants to ensure the production of important foodstuffs. As an example, Japan was cut off from imports of a variety of foods during World War II. To guarantee domestic rice production, the Japanese government supports this industry through subsidies to farmers and by placing a nearly complete ban on imported rice.

National Priorities. Closely associated with food security is a nation's desire to protect or support a particular domestic industry. Frequently, this desire manifests itself in efforts toward saving small farms, preserving rural communities, or supporting farmers' incomes. Government protection may be needed because foreign farmers can provide the product more cheaply or efficiently. The U.S. sugar industry is an example of a protected industry. Other U.S. commodities industries receive direct government payments for raising program crops.

Governments also intervene in agriculture to protect the health of their citizens and to protect domestic crops and livestock from harmful biological agents, such as bacteria. Laws regarding agricultural production and food processing spell out what products can and cannot be used on food. Inspection services are often a governmental function that ensures adherence to grade and quality standards. These services allow for an efficient operation of the market for these commodities and permit buyers to determine what they are buying. Import restrictions sometimes center on concerns about quality of food.

Food assistance programs in many countries allow for qualifying participants to receive food free or at reduced cost. Providing nutrition and food education is another role that many governments assume regarding food products. This role may take the form of setting standards and requirements for food labeling, whereby food ingredients and nutritional content are included on labels.

Agricultural production is subject to the vagaries of weather, pests, and disease. Many governments therefore provide DISASTER RELIEF to farmers who have suffered serious loss resulting from natural calamities.

Government Regulation. Growing awareness of the environmental impact of farming has led to increased government regulation of agricultural practices. More stringent requirements have been placed on the research, testing, and marketing of herbicides, insecticides, and animal health products. Some countries encourage tillage methods, crop rotations, and other techniques that conserve soil and reduce fuel use.

Governments also involve themselves in agriculture to promote political agendas. The phrase "food as a weapon" was coined to describe the use of agricultural production to achieve foreign policy objectives. Food and technical agricultural assistance are given as a reward for favors and withheld as a retaliatory action. In the United States, Public Law 480, commonly known as the "Food for Peace" program, has been the source of millions of tons of commodities given to foreign nations. Politicians have also used export embargoes to punish countries for certain behaviors. The Soviet grain embargo of 1980, in which the United States placed an embargo on the export of selected products to the Soviet Union after its invasion of Afghanistan, is an example of this type of policy.

Imports and Exports. Governments have numerous ways to intervene in agriculture, depending upon the goals that are to be achieved. For example, they might impose charges, known as TARIFFS, on imports to protect domestic industries. The effect of such duties is to raise commodity prices relative to domestically produced goods—with the goal

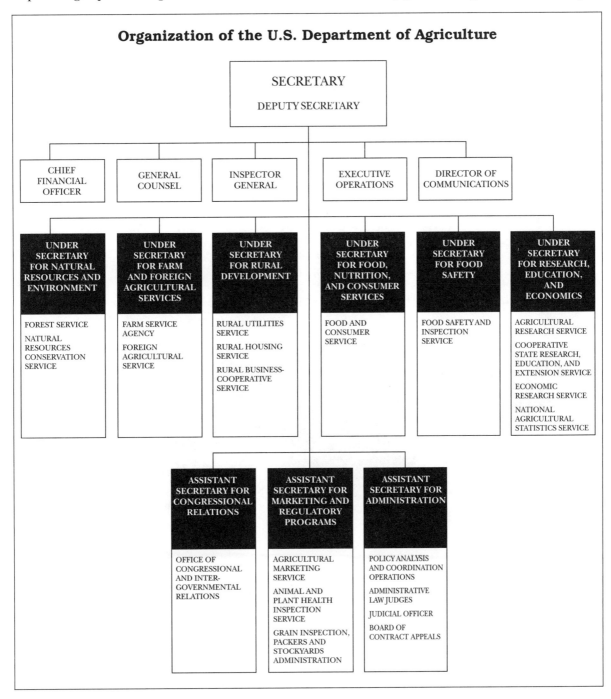

Organization of the U.S. Department of Agriculture

SECRETARY

DEPUTY SECRETARY

CHIEF FINANCIAL OFFICER

GENERAL COUNSEL

INSPECTOR GENERAL

EXECUTIVE OPERATIONS

DIRECTOR OF COMMUNICATIONS

UNDER SECRETARY FOR NATURAL RESOURCES AND ENVIRONMENT

FOREST SERVICE

NATURAL RESOURCES CONSERVATION SERVICE

UNDER SECRETARY FOR FARM AND FOREIGN AGRICULTURAL SERVICES

FARM SERVICE AGENCY

FOREIGN AGRICULTURAL SERVICE

UNDER SECRETARY FOR RURAL DEVELOPMENT

RURAL UTILITIES SERVICE

RURAL HOUSING SERVICE

RURAL BUSINESS-COOPERATIVE SERVICE

UNDER SECRETARY FOR FOOD, NUTRITION, AND CONSUMER SERVICES

FOOD AND CONSUMER SERVICE

UNDER SECRETARY FOR FOOD SAFETY

FOOD SAFETY AND INSPECTION SERVICE

UNDER SECRETARY FOR RESEARCH, EDUCATION, AND ECONOMICS

AGRICULTURAL RESEARCH SERVICE

COOPERATIVE STATE RESEARCH, EDUCATION, AND EXTENSION SERVICE

ECONOMIC RESEARCH SERVICE

NATIONAL AGRICULTURAL STATISTICS SERVICE

ASSISTANT SECRETARY FOR CONGRESSIONAL RELATIONS

OFFICE OF CONGRESSIONAL AND INTER-GOVERNMENTAL RELATIONS

ASSISTANT SECRETARY FOR MARKETING AND REGULATORY PROGRAMS

AGRICULTURAL MARKETING SERVICE

ANIMAL AND PLANT HEALTH INSPECTION SERVICE

GRAIN INSPECTION, PACKERS AND STOCKYARDS ADMINISTRATION

ASSISTANT SECRETARY FOR ADMINISTRATION

POLICY ANALYSIS AND COORDINATION OPERATIONS

ADMINISTRATIVE LAW JUDGES

JUDICIAL OFFICER

BOARD OF CONTRACT APPEALS

of increasing consumption of the domestic commodities.

Nontariff barriers to trade cover all restrictions on imports and exports other than tariffs. Import quotas, the most widely used nontariff barrier, limit quantities of products that may be imported. They tend to have the effect of raising the price of the commodities in the importing country.

An export quota is the opposite of an import quota. It imposes a limit on the quantity of a good that can be exported. Its purpose may be to stabilize the export earnings of the exporting country by restricting the supply of the commodity, thereby sustaining the price. This approach will work only if the commodity in question has no substitutes and the exporting country has few competitors in the export market.

Embargoes are often used for political reasons, such as holding down domestic prices of commodities or preventing the accidental importation of disease. An embargo is a complete stoppage of either the import or export of a

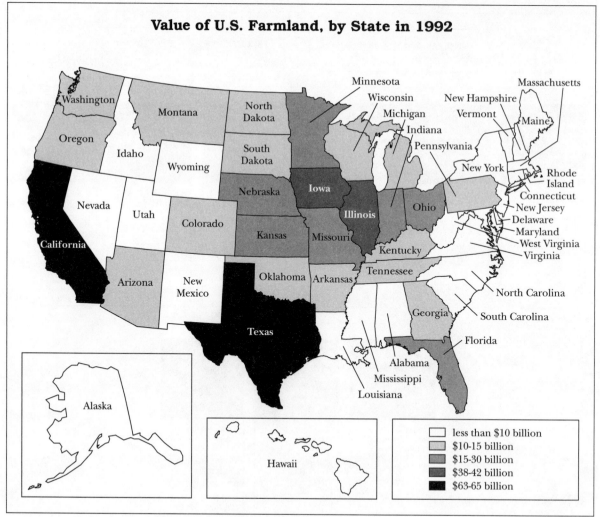

Value of U.S. Farmland, by State in 1992

Legend:
- less than $10 billion
- $10-15 billion
- $15-30 billion
- $38-42 billion
- $63-65 billion

Source: U.S. Bureau of the Census, *Statistical Abstract of the United States: 1997.* 117th ed. Washington, D.C.: U.S. Government Printing Office, 1997.

Note: Dollar figures are based on total estimated worth of farmland and structures in each state.

As Secretary of Agriculture Dan Glickman looks on in April, 1996, President Bill Clinton signs a Republican-passed farm bill ending the link between major crop prices and government subsidies. (AP/Wide World Photos)

commodity. One of the problems with implementing embargoes is that they are effective only if the exporting country has few competitors in the international market.

Export subsidies are a fixed government payment per unit of product exported. They may be used to help reduce burdensome supplies of surplus commodities. The United States has sometimes sold dairy products in the export market at a price lower than the domestic price support level, to move surplus product. Export subsidies may also be put into place for humanitarian reasons, such as making it easier for poor countries to purchase desperately needed foodstuffs.

Sanitary regulations provide another non-tariff method to limit imports. Such regulations are designed to make imported commodities meet certain health, appearance, or quality standards. In many cases these regulations are in place for legitimate reasons. However, these rules are sometimes implemented to limit imports and protect domestic industries.

Domestic Government Programs. Governments also intervene in agriculture through domestic programs. In the United States, major program products include wheat, corn, rice, cotton, and dairy foods. For crops, typical support has been through a target price and deficiency payment program. This works in the following way: A target price is established for the program crop. If the market price drops below the target price, an amount equal to the difference, known as the deficiency payment, is paid in cash or in kind. For dairy farmers, a mandated milk price, set by the government, is what milk processors must pay. If such a price results in a surplus of processed products on the market, the government purchases this surplus in the form of cheese and butter.

Grading and inspection services are often a government function. In the United States, the Federal Grain Inspection Service, a branch of the U.S. Department of Agriculture (USDA), sets standards for and inspects and grades all grain shipped for export. For domestic consumption, the USDA inspects and grades meat, milk, eggs, and some fruits.

The scope of government intervention varies greatly among and within countries. Almost every nation supports agricultural research. Many provide indirect assistance to farmers in the form of special credit institutions and support for farm supply and marketing cooperatives. The principal differences among nations are found in the degree to which they intervene in supporting farm product prices and in subsidizing food consumption and exports. Japan is at one end of the spectrum among industrial nations. Most farm and food prices in Japan are strongly influenced by government decisions. Japanese farmers are almost completely insulated from world market forces. New Zealand lies close to the other extreme. Its farm prices are influenced little by government intervention; they are dictated mainly by world supply-and-demand conditions. The United States falls somewhere between these extremes. In the United States, government action strongly influences the prices of some commodities but not others.

Bibliography

Hallberg, Milton C. *Policy for American Agriculture: Choices and Consequences.* Ames: Iowa State University Press, 1992.

MacKenzie, David R. *Principles of Agricultural Research Management.* Lanham, Md.: University Press of America, 1996.

Robinson, Kenneth L. *Farm and Food Policies and Their Consequences.* Englewood Cliffs, N.J.: Prentice-Hall, 1989.

Runge, C. Ford, John A. Schnittker, and Timothy J. Penny. *Ending Agricultural Entitlements: How to Fix Farm Policy.* Washington, D.C.: Progressive Foundation, 1995.

Sanderson, Fred H., ed. *Agricultural Protectionism in the Industrialized World.* Washington, D.C.: Resources for the Future, 1990.

John C. Foltz

Ambassadors and Embassies

Ambassadors represent their home states in foreign lands, furthering the interests of their governments and fellow citizens abroad. The official headquarters of ambassadors and their staffs are embassies.

No matter how large a country is or what its natural and economic resources are, it cannot isolate itself from the global community. To survive and prosper, it must actively participate in world events. Active involvement in the world cannot be accomplished without diplomacy.

In many ways, the methods of diplomacy currently in use differ little from those of past generations. The modern ambassadorial system arose during the fourteenth century in Italian city-states. Their permanent embassies were so successful that others were soon established throughout Europe. During that time, there were no formalized rules regarding the classification of diplomatic agents or the treatment of diplomats. Diplomatic titles and rankings varied from state to state. It was not until the late Middle Ages that some diplomats came to be called ambassador.

The Rise of Diplomacy. By the early nineteenth century, efforts were under way to classify diplomatic agents according to office and to formalize their functions. Although there have been minor adjustments in ranking since the modern art of diplomacy began, the top-ranking diplomatic officials exchanged by states remain as follows: ambassadors, ministers, minister residents, chargés d'affaires, and consuls. The current general guidelines of diplomatic practice were not officially agreed upon by most states, however, until the mid-twentieth century.

Key Terms

AMBASSADOR: senior diplomatic officer stationed at an embassy

CONSUL: representative of a state who lives abroad to promote the business interests of and provide selected services to citizens living or traveling abroad

CONSULATE: extension of an embassy serving to protect its citizens abroad and to perform administrative tasks

DIPLOMACY: methods used by states to pursue objectives related to their international interests

DIPLOMAT: official deputy, appointed by a head of state, who represents his or her country under the direction of that head of state

EMBASSY: group of diplomats headed by an ambassador, or their official headquarters

FOREIGN POLICY: state's goals and objectives when dealing with a foreign state and the strategy by which those goals are realized

FOREIGN SERVICE: division of the government that maintains embassies, missions, and consulates in other states

STATE DEPARTMENT: department within the executive branch of the U.S. government that is responsible for diplomatic relations

---

A basic tenet of diplomacy is that it cannot begin unless two parties agree to discuss their mutual concerns and goals. Before an ambassador or other representative of a state is sent to a foreign land in an effort to begin a dialogue, the host state needs to agree to recognize that person as the legitimate delegate. Even after both parties agree on an ambassador, that person may at any time be declared unacceptable (*persona non grata*).

Embassy Staffing. Upon arrival in the host state, an ambassador and all accompanying staff are considered representatives of their head of state. For example, a U.S. ambassador is part of the executive branch of government. As the U.S. president's deputy abroad, the ambassador represents that office. Major contributors to presidential campaigns are often appointed to such positions despite their lack of qualifications. Many argue that such political appointees are merely figureheads who do little to further the interests of their country.

Prior to the advent of modern communications, a country's ambassador and staff were a critical part of the decision-making process. Treaties and agreements were often negotiated by ambassadors without prior approval of their superiors. The role of modern ambassadors has become more ceremonial and less critical to the decision-making process. Live news coverage of political turmoil, war, and negotiations has greatly complicated ambassadors' jobs.

The real work of embassies is carried out by foreign service officers. These people are often required to deal with a variety of issues that demand an expertise in a variety of fields, including history, international law, politics, economics, diplomacy, and military science. Occasionally, the avoidance of war depends on the capabilities of these officers. Many embassies now have several hundred full-time personnel.

The emergence of a global economic system has placed greater demands on embassies.

Countries may wish to establish diplomatic posts in more than one city in a foreign country. For example, an Asian country may wish to establish a consulate in Los Angeles, as well as an embassy in Washington, D.C., to facilitate trade. Consulates are considered extensions of the embassy. Their primary function is to protect citizens abroad. They also promote trade and issue visas to foreigners.

Diplomatic Privileges. The activities of diplomats and embassies give them considerations and privileges not normally given to visitors in foreign lands. An embassy is considered an extension of the ambassador's native soil. Any effort to enter embassy grounds without permission may be considered a violation of sovereignty. The laws enforced in an embassy are thus those of the foreign nation. The existence of these rules has often resulted in the use of embassies as havens for those who seek political asylum.

Diplomats and their families are also given diplomatic immunity. Like sovereignty, immunity is a basic principle of diplomatic practice. It exempts diplomats and their families from the host state's civil or criminal laws. Without such immunity negotiations cannot be freely conducted. Although officially protected by the traditions of diplomatic practice, ambassadors and their personnel are not always guaranteed safety, however. As a country's official representative in a foreign land, the embassy is particularly susceptible to attacks by those displeased with the policies of the country that embassy represents.

The U.S. government maintains embassies and consulates in more than 150 countries. Each post reports to the State Department and carries out instructions and policies of the president. The United States also has established special missions to the North Atlantic Treaty Organization, European Community, United Nations, European office of the United Nations, Organization for Economic Cooperation and Development, and Organization of American States.

As the head of the U.S. State Department, Secretary of State Madeleine Albright directs the work of all diplomatic personnel. (Reuters/Robert Giroux/ Archive Photos)

Bibliography
Mayers, David A. *The Ambassadors and America's Soviet Policy.* New York: Oxford University Press, 1995.
Miller, Robert Hopkins, ed. *Inside an Embassy: The Political Role of Diplomats Abroad.* Washington, D.C.: Congressional Quarterly, 1992.
Steiner, Zara, ed. *The Times Survey of Foreign Ministries of the World.* London: Times Books, 1982.

Donald C. Simmons, Jr.

American Indians

Many descendants of the original inhabitants of the Americas are members of distinct political communities that still have limited sovereignty. Tribal American Indians share a legal status unique among American citizens.

When Europeans found the Americas, they encountered peoples whose ancestors had occupied the Western Hemisphere for perhaps fifteen centuries. Numerous North American tribes utilized many different legal systems which functioned successfully under natural law without police, formal courts, or prisons. Decisions affecting individual rights were resolved in a manner that gave considerable weight to the best interests of the group and sought restoration of community harmony and balance. After the fifteenth century the indigenous peoples encountered Europeans holding different views of legal rights. These newcomers posed serious threats to Indian sovereignty and rights.

The Colonial Legacy. North America's English colonizers generally pursued the treaty-making process as the chief means for acquiring land. Their diplomacy recognized Indian tribes as sovereign, or self-ruling, foreign nations. When the American Revolution ended British rule in the thirteen seaboard colonies, the new American republic displaced England. It continued the old colonialism in its diplomatic relationships with the tribes. The United States initially viewed American Indians as members of small nations who would permanently exist outside American political institutions.

Early American statesmen, including Thomas Jefferson, formulated ideal rules for the peaceful and voluntary extinction of Indian title through legal land purchases. Government policy encouraged Native Americans to enter the mainstream of the dominant culture and live alongside white settlers.

The United States abandoned this policy when it concluded that the tribal lands were too valuable to recognize Indian rights within them. Successive presidential administrations responded to pressure from anti-Indian frontiersmen and the desire of new southern states to appropriate Indian lands and dismantle tribal governments. Between 1815 and 1840, most eastern and southern tribes were removed to the southern plains region designated Indian Territory.

As removal proceeded, a defining moment in the legal relationship between tribes and the United States came with the Cherokee court cases of the 1830's. The Cherokee, a culturally advanced southeastern tribe that was implementing Jefferson's advice, sought justice through the U.S. legal system. They resisted removal from Georgia and the state's effort to dissolve their government and subject them to its laws. In *Cherokee Nation v. Georgia* (1831), Chief Justice John Marshall ruled that the case could not be heard by the U.S. Supreme Court because Indian tribes were not sovereign foreign nations. This decision characterized tribes as "domestic dependent nations" whose relationship with the U.S. government was that of wards to a guardian.

In a second case, *Worcester v. Georgia* (1832), Marshall reached different conclusions. He

Much of the political energy of American Indians has been channeled into adapting to changing relationships between tribal governments and the federal government. This photograph captures a Navajo tribal council meeting held in Arizona in 1935, after passage of the federal Indian Reorganization Act forced the Navajo to reorganize their own government. (Museum of New Mexico, Norman B. Conway)

cited earlier treaties with the Cherokee recognizing their national character and right to self-government as distinct, independent political communities retaining natural rights as the original possessors of the soil. Georgia's actions interfered with the federal government's exclusive authority to make treaties with Indian tribes and were therefore invalid. The Cherokee legal victory was short-lived, however, as President Andrew Jackson refused to enforce the ruling. The tribe was soon forcibly removed to Indian Territory. Nevertheless, on this important decision, cited frequently in later cases, hinged issues such as Indian title to lands, tribal independence, and the validity of treaty rights.

Dispossession and Warfare, 1840-1870's. Unexpectedly rapid American expansion westward beginning in the 1840's jeopardized the political autonomy and security of the

In late 1969 American Indian activists from across the nation tested an old federal law permitting Indians to claim unused federal lands by occupying Alcatraz Island in San Francisco Bay after its federal penitentiary was closed down. The Indians were forced to leave the island in mid-1971, succeeding only in heightening public awareness of their grievances. (AP/Wide World Photos)

tribes in their new lands. A final round of violent confrontation played out after 1860. As American movement into tribal lands of the West and Great Plains forced further cessions and destroyed the tribes' traditional economic base. Tribal sovereignty received a new setback in 1871. That year the United States ceased negotiating treaties with tribal nations. Although previous treaties were to remain valid, from this point onward the federal government would unilaterally subject the tribes to congressional legislation and presidential orders.

The New Colonialism, 1870's-1920's. Under this new colonialism, the situation of American Indians reached its lowest point. Tribal peoples were confined to reservations under authoritarian paternalistic control. There the government ruthlessly pursued assimilation goals through forced acculturation, while corrupt U.S. Indian agents plundered tribal resources. Furthermore, the General Allotment Act of 1887 forced tribal members to break up communal holdings and opened unallotted reservation land to all comers. The practical effect of this allotment policy was to dissolve tribal communities.

After 1870, court rulings and congressional legislation further refined and narrowed the scope of tribal sovereignty. Moreover, the BILL OF RIGHTS did not protect tribal people's rights. In legal disputes with the government, Indians were denied freedom of choice of counsel. The First Amendment right to assemble was violated through forced confinement on reservations, which Indians were unable to leave without permission.

The late 1870's and early 1880's witnessed the creation of tribal police forces and courts as instruments to enforce the government's determined assault on Indian culture. In 1885, Congress passed the Major Crimes Act, which placed seven categories of serious CRIME under federal jurisdiction even when they were committed on reservation land. This list of crimes was expanded in the twentieth century, leaving tribal courts with jurisdiction over only minor offenses.

A devastating blow to sovereignty came in the court case *Lone Wolf v. Hitchcock* (1903). This litigation involved the Kiowa tribe's attempt to halt the sale of "surplus" reservation lands based on a former treaty guarantee. Ignoring the Constitution's Fifth Amendment protection of life, liberty, and property, the Supreme Court upheld lower court opinions that Congress had full authority over tribal land which superseded treaty guarantees.

In 1924 the government bestowed U.S. citizenship on American Indians. This gesture did not halt the loss of lands to whites or the campaign to suppress Indian culture. Moreover, some states successfully prevented these new citizens from voting.

The Indian New Deal, 1934-1946. A major policy shift followed the election of President Franklin D. Roosevelt in 1932. The Indian Reorganization Act (IRA), or "Indian New Deal," the inspiration of Roosevelt's Bureau of Indian Affairs chief, John Collier, ended allotment, helped tribes purchase some lost land, encouraged the recovery of traditional native culture, and attempted to revitalize the tribal system of self-government. The IRA improved conditions for Native Americans and gave them new hope; it is still considered the most important piece of Indian legislation in U.S. history. About half of the tribes refused participation, however. They preferred traditional forms of self-rule.

Termination, 1946-1960. After World War II, a conservative Congress mounted the most serious threat to date against tribal sovereignty under the label "termination." Under this policy Congress authorized termination of various designated tribes, thereby liquidating federal treaty obligations and payments. Public Law 280 authorized states to assume jurisdiction over criminal and civil cases involving Indians.

Twentieth Century Legislation Affecting Civil Rights of American Indians

Date	Federal Legislation	Purpose
1934	Indian Reorganization Act	Provides for formal, legal organization of tribes.
1961	Area Redevelopment Act	Provides aid to depressed areas.
1964	Economic Opportunity Act	Provides aid to depressed areas.
1965	Voting Rights Act	Specifically outlaws voting practices that discriminate against minorities.
1968	American Indian Civil Rights Act	Extends Bill of Rights provisions to tribal members.
1972	Indian Education Act	Provides financial grants to schools with significant numbers of Indian students.
1975	Indian Self-Determination and Education Assistance Act	Allows tribes to assume responsibilities previously held by federal government agencies.
1975	Voting Rights Act (renewal)	Outlaws manipulating voting districts (gerrymandering) and requires bilingual ballots where needed.
1978	Tribally Controlled Community College Assistance Act	Provides incentives for the establishment of community colleges to teach native languages and traditions.
1978	American Indian Religious Freedom Act	Protects and encourages the expression of traditional Native American religious beliefs.
1986	Indian Civil Rights Act	Amends 1968 act to allow tribal courts to impose fines and jail time for criminal offenses.
1988	Indian Education Act	Provides financial assistance to local educational agencies serving Indian children.
1988	Tribally Controlled School Grants Act	Assures maximum Indian participation in provision of educational services.
1988	Indian Gaming Regulatory Act	Allows gambling on Indian land to promote tribal economic self-sufficiency.
1990	Indian Child Protection and Family Violence Prevention Act	Authorizes procedures to ensure child protection and to provide programs to prevent and treat family violence.
1991	Criminal Jurisdiction Act	Establishes that tribes can exercise criminal jurisdiction over members.
1992	Indian Resources Act	Provides assistance to foster tribal control in developing and administering natural resources.

Termination failed badly. States faced escalating welfare costs and were often reluctant to assume the added expense of policing or taking control of judicial matters in Indian country. As the injustice and impracticality of this policy became clear, it was put on hold after 1960. Congress eventually restored the status of most terminated tribes. Public Law 280 was amended to the point where it ceased to be a threat to tribal sovereignty.

Indian Civil Rights Act of 1968. Earlier rulings recognizing tribes as distinct political entities exempted their courts from external regulation. Concern that basic rights guaranteed to other Americans were sometimes violated in tribal judicial proceedings prompted passage of the Indian CIVIL RIGHTS ACT. The legislation extended many constitutional protections to tribal members. Some Indians welcomed this measure. Most tribal courts already adhered to its provisions. Traditionalists, however, saw it as another attempt to force white culture on tribal peoples. The legislation gave rise to situations in which procedures consistent with Native American culture were challenged in court by both Indian and non-Indian litigants.

Post-1970 Developments. The late 1960's gave rise to political militancy among urban Indians, who reacted against racism and sought to reconnect with their roots. Pride in being Indian and efforts to seek renewal through the recovery of language, religion, and other traditions, nearly eradicated by past U.S. policy, contributed to a Native American cultural rebirth.

President Richard Nixon denounced termination and handed the Taos Pueblo tribe a major victory with the return of its sacred Blue Lake area. Renewed tribalism and self-determination empowered tribes by allowing them to contract with the government to assume management of numerous government programs and services on the reservation. Although contested at every step, tribes have also

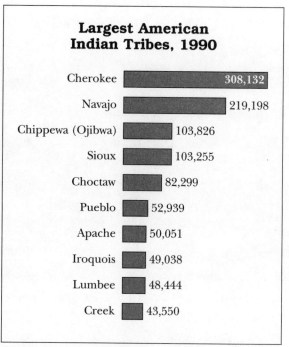

Source: U.S. Bureau of the Census, *We, the First Americans.* Washington, D.C.: U.S. Government Printing Office, 1993.

had some success in asserting control over natural resources.

During the Reagan presidency, Indian rights suffered a setback in Supreme Court rulings that restricted First Amendment religious freedoms. The new conservative Court majority ruled against Native American efforts to protect sacred sites from development. A 1990 decision threatened the traditional use of the sacramental plant and drug peyote in religious ceremonies of the Native American Church, likened to the use of wine in the Christian Communion rite.

After 1990, progress occurred on the sensitive issue of repatriating the remains of tribal people from museums and private and government collections. Nevertheless, the exercise of tribal sovereignty and treaty rights continues to bring tribes into conflict with state and local interests. Also uncertain is the future of tribally owned gambling casinos on reservation land, a financially successful business venture for many tribes regulated under the Indian Gaming Act of 1989.

Bibliography

Johnson, Troy R., Joane Nagel, and Duane Champagne. *American Indian Activism: Alcatraz to the Longest Walk.* Urbana: University of Illinois Press, 1997.

Markowitz, Harvey, ed. *Ready Reference: American Indians.* 3 vols. Pasadena, Calif.: Salem Press, 1995.

Olson, James S., and Mark Baxter, eds. *Encyclopedia of American Indian Civil Rights.* Westport, Conn.: Greenwood Press, 1997.

Wilkins, David E. *American Indian Sovereignty and the U.S. Supreme Court: The Masking of Justice.* Austin: University of Texas Press, 1997.

Wunder, John R. *Retained by the People: A History of American Indians and the Bill of Rights.* New York: Oxford University Press, 1994.

David A. Crain

American Revolution

Separation from Great Britain led to the creation of the United States as an independent state with its own system of government.

The American Revolution was the culmination of a number of trends that finally resulted in open conflict in 1775 at the Battle of Lexington and Concord. Those trends were a mixture of economic, social, and constitutional matters that stretched back to the settlement of the colonies. These matters became seriously divisive in 1763 with the conclusion of the French and Indian War.

The British War Debt. The Peace of Paris of 1763 left Britain with an enormous empire and with what for the day seemed an enormous debt. The government determined to both economize and increase revenues to deal with its problems. To reduce the cost of defense against Indians in North America, the British government issued the Proclamation of 1763 to forbid westward expansion. This act was intended to buy time for resolving the question of Indian resistance. The colonists, who generally regarded Indians with disdain, saw expansion as their right and were outraged.

Raising revenue provoked more questions about the rights of the colonists. The mercantilist economic philosophy of the day required governmental involvement in commerce, and there was no question that taxes could be used to regulate trade. The colonists, however, argued that they had the right to consent to any taxation for revenue. Although many Whig Party political leaders, including William Pitt, agreed, the chief ministers of the 1760's did not. A series of revenue measures provoked increasing colonial defiance and assertion of rights.

Sugar and Stamp Acts. The first effort to tax for revenue came with the Sugar Act (1764). It actually lowered duties on colonial sugar and molasses but contained a provision for effective enforcement. Earlier duties, though higher, had been ineffectively enforced, and colonists had come to regard smuggling as virtually a right. The next year the Stamp Act required tax stamps on a variety of luxury items, publications, and legal documents. The latter two hit journalists and lawyers, groups particularly well situated to protest. Groups called the Sons of Liberty formed, a Stamp Act Congress drew delegates from most of the colonies, and an effective boycott of British goods was established.

The loss of trade quickly led to the repeal of the Stamp Act, but Parliament passed a Declaratory Act (1766), asserting the British right to tax colonies. Since the British constitution is not single document, but rather all the acts of Parliament and customs of the realm, this act technically made such taxation

When Patrick Henry proclaimed, "Give me liberty or give me death," before the Virginia Assembly on March 23, 1775, he laid down a war cry for the American Revolution. (Library of Congress)

constitutional. The colonists, accustomed to not being taxed and used to considerable autonomy, ignored the technicality.

When new duties were imposed in 1767, another boycott was established. Once again the duties were repealed, except the one on tea; it was retained to establish the principle. This was the worst possible move the English government could have made. Although the colonists could smuggle tea to avoid paying the duty, they did not miss the implication of the remaining toll. All the British had hoped to gain from taxing the colonists was future defense costs in North America, but the revenue from the one duty on tea would have come nowhere near paying it. The government had, in other words, ensured the continuing animosity of the colonists without achieving even

the possibility of meaningful revenue collection.

The Road to Confrontation. In 1770, the year that the second duties were repealed, a tragic incident further marred British-American relations. Modern police forces had not yet been developed, so soldiers commonly maintained order. To the outrage of its citizens, the British established a garrison in Boston. In March, a mob led by, among others, the black freedman Crispus Attucks was harassing some of the British Redcoats, who fired on them, killing several, including Attucks. The violence gave both sides pause, but in a failure of leadership, no compromise was advanced. In the next several years Committees of Correspondence appeared in colony after colony with the goal of maintaining communications

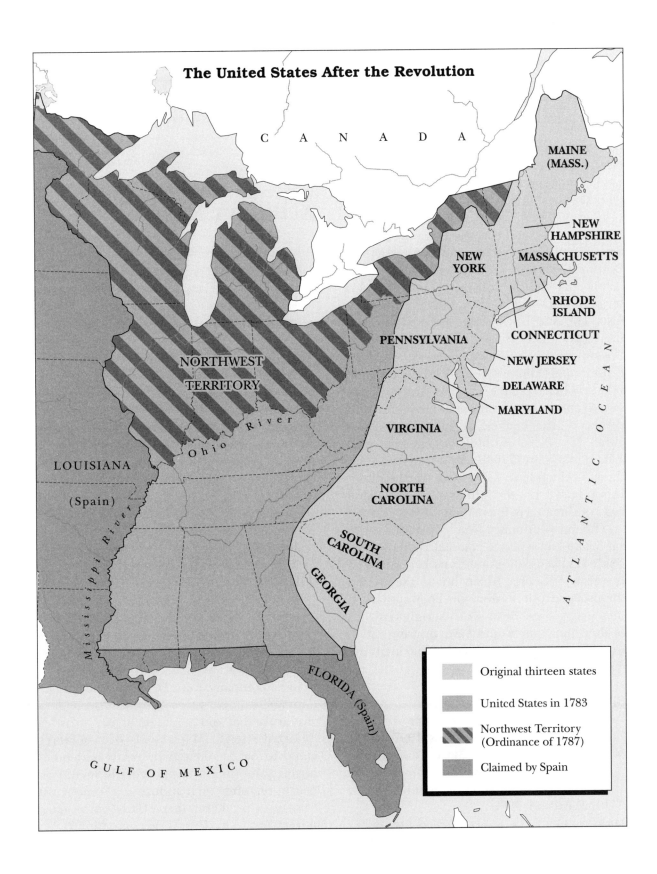

The United States After the Revolution

CANADA

MAINE
(MASS.)

NEW
HAMPSHIRE

NEW
YORK

MASSACHUSETTS

RHODE
ISLAND

CONNECTICUT

PENNSYLVANIA

NEW JERSEY

DELAWARE

MARYLAND

NORTHWEST
TERRITORY

VIRGINIA

Ohio River

LOUISIANA

(Spain)

NORTH
CAROLINA

SOUTH
CAROLINA

GEORGIA

Mississippi River

FLORIDA (Spain)

ATLANTIC OCEAN

GULF OF MEXICO

	Original thirteen states
	Unitcd States in 1783
	Northwest Territory (Ordinance of 1787)
	Claimed by Spain

in case of renewed disputes.

A final incident precipitated the actual military confrontation. The East India Company, holder of the British monopoly of trade in and around India, was exempted from the navigation laws and allowed to ship tea directly to North America. This tea, even with the duty paid, would undercut both legal and smuggled supplies already in the colonies. In December, 1773, colonists seized several ships in Boston harbor and threw the tea overboard. This act of defiance became famous as the Boston Tea Party. London insisted that the colony pay for the lost cargo and passed a series of acts—called "intolerable" by the colonists. The British also closed the port, revoked the colonial charter, and quartered troops in Boston. The colonists responded with the First Continental Congress in 1774. When, the next year, colonial irregulars fired on British troops sent to confiscate munitions at Lexington and Concord, the chance of compromise was gone. The British would not negotiate with armed rebels. In 1776 the Americans declared their independence, asserting "unalienable" rights based on the philosophy of natural rights expressed in the writings of John Locke.

The Revolutionary War continued until 1783, but the issue of colonial rights was already resolved. The Americans had declared British king George III a tyrant and separated themselves from his domain. They embarked on a struggle to determine what rights citizens of their new state would have, drawing much from the English experience but making innovations as well.

Bibliography

Fleming, Thomas J. *Liberty! The American Revolution*. New York: Viking Press, 1997.

Martin, James Kirby, and Mark Edward Lender. *A Respectable Army: The Military Origins of the Republic, 1763-1789*. Arlington Heights, Ill.: Davidson, 1982.

Middlekauff, Robert. *The Glorious Cause: The American Revolution, 1763-1789*. New York: Oxford University Press, 1982.

Namier, Lewis. *The Structure of Politics at the Accession of George III*. 2d ed. London: Macmillan, 1968.

Fred R. van Hartesveldt

Antitrust Law

A body of laws and court decisions that regulate and limit business mergers, practices, and behavior, U.S. antitrust laws are unparalleled in the world. No other capitalist nation has legislated marketplace competition on such a large scale.

After the Civil War, the United States enjoyed rapid economic growth. The nation was transformed from an agrarian society with high transportation costs and limited internal markets into one with a national railroad system, an emerging modern capital market, and national markets for many industrial goods. Because of these changes, many small regional manufacturers began facing large national competitors. The latter enjoyed lower costs of production because of such economies of scale as the ability to buy raw goods at lower unit costs. Small regional producers could either quit or merge with other firms.

A popular way to join forces was to form "trusts." The stock certificates of several corporations were turned over to a trust in exchange for shares in the trust. The trust would then operate the various firms as though they were a single company. John D. Rockefeller's Standard Oil Company was a notoriously aggressive trust that did much to make "trust" a pejorative term. Many areas of commerce came to be dominated by trusts and other business monopolies, particularly in the tobacco, oil, and sugar industries. Some trusts were more predatory than others, but all acted in restraint of trade to stifle competition.

The federal Sherman Antitrust Act of 1890 declared that contracts or combinations forming trusts that restrained trade were illegal. It also made trying to monopolize trade among the states or with foreign nations a felony offense. The law provided for heavy fines and prison sentences for convicted offenders.

Enforcement of the Sherman Act was never vigorous until the "trust-busting" era of President Theodore Roosevelt during the first decade of the twentieth century. However, the act was used most successfully against labor unions, rather than against trusts and other business monopolies. Also, its language was too brief and too general to be effective. In addition, the courts had considerable latitude in interpreting and applying the law.

Clayton Antitrust Act and the Federal Trade Commission. Enactment of the Clayton Antitrust Act in 1914 outlawed certain specific practices, while exempting labor unions from federal antitrust laws. The FEDERAL TRADE COMMISSION (FTC), created the same year, was designed to act against anticompetitive business practices and to enforce federal antitrust laws. Thereafter, the FTC put U.S. antitrust policy under the continuous supervision of an independent, partly judicial commission. Other sections of the Clayton Act outlawed price discrimination, kickbacks or bribes in the form of unearned commissions, interlocking directorates, and agreements tying purchase or lease of one item to another.

The Sherman and Clayton Antitrust Acts have been enforced by both the U.S. Department of Justice and the Federal Trade Commission. Both criminal and civil actions can be brought under these statutes. Courts may award triple damages plus attorney fees in civil cases. The FTC was empowered to enforce the Sherman and Clayton Acts because the Department of Justice is a highly politicized agency. The head of the department, the attor-

President Theodore Roosevelt's vigorous enforcement of antitrust laws during his administration earned the first decade of the twentieth century the nickname of "trust-busting" era. (Library of Congress)

ney general, is a member of the president's cabinet, and, as such, follows the political philosophy of whatever administration is in office.

The FTC, by contrast, is an independent, quasi-judicial agency. It consists of five commissioners appointed by the president for staggered seven-year terms, with the advice and consent of the U.S. Senate. Presidents can remove members of the commission only for "inefficiency, neglect of duty, or malfeasance in office."

The Robinson-Patman Act of 1936. During the 1920's chain stores and other mass distributors grew in importance. The Great Depression of the 1930's and the aggressive tactics used by mass merchandisers put independent retailers and wholesalers under pressure. A politically well-organized group of these independents helped force passage of the Robinson-Patman Act in 1936, sometimes referred to as the "anti-chain store act." The law amended the Clayton Act. It was aimed at limiting price discrimination among buyers in cases in which price differences give an unfair competitive advantage that hurts competition.

Other Federal Legislation. The twentieth century saw the development of advertising and brand-name loyalty. Many consumers

Major Antitrust Cases and Legislation

Date	Action	Significance
1890	Sherman Antitrust Act	Banned every "contract, combination . . . or conspiracy" in restraint of trade or commerce.
1898	*United States v. Addyston Pipe and Steel Co.*	Ruled that an agreement to set prices was illegal because it gave the parties power to set unreasonable prices.
1904	*Northern Securities v. United States*	Supreme Court ruled against holding companies that control the stock of competing companies.
1911	*Standard Oil Co. v. United States*	Supreme Court ordered the breakup of Standard Oil.
1911	*United States v. American Tobacco Co.*	Supreme Court ordered the breakup of American Tobacco Company. Along with the Standard Oil case, established the "rule of reason" approach to antitrust prosecution.
1914	Clayton Antitrust Act	Specified actions that are subject to antitrust prosecution.
1914	Federal Trade Commission Act	Established the Federal Trade Commission as an administrative agency to police "unfair methods of competition."
1920	*United States v. U.S. Steel Corp.*	Supreme Court ruled that size alone, in the absence of abuse of power, did not make a monopoly illegal.
1921	*American Column and Lumber Co. v. United States*	Ruled that competitors could be convicted if they had discussed prices and later set identical prices, even if no agreement to do so had been reached.
1936	Robinson-Patman Act	Specified the types of price discrimination that are illegal.

came to associate quality with price. The aggressive price competition of the mass merchandisers of the 1930's led independent retailers to press for passage of "fair trade" or retail price maintenance laws. Most states passed such legislation during the 1930's. The manufacturers of the day went along with independent retailers for their own reasons. The Miller-Tydings Act of 1937 exempted retail price maintenance laws, which prohibited retailers from discounting brand-name products, from all federal antitrust laws.

The Clayton Antitrust Act prohibited corporations from merging if the effect of a merger would be substantially to reduce competition or tend to create a monopoly. However, corporations could still simply buy the physical assets and equipment of competitors. In 1950 the Celler-Kefauver Act amended the Clayton Act to prohibit such purchases if they had the effect of lessening competition or creating monopolies.

American Telephone and Telegraph Cases. In November, 1974, the U.S. JUSTICE DEPARTMENT brought an antitrust action against American Telephone and Telegraph (AT&T), which it accused of monopolizing the telecommunications business. The Justice Department

1936	*International Business Machines Corp. v. United States*	Established conditions under which it is illegal to tie the sale of one product to the sale of another.
1937	Miller-Tydings Act	Exempted manufacturers and retailers from prosecution for agreeing to set minimum prices if the states in which they operate allow such agreements.
1938	Wheeler-Lea Act	Strengthened enforcement powers of the Federal Trade Commission.
1945	*United States v. Aluminum Co. of America* (Alcoa)	Supreme Court ordered breakup of Alcoa, ruling that a monopoly is illegal even if not accompanied by abuse of power.
1948	*Federal Trade Commission v. Cement Institute*	Supreme Court ruled illegal agreements by producers to base prices on manufacturing costs plus transportation from a given location (base-point pricing).
1950	Celler-Kefauver Act	Clarified the Clayton Antitrust Act, making it enforceable against mergers accomplished by sale of assets in addition to those accomplished by sale of stock.
1967	*Federal Trade Commission v. Procter & Gamble Co.*	Supreme Court forced Procter & Gamble to divest itself of Clorox because P&G's market power could have allowed Clorox to dominate the bleach market.
1976	Antitrust Improvements Act	Allows state attorneys general to sue on behalf of residents.
1976	*United States v. American Telephone and Telegraph Co.*	Ruled that even though the company was subject to regulation it still was subject to antitrust prosecution. The decision led to the breakup of AT&T.

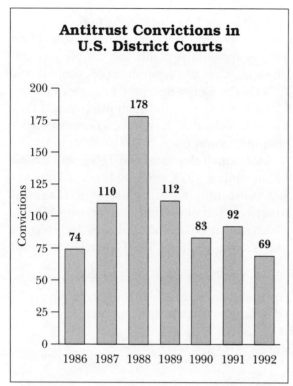

Antitrust Convictions in U.S. District Courts

Source: U.S. Department of Justice, Bureau of Justice Statistics, *Sourcebook of Criminal Justice Statistics—1993.* Washington, D.C.: U.S. Government Printing Office, 1994.

wanted AT&T to divest itself of its manufacturing subsidiary, Western Electric, and either divest itself of some or all regional Bell Telephone companies or leave the long-distance telephone business. In 1983 an out-of-court settlement split AT&T into eight separate companies in the largest antitrust divestiture in history.

AT&T had long been considered a "natural monopoly" because the cost of duplicating its thousands of miles of copper telephone wiring would have been both expensive and a waste of resources. The development of microwave transmission and communications satellites, however, made a competitive market structure possible.

Evolving Government Attitudes. The 1980's were quiet for antitrust enforcement. Few cases were initiated during the decade. In

1989, however, James F. Rill was appointed to head the Justice Department's Antitrust Division, and antitrust enforcement came back with a vengeance. Ivy League universities, airlines, the Salomon Brothers, and Arizona dentists were investigated by the Justice Department. In 1990 the Justice Department brought actions against eleven proposed mergers, the greatest number of cases filed in any year since 1973. In the late 1990's the government took strong antitrust action against the Microsoft Corporation—a giant in the computer software industry, which had not even existed a few decades earlier. Congress substantially increased the budget for antitrust activities and stiffened the penalties for violations.

Bibliography

Bork, Robert H. *The Antitrust Paradox: A Policy at War with Itself.* New York: Basic Books, 1978.

Breit, William, and Kenneth G. Elzinga. *The Antitrust Casebook: Milestones in Economic Regulation.* Chicago: Dryden Press, 1982.

Shenefield, John H. *The Antitrust Laws: A Primer.* 2d ed. Washington, D.C.: AEI Press, 1996.

Daniel C. Falkowski

Armed Forces

As extensions of national governments, armed forces act as deterrents against foreign attack, as tools for national expansion, and sometimes as arbiters of foreign policy.

National armed forces function in different ways, depending on the types of government in place. Most nations' militaries are directly under civilian leadership and answer directly to heads of state. The basic function of any military is to prepare for and defend against threats to national security, but the power of the military branch of a government can be a threat to the sovereignty of a government. Because of this, even the world's most despotic governments have subordinated the military to civilian leadership.

The U.S. Military. In the United States, the military answers to the secretary of defense, a civilian office. That officer is a cabinet member who answers directly to the president—who is commander in chief of all the armed forces. At the state level, the National Guard in each state responds directly to the governor of the state. The National Guard is strictly limited in the types of actions in which it can become involved and normally functions as a reserve force for the national military.

In the Soviet Union, during the height of the tyranny of Joseph Stalin, the military was a separate organization from the government. Internal policies were carried out by the Ministry of State Security, or KGB, rather than by the defense ministry. This pattern has been true for most totalitarian regimes throughout history.

Regardless of the types of government, military forces require large outlays of money. They must recruit members; pay, feed, and house them; care for their health; and supply them with weapons and training. Armed forces use funds rather than create them. Many argue, however, that preventing war is a worthwhile investment. When a nation maintains a large standing military force, aggressive nations may be deterred from attacking it.

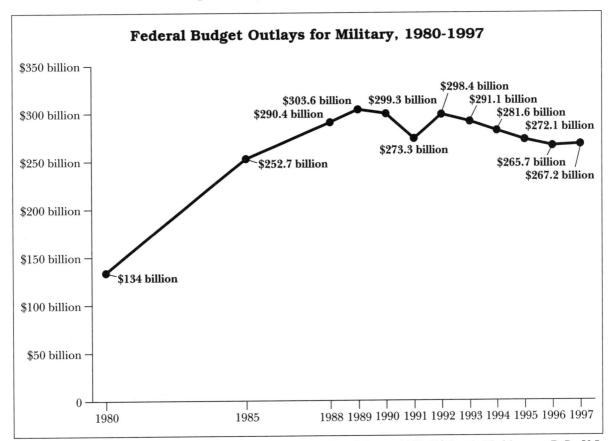

Federal Budget Outlays for Military, 1980-1997

Source: U.S. Bureau of the Census, *Statistical Abstract of the United States: 1997.* 117th ed. Washington, D.C.: U.S. Government Printing Office, 1997.

Note: 1997 figure is estimated.

Maintaining the peace allows the country to conduct business without outside interference. On the other hand, maintaining a large standing military force drains a national economy. The breakup of the Soviet Union in 1991 may have been caused in part by excessive military spending.

Armed Forces Personnel of Selected Countries in 1995

Country	Armed Forces Personnel (1,000)	Armed Forces per 1,000 Population
United States	1,620	6.2
Argentina	65	1.9
Australia	58	3.2
Brazil	285	1.8
Canada	70	2.5
China	2,930	2.4
Croatia	60	12.1
Cuba	70	6.4
Egypt	430	6.9
France	504	8.7
Germany	352	4.2
Iran	440	6.8
Iraq	390	18.9
Israel	185	34.9
Italy	435	7.6
Japan	240	1.9
Korea, North	1,040	44.3
Korea, South	655	14.5
Kuwait	20	11.0
Libya	76	14.5
Mexico	175	1.9
Russia	1,400	9.4
Saudi Arabia	175	9.3
South Africa	100	2.4
Sweden	51	5.8
Taiwan	425	20.0
Ukraine	476	9.3
United Kingdom	233	4.0
Vietnam	550	7.6

Source: U.S. Bureau of the Census, *Statistical Abstract of the United States: 1997*. 117th ed. Washington, D.C.: U.S. Government Printing Office, 1997.

Multinational Alliances. Some countries join multinational alliances, such as the North Atlantic Treaty Organization (NATO) or the Warsaw Pact, to avoid maintaining large military forces of their own. Such alliances allow member nations to focus more on economic development by combining their military force with the armed forces of the other member countries if one of the countries is attacked.

The differences between NATO and the former Warsaw Pact help illustrate differences among governments. NATO members choose to join and take an active part in determining the objectives of the organization, whereas the Warsaw Pact members were allowed only nominal control over the use of their forces. NATO forces are committed to the mutual benefit of all. Warsaw Pact forces were there by direction of the central committee of the Soviet Union, and member nations had little voice in the use of their own forces.

Membership in a treaty organization can have disadvantages. For example, a country can become involved in a war not in its best interest. Situations can arise that put the member at an unacceptable risk, such as the deployment of intermediate-range nuclear weapons in Western Europe under NATO.

Maintaining an independent and large, well-equipped military enables a government to negotiate with other countries from a position of strength, as well as impose its will on small nations. Used effectively, military strength can drastically shorten the process of negotiation. Used badly, it can foster lasting ill will.

Civilian Leadership. Because of the military's destructive power, it is essential to have national leadership that approaches problems from a diplomatic perspective, rather than one of force. Many critics argue against large militaries, con-

As president of the United States, Bill Clinton is commander in chief of all military forces. Here he inspects a U.S. guardpost at the Demilitarized Zone separating North and South Korea in 1993. (AP/Wide World Photos)

The United States and Haiti

Governments have used the military as extensions of their diplomacy throughout history. A modern example is the situation that existed between the United States and Haiti from 1991 to 1994. After Haiti's elected president had been forced out of office, an army general took over the government, and there were widespread abuses of power by the police and the military. To counteract this situation, U.S. president Bill Clinton warned Haiti's military leaders that their violations of civil rights were unacceptable and that they had to reinstate their ousted president, Jean-Bertrand Aristide.

When Clinton realized that ordinary diplomacy would not work, he notified Haiti's military leadership that if they continued to commit civil rights abuses, the United States would remove them by force. Two days before the deadline for action on the part of the military leadership, U.S. negotiators asked Haiti's military leaders to step down. The negotiations ended after two days when the Haitian government learned that U.S. military forces were en route to Haiti. The military government agreed to step down, avoiding a potentially bloody confrontation. In this instance, the existence of a large military force was the key ingredient in a diplomatic endeavor.

U.S. troops in Haiti in 1994. (AP/Wide World Photos)

tending that using armed forces is an inappropriate way to achieve national goals. Achieving objectives by force rather than negotiating a mutually beneficial agreement invariably leaves the receiving party with bad feelings toward the aggressor and can cause future problems with any negotiation.

Armed forces exist as extensions of national will. Depending on that will, the armed forces can be the savior of a country or the cause of its destruction. For example, if Germany had not developed such a large armed force in the late 1930's, it probably would not have instigated World War II, which resulted in the country's being politically divided for forty years. Likewise, if Joseph Stalin had not developed a large armed force, the Soviet Union probably would not have controlled a large segment of Eastern Europe for more than seventy years.

The success or failure of a country depends more on competent government than on a large military. Badly used, the military can become an aggressive, destructive force that drains the national economy and stifles growth. Used properly, the armed forces can be an effective extension of the national will, helping the country to achieve many goals that would otherwise be out of its reach and enabling the country to continue its economic growth and maintain its stability and security.

Bibliography

Kaufmann, J. E. *The Sleeping Giant: American Armed Forces Between the Wars.* Westport, Conn.: Praeger, 1996.

Morris, James M. *America's Armed Forces: A History.* 2d ed. Upper Saddle River, N.J.: Prentice Hall, 1996.

Sarkesian, Sam C., and Robert E. Connor. *America's Armed Forces: A Handbook of Current and Future Capabilities.* Westport, Conn.: Greenwood Press, 1996.

Carl A. Thames

Asian American Politics

The fastest-growing component of the U.S. population, Asian Americans began engaging in electoral and mass-protest politics during the 1960's.

Asian Americans are a rapidly expanding minority group in the United States. In 1970 almost all of the country's 1.5 million Asian Americans lived in Hawaii and California. By 1990 there were almost 7.9 million Asian Americans, and the census projected that the Asian American population would be 20 million by the year 2020.

Asian Immigration. Between the 1850's and the 1930's almost a million Chinese, Japanese, Koreans, Filipinos, and Indians immigrated to the United States and Hawaii. By comparison, almost 35 million European immigrants arrived in the country during those same years. A second wave of Asian emigration from Southeast Asia took place in the 1970's as a consequence of American involvement in the Vietnam War.

Early Asian American IMMIGRATION was a response to socio-political forces in Asia. Chinese immigrants, the first to arrive, were driven out of their home country by political and social instability around the same time that gold discoveries in the western United States created new economic opportunities. Early immigrants from Japan, Korea, and the Philippines were recruited by agents to work in Hawaii sugar plantations. Immigrants from India were attracted by job opportunities in North America. American recruiters found it profitable to turn to Asian countries for an abundant supply of cheap labor.

Concern about the numbers of Asian immigrants led to systematic American attempts to exclude them. These exclusionary acts included economic discrimination, political disfranchisement, physical violence, immigration exclusion, social segregation, and incarceration. The Chinese faced prejudice

Campaign poster for a Korean American candidate for the city council of Los Angeles, which has the largest concentration of Korean residents in the United States. (Korea Society)

to enact the 1882 Chinese Exclusion Act, which suspended the entry of Chinese labor for ten years. The Immigration Acts of 1917 and 1924 were used to ban other Asian groups, such as Indians and Japanese, from the country. Efforts were also made to segregate Asian Americans in public schools, while antimiscegenation laws prevented social interaction and intermarriage between whites and Asians in many states.

Asian American Associations. Efforts to segregate and exclude Asian Americans from all spheres of American life led to attempts at political organization among Asians at the turn of the century. Chinese and Japanese tended to form associations based on shared languages, residence, and occupation, among other criteria. A group of six Chinese associations became known as the Chinese Six Companies, which were the first to challenge anti-Chinese legislation using European American lawyers. The Japanese Association of America was similarly formed in 1908 to counter anti-Japanese sentiment in California.

actively propagated by diplomats, merchants, and missionaries, who helped create negative images of the Chinese in the United States.

Discriminatory Legislation. Many states passed laws to prevent aliens from leasing land, and Asian immigrants were also denied the right of naturalization, which meant that they could not vote. Deprived of political rights, Asians were also subjected to organized and spontaneous violence. The dislike of Asian immigrants finally led the U.S. Congress

Chinese and Japanese consuls played important roles in sponsoring and aiding the activities of these groups. The Asian American associations thus maintained close connections with their home countries. In fact, in the case of Koreans and Indians, the earliest political organizations in the United States were responses to political problems in the countries of origin. Koreans were probably the most political of all Asian communities, their chief organization being the church. Their initial concerns were focused on the Japanese occupation of Korea, and their political efforts were geared toward publicizing the plight of their homeland. In a similar vein, Asian Indians of the Sikh faith organized to fight for Indian independence. Filipinos, too, had their own organization geared toward fighting for independence.

The political ACTIVISM that originated in concerns for Asian American homelands became the vehicle later for protesting the weak position of Asian Americans in the U.S. economy. For example, Chinese garment and laundry workers organized strikes and engaged in litigation to improve their economic and social status.

During the 1950's and 1960's young activists inspired by Chinese communist methods tried to organize garment and restaurant workers. Other, less radical individuals aimed at setting up legal aid organizations, health care clinics, and language instruction programs. At the same time, Asian community groups across the United States began to join forces on issues that concern all Asian Americans. The work of such groups led the U.S. Civil Rights Commission to recognize in 1986 that violence against Asian Americans was a problem national in scope.

Electoral Politics. Asian Americans participated in electoral politics as early as the 1920's and 1930's. Japanese

American participation in Hawaiian politics increased dramatically after World War II, when war veterans used the G.I. Bill to study law and later enter politics. Between the 1950's and 1980's about 55 percent of the leadership positions in the Hawaiian state legislature were held by Japanese Americans.

Chinese and Indian immigrants were also successful in U.S. electoral politics. In the mainland states, however, Asian Americans

A Sikh resident of New York campaigns for a civil court judgeship. (Richard B. Levine)

have had a harder time gaining visibility since they are small fractions of local populations there. Nevertheless, those who have made it into political office have been instrumental in increasing national awareness regarding discrimination and prejudice against Asian Americans.

Post-1970 Immigrants. The wave of Asian immigrants in the 1970's consisted mostly of Chinese Vietnamese, Cambodians, Hmong, and Laotians. In general, these refugees had difficult resettlement experiences. Many were former soldiers, officers of regular armies, or white-collar workers with occupational skills not easily transferred to the U.S. economy. Moreover, most had little or no knowledge of English. In states, such as California, that have attracted large numbers of these immigrants, there has been growing public resentment of immigration as a drain on the economy in general and on public assistance programs in particular.

Political activism by Asian Americans has led to increased awareness regarding their problems. Violence directed against Asian Americans may have helped to mobilize Asian

On August 10, 1988, President Ronald Reagan signed the Civil Liberties Act of 1988 as government officials and Japanese American community leaders look on. The law was designed to redress violations of the civil liberties of Japanese Americans who, solely because of their ancestry, were interned during World War II, when the United States fought against Japan. (Ronald Reagan Library)

Americans, but many other issues have been addressed by individuals and organizations that make up the community.

Asian American Consciousness. In the 1960's and 1970's, increased immigration from Asian countries led to an influx of Asian students into elite colleges and universities on the East and West Coasts. Administrators at these schools began to think that Asians were "overrepresented." At some schools, such as the University of California at Berkeley, administrative changes might have helped discourage Asian American students from applying for admission. The result has been that more and more Asian American parents, regardless of ideological differences, are joining to guarantee better educational opportunities for their children.

There has also been activism on behalf of immigrants from Vietnam, Cambodia, and Laos, many of whom do not speak English and who are confined to urban ghettos where opportunities for employment are limited. The result of this poverty and lack of opportunity has been an outbreak of Asian gangs and drug-related violence. Growing discrepancies in education, wealth, and opportunities between descendants of early and recent immigrants are worrisome to groups that traditionally focus on group success. There is only a limited sense of "Asian American" identity, however; Asian Americans have tended to see themselves as Korean Americans, Japanese Americans, Asian Indians, and so on. Leadership is correspondingly fragmented, and until this changes the political successes are likely to be limited to those areas where self-interest urges cooperation.

Bibliography
Aguilar-San Juan, Karin, ed. *The State of Asian America: Activism and Resistance in the 1990's.* Boston, Mass.: South End Press, 1994.

Chan, Sucheng. *Asian Americans: An Interpretive History.* Boston: Twayne, 1991.

Lowe, Lisa. *Immigrant Acts: On Asian American Cultural Politics.* Durham, N.C.: Duke University Press, 1996.

Ng, Franklin, ed. *The Asian American Encyclopedia.* 6 vols. New York: Marshall Cavendish, 1996.

Wei, William. *The Asian American Movement.* Philadelphia: Temple University Press, 1993.

Sudha Ratan

Attorney General of the United States

The cabinet-level officer heading the Department of Justice, the attorney general of the United States is a politically appointed officer responsible for impartial enforcement of federal law. The office has evolved into something quite different from what it was at the time of its creation.

Evolution of the Office. A major enactment of the first Congress under the U.S. CONSTITUTION was the Judiciary Act of 1789. It set forth the structure of the federal court system and created the office of attorney general. The law set forth no qualifications for the position other than that the person appointed be learned in the law. George Washington, the first president, was to appoint an attorney general, subject to the consent of the Senate.

Washington wanted to appoint Edmund Randolph of Virginia to be the first attorney general, but the latter was not eager to have the position because Congress authorized only a low salary. Moreover, Congress had created no department for the attorney general to head. If Randolph were to need help, expenses must come out of his pocket. Congress apparently regarded the new office merely as legal adviser to the president. Randolph accepted the appointment after Washington convinced him that his private law practice

President Bill Clinton watches as Janet Reno is sworn in as the first woman attorney general of the United States in March, 1993. (AP/Wide World Photos)

would benefit from the office's prestige.

Since the attorney general did head an executive department, Randolph was not initially a member of the president's cabinet. However, cabinet discussions so often revolved around legal issues that Washington put Randolph in his cabinet, setting a precedent for future attorneys general.

The office of attorney general underwent its greatest change when the Department of Justice was created in 1870. At the same time, the position of solicitor general of the United States was also created. The solicitor general became the official who represented the United States before the Supreme Court, with strong ties to the Court as well as to the Department of Justice. Attorneys general then stopped representing the United States regu-

larly before the Court and became primarily administrators and presidential advisers.

By the late twentieth century, the attorney general headed a large and complex organization. Among the major units of the JUSTICE DEPARTMENT in the 1990's were the Criminal Division, Civil Division, Civil Rights Division, Antitrust Division, Tax Division, Immigration and Naturalization Service, FEDERAL BUREAU OF INVESTIGATION, and DRUG ENFORCEMENT ADMINISTRATION.

Politics and the Attorney General. Many twentieth century attorneys general were politically active persons who played major roles in the campaigns of the presidents who appointed them. Attorney General Robert F. Kennedy, for example, had no legal experience. His brother, President John F. Kennedy, appointed him because he relied on his advice and loyalty. President Richard Nixon appointed John Mitchell, a former law partner, who had managed his campaign.

After Mitchell was later discredited because he had been a major participant in the Watergate scandal, Presidents Gerald Ford and Jimmy Carter therefore sought attorneys general less involved in partisan politics.

President Bill Clinton appointed Janet Reno, the first woman to hold the office of attorney general. Reno took an interest in children's issues and in supporting the Immigration and Naturalization Service's efforts to prevent illegal immigrants from entering the United States. She sometimes displayed a degree of independence from the president who appointed her.

Bibliography

Baker, Nancy V. *Conflicting Loyalties: Law and Politics in the Attorney General's Office, 1789-1990.* Lawrence: University Press of Kansas, 1992.

Clayton, Cornell W. *The Politics of Justice: The Attorney General and the Making of Legal Policy.* Armonk, N.Y.: M. E. Sharpe, 1992.

U.S. Department of Justice. *Attorneys General of the United States, 1789-1979.* Washington, D.C.: U.S. Government Printing Office, 1980.

Patricia A. Behlar

B

Bill of Rights

In protecting civil and legal rights against encroachment by the federal or state governments, the U.S. Bill of Rights is a fundamental guarantee of rights enjoyed by American citizens.

James Madison, the principal architect of the Bill of Rights and fourth president of the United States. (Library of Congress)

The first ten amendments to the Constitution of the United States form the federal Bill of Rights. A bill of rights was not included in the Constitution when it was framed in 1789 because the Framers did not believe it necessary. Since the federal government was a limited government, there was no need to protect the rights of the citizens. The Framers also believed that the greatest danger to the rights of the citizens came from the states, not the federal government, and most of the states had a bill of rights in their own constitutions.

When the U.S. CONSTITUTION was submitted to the states for ratification, the greatest objection to it was its lack of a bill of rights. Supporters of the Constitution, led by James Madison, agreed to submit to the states such a bill after the Constitution was adopted. Twelve proposed amendments passed the House of Representatives and the Senate and were sent to the states. Ten of them were ratified and became the Bill of Rights in December, 1791.

The Ten Amendments. The First Amendment guarantees the fundamental freedoms of speech, press, petition, and religion. The RIGHT TO BEAR ARMS is expressed in the Second Amendment. The Third Amendment prohibits quartering of troops in private homes. The Fourth Amendment provides for people to be secure in their person, homes, and papers against unreasonable SEARCH AND SEIZURE, and sets limits for search warrants.

Procedural rights are guaranteed in the Fifth, Sixth, Seventh, and Eighth Amendments. Indictment by a grand jury in criminal cases, protection against double jeopardy or self-incrimination, and prohibitions against depriving persons of life, liberty, or property except by DUE PROCESS and against taking private property without just compensation are examples of rights guaranteed by the Fifth Amendment. The Sixth Amendment includes the right to a speedy and public trial by an impartial jury in a court previously established by law in the state and district where the crime occurred. It also guarantees that the accused shall be informed of the charges, be confronted with the witnesses, have subpoena power, and be allowed counsel. The right of trial by jury in civil cases is included in the Seventh Amendment. The Eighth Amendment prohibits excessive bail and cruel and unusual punishment.

The Ninth and Tenth Amendments ensure that the Bill of Rights is not used to deprive the people or the states of their implied rights or reserved powers. The Ninth Amendment

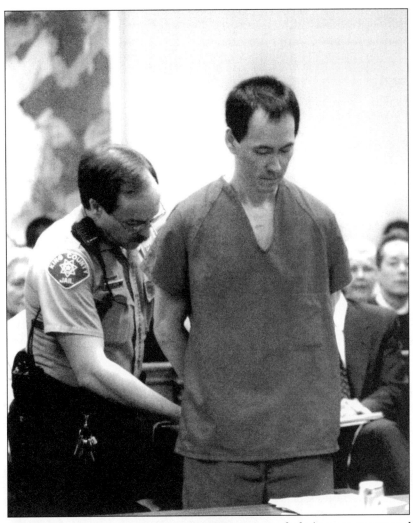

Many of the procedural rights protecting persons accused of crimes are guaranteed by the Fifth through Eighth Amendments to the U.S. Constitution. (AP/Wide World Photos)

states that the enumeration of rights does not mean that others, not included in the document, are denied. Powers neither delegated to the federal government nor denied to the states are reserved to the states or to the people by the Tenth Amendment.

The Supreme Court and the Bill of Rights. From the adoption of the Bill of Rights until the 1830's, cases involving Bill of Rights guarantees were not taken to the Supreme Court because it was believed that the justices on the Court would not rule favorably. Even the Alien and Sedition Acts, which were a clear violation of citizen rights, were not tested.

In the 1830's the Supreme Court began accepting cases involving the Bill of Rights.

Chief Justice John Marshall's decision in *Barron v. Baltimore* in 1833 established the principle that the Bill of Rights did not apply to the states. This view was universally accepted until

The Bill of Rights

Amendment I

Congress shall make no law respecting an establishment of religion, or prohibiting the free exercise thereof; or abridging the freedom of speech, or of the press; or the right of the people peaceably to assemble, and to petition the Government for a redress of grievances.

Amendment II

A well regulated Militia, being necessary to the security of a free State, the right of the people to keep and bear Arms, shall not be infringed.

Amendment III

No Soldier shall, in time of peace be quartered in any house, without the consent of the Owner, nor in time of war, but in a manner to be prescribed by law.

Amendment IV

The right of the people to be secure in their persons, houses, papers, and effects, against unreasonable searches and seizures, shall not be violated, and no Warrants shall issue, but upon probable cause, supported by Oath or affirmation, and particularly describing the place to be searched, and the persons or things to be seized.

Amendment V

No person shall be held to answer for a capital, or otherwise infamous crime, unless on a presentment or indictment of a Grand Jury, except in cases arising in the land or naval forces, or in the Militia, when in actual service in time of War or public danger; nor shall any person be subject for the same offence to be twice put in jeopardy of life or limb; nor shall be compelled in any criminal case to be a witness against himself, nor be deprived of life, liberty, or property, without due process of law; nor shall private property be taken for public use without just compensation.

Amendment VI

In all criminal prosecutions, the accused shall enjoy the right to a speedy and public trial, by an impartial jury of the State and district wherein the crime shall have been committed, which district shall have been previously ascertained by law, and to be informed of the nature and cause of the accusation; to be confronted with the witnesses against him; to have compulsory process for obtaining Witnesses in his favor, and to have the assistance of counsel for his defence.

Amendment VII

In Suits at common law, where the value in controversy shall exceed twenty dollars, the right of trial by jury shall be preserved, and no fact tried by a jury, shall be otherwise reexamined in any Court of the United States, than according to the rules of the common law.

Amendment VIII

Excessive bail shall not be required, nor excessive fines imposed, nor cruel and unusual punishments inflicted.

Amendment IX

The enumeration in the Constitution, of certain rights, shall not be construed to deny or disparage others retained by the people.

Amendment X

The powers not delegated to the United States by the Constitution, nor prohibited by it to the States, are reserved to the States respectively, or to the people.

1868, when the Fourteenth Amendment was ratified. That amendment states:

> All persons born or naturalized in the United States, and subject to the jurisdiction thereof, are citizens of the United States and of the State wherein they reside. No State shall make or enforce any law which shall abridge the privileges or immunities of citizens of the United States; nor shall any State deprive any person of life, liberty, or property, without due process of law; nor deny to any person within its jurisdiction the equal protection of the laws.

It is possible to read the Fourteenth Amendment and conclude that the states could no longer violate the rights included in the federal Bill of Rights. This interpretation is controversial and has never been accepted by the Supreme Court. Later the Court gradually incorporated most of the guarantees of the Bill of Rights under the due process clause.

The Privileges and Immunities Clause. The first time that the Supreme Court considered the definition of the privileges and immunities clause of the Fourteenth Amendment was in the *Slaughterhouse* cases of 1873. Although the cases did not directly address the question of incorporation of the Bill of Rights, most justices on the Court declared that the Thirteenth, Fourteenth, and Fifteenth Amendments were intended to protect the rights of the newly freed slaves, not the fundamental rights of the citizens, against state actions. The decision mentioned travel to and from the capital and on the high seas and protection of the citizen on the high seas and in foreign countries as fundamental rights protected by the amendment. Other fundamental rights included in the Bill of Rights remained subject to the police powers of the states.

The Due Process Clause. In 1897 the Supreme Court used the due process clause of the Fourteenth Amendment to apply Fifth Amendment property rights to the states. In 1925, in *Gitlow v. New York*, the Court said:

> For present purposes we may and do assume that freedom of speech and of the press—which are protected by the First Amendment from abridgement by Congress—are among the fundamental personal rights and "liberties" protected by the due process clause of the Fourteenth Amendment from impairment by the States.

"Incorporation" of the Bill of Rights. During the 1930's the Court began the "modernization" of the Bill of Rights by incorporating most of the Bill of Rights in the Fourteenth Amendment. By this process the Court applied the federal guarantees to the states. In 1931 two cases, *Near v. Minnesota* and *Stromberg v. California*, applied the First Amendment rights of FREEDOM OF SPEECH AND PRESS to the states. Additional Bill of Rights guarantees were applied to the states in succeeding cases. In 1932 in *Powell v. Alabama* the Supreme Court declared that the right to counsel granted in the Sixth Amendment was a right the states must grant in state courts, and in 1937 in *DeJonge v. Oregon* the Court gave federal protection to FREEDOM OF ASSEMBLY.

When the Court decided *Palko v. Connecticut* in 1937, the rights protected by the due process clause of the Fourteenth Amendment had been expanded without reference to the privileges and immunities clause. With *Palko*, however, the Court addressed the relationship between the privileges and immunities clause and the due process clause. Even though the prohibition against double jeopardy in the Fifth Amendment was extended to the state courts, the Supreme Court stated in its decision that all the guarantees in the Bill of Rights apply to the federal government but not to the states.

Many of the procedural guarantees in the Bill of Rights did not limit state courts, but

The First Amendment did nothing to protect members of the young Church of Jesus Christ of Latter-day Saints (Mormons) from persecution as they moved from state to state seeking freedom to practice their religion. Meanwhile, anti-Mormon feelings culminated in the assassination of the church's founder, Joseph Smith, in Illinois in 1844. (Library of Congress)

such fundamental rights as freedom of speech and press, the free exercise of religion, peaceable assembly, and benefit of counsel were protected from state encroachment by the due process clause of the Fourteenth Amendment. The Court ruled that the rights in the Bill of Rights are "privileges and immunities," only some of which are so important they cannot be violated by either the federal government or the states. The importance of each right must be decided by the Court on a case-by-case basis.

The Franklin Roosevelt Administration. During the 1930's President Franklin D. Roose-

velt appointed more liberal justices to the Court. The new justices argued that all the Fourteenth Amendment privileges and immunities limited the states. Even though this principle was a minority opinion of the Court and not accepted as the basis for decisions, the Court continued to include more Bill of Rights guarantees in the protection of the due process clause. During World War II, however, some restrictions upon these rights were permitted in the interest of national security.

In the 1950's incorporation of the Bill of Rights made greater strides. Federalism was given less consideration, and the rights of individuals, especially minorities, became more important. By the end of the 1960's, most of the Bill of Rights had been applied to the states. The Court continued to use the due process clause, rather than the privileges and immunities clause, to justify the application.

Unincorporated Rights. By 1991 most of the rights included in the first eight amendments were protected from state encroachment. Exceptions were the Second Amendment right to keep and bear arms, the Third Amendment right that prohibits quartering of troops in private homes, the Fifth Amendment right to a grand jury indictment, the Sixth Amendment right of twelve jurors in a criminal trial, and the Seventh Amendment right of a civil jury. The Supreme Court has held that state procedures are adequate to protect the values inherent in those federal Bill of Rights guarantees.

The Bill of Rights was originally adopted to protect the rights and liberties of the citizens against actions by the federal government. The adoption of the Fourteenth Amendment in 1868 provided a basis for incorporation, that is, the application of the guarantees of the Bill of Rights to the states. The due process clause of the Fourteenth Amendment was interpreted by the Supreme Court to require the incorporation of fundamental rights, but few rights were incorporated until the 1920's and 1930's, when the fundamental freedoms were defined as freedom of speech, press, religion, and assembly.

Incorporation of Procedural Rights. During the 1960's incorporation of the procedural rights in the Fourth through Eighth Amendments took place. The Supreme Court reflected the citizens' concerns with civil rights and with discrimination against minorities and women. Later, the public became concerned with law and order and with morality. The more conservative justices appointed after 1968 began to increase the police powers of the states and to limit Bill of Rights guaran-

tees at both the federal and the state levels.

The Supreme Court is not directly influenced by public opinion in making its decisions, but the climate of the times is often reflected in Court opinions. The Court is influenced by the country's political and social thinking in several ways. Various interest groups participate in cases before the justices as friends of the court. Presidents use new appointments to attempt to get their political points of view represented on the Court. Although the president can never be sure how an independent justice will decide an issue, the Court is influenced by new justices and especially by chief justices with leadership ability. Consequently, the opinions of the Court do follow public opinion and concerns.

Bibliography
Abraham, Henry J., and Barbara A. Perry. *Freedom and the Court.* 6th ed. New York: Oxford University Press, 1994.
Center for Civic Education. *We the People: The Citizen and the Constitution.* Calabasas, Calif.: Author, 1995.
Hickok, Eugene W., Jr., ed. *The Bill of Rights: Original Meaning and Current Understanding.* Charlottesville: University of Virginia Press, 1991.
Leahy, James E. *The First Amendment, 1791-1991: Two Hundred Years of Freedom.* Jefferson, N.C.: McFarland, 1991.
Mendelson, Wallace. *The American Constitution and Civil Liberties.* Homewood, Ill.: Dorsey Press, 1981.

Robert D. Talbott

Birth Control

Birth control is the employment of methods or objects that help regulate or prevent pregnancy. Following evolving definitions of individual liberties and the right to privacy, the American justice system has been involved in changing notions of the permissibility of individual citizens' use of birth control.

Throughout American history, midwives and health professionals have always recorded ways in which couples could restrict or prevent pregnancies. In the nineteenth century, however, increasingly stringent moral standards and emphasis on women's domesticity led re-

Margaret Sanger struggled against laws equating birth control education with pornography. Here she is seen emerging from a Brooklyn courthouse in 1916 after she was arraigned on pornography charges for lecturing on birth control. (AP/Wide World Photos)

formers to identify the prevention of pregnancy as a moral evil. Such moral views were made a legal formality in 1873, when Anthony Comstock pressed for legislation that made illegal the possession, sale, or gift of any obscene materials or articles for the prevention of conception. Comstock was made an assistant postal inspector, which gave him expanded power to investigate and prosecute the dissemination of literature dealing with planned parenthood through the mail.

In the 1870's and 1880's, several states passed similar laws, making the use of contraceptives and the spread of information about pregnancy prevention punishable under obscenity statutes.

The Birth Control Movement. Some reformers, however, viewed this legislation as damaging to the development of American families. Pointing to large immigrant families and to mothers who were always in ill health, they suggested that the spread of information about contraception would help to prevent unchecked growth of American cities. One reformer in particular, Margaret Sanger, was joined by Protestants, social reformers, population-control advocates, and others who believed that American cities suffered from unchecked population growth. Sanger chose to confront the Comstock Law. She founded planned parenthood clinics and mailed contraception information to women.

Although doctors could then legally prescribe birth-control devices for health reasons—such as disease prevention—Sanger and other reformers were arrested and jailed under the Comstock Law. Despite numerous penalties and court appearances, she continually agitated for changes in the laws to permit the use of contraception by married couples. Eventually, ACTIVISTS in the state of Connecticut made a direct challenge to the legal validity of such statutes.

In 1935 the Birth Control League of Connecticut began to operate clinics for married women who could not afford doctors. Because this action violated Connecticut's obscenity statutes, the clinics' directors were arrested and found guilty, and the clinics were closed.

During the 1960's Estelle Griswold, executive director of the Planned Parenthood League of Connecticut, opened another Planned Parenthood center for married women in the state. In a court case that ensued, *Griswold v. Connecticut* (1965), what was at issue were fundamental principles of individual freedoms and rights to PRIVACY within the home. Griswold and her coworker both maintained that they had the right to practice their occupations and that the state's effort to limit their right to property was arbitrary. Even more important, attorneys maintained that obscenity statutes violated due process, since they unfairly invaded the privacy of the home and the private decisions of couples regarding their sexual practices and family planning. The Supreme Court, in a 7-2 ruling, agreed that laws passed under the terms of the Comstock Law were unfair invasions of privacy.

Privacy and Birth Control After *Griswold*. *Griswold* was one of several federal court decisions dealing with privacy rights. In other cases, such as *Mapp v. Ohio* (1961), *Bowers v. Hardwick* (1986), and *Roe v. Wade* (1973), courts have addressed the extent to which the judicial system protects individual liberties and citizens' rights to privacy.

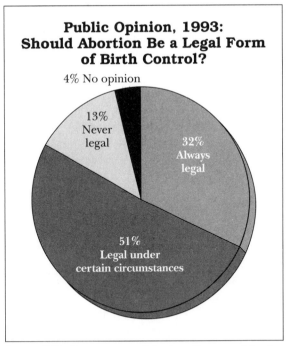

Public Opinion, 1993: Should Abortion Be a Legal Form of Birth Control?

4% No opinion

13% Never legal

32% Always legal

51% Legal under certain circumstances

Source: U.S. Department of Justice, Bureau of Justice Statistics, *Sourcebook of Criminal Justice Statistics—1993.* Washington D.C.: U.S. Government Printing Office, 1994. Primary source, *The Gallup Poll Monthly*, April, 1993.

Note: The question asked was, "Do you think abortions should be legal under any circumstances, legal only under certain circumstances, or illegal in all circumstances?"

After the *Griswold* case contraception became widely available, through both private purchases and public programs. In later years the spread of venereal disease and acquired immunodeficiency syndrome (AIDS) has added to public acceptance of the use of contraceptives. Nevertheless, public funding for the dissemination of information about contraception, condoms, and other preventive devices has come under increasing criticism.

Some groups have organized protests against the use of public funds for private relations. In particular, Roman Catholics and Christian Fundamentalists protest the spread of information and contraceptives for moral and religious reasons. Some cities have engaged in debates regarding whether the desire to protect public health outweighs the need to respect the religious and moral convictions of those opposed to the use of condoms and of family planning in general.

Bibliography

Critchlow, Donald T., ed. *The Politics of Abortion and Birth Control in Historical Perspective.* University Park: Pennsylvania State University Press, 1996.

Moskowitz, Ellen H., and Bruce Moskowitz. *Coerced Contraception? Moral and Policy Challenges of Long-acting Birth Control.* Washington, D.C.: Georgetown University Press, 1996.

Riddle, John M. *Eve's Herbs: A History of Contraception and Abortion in the West.* Cambridge, Mass.: Harvard University Press, 1997.

Tone, Andrea. *Controlling Reproduction: An American History.* Wilmington, Del.: SR Books, 1997.

Sarah E. Heath

Business and Government

Governments promote and regulate business activity. The relationship between business and government is affected by a variety of factors, including cultural attitudes, state of the economy, and existence of competing interest groups.

Operating in all but the most technologically primitive societies, businesses are economic enterprises seeking to profit from the sale of goods or services. They range in size from firms owned and operated by single persons to large corporations run by professional managers and owned by many shareholders.

Business and Government Policy. Government policies toward business fall into two categories: promotion and regulation. Governments promote business indirectly by creating a political and legal environment condu-cive to risk-taking. Bankruptcy laws, for example, may encourage risk-taking by entrepreneurs because failure will not reduce them to lifelong poverty. Similarly, government charters of incorporation may serve to encourage investors to risk capital in a new enterprise by limiting their debt liability if the company fails. Governments protect the property rights of business owners by giving them legal sanction. Under patent law this protection extends to intellectual property.

Governments can also shield business from public hostility by enacting symbolic legislation giving vent to public anger about business practices. For example, passage of ANTITRUST LAW defused popular discontent with American big business while posing no real threat to large corporations.

Direct government promotion of business can take many forms: subsidies (cash payments), tariff protection, government-approved monopolies, tax reductions, and financing (through direct and guaranteed loans). In addition, governments purchase many of the goods and services produced by business. Defense firms, in particular, depend upon government orders for their existence.

Government Regulation. Governments also regulate business activity. In industries vital to the public interest (such as utilities and transportation), governments may regulate the price of goods or establish state-owned monopolies to produce that good for public consumption. Governments sometimes impose restrictions on businesses when they commit acts, such as price fixing, that threaten the general welfare. Government regulation of business also stems from concerns with reducing pollution, protecting the consumer, preserving opportunity for small businesses, or guarding national security.

Indeed, most industrialized nations have few limits on government regulation of business. Government regulation affects hiring (equal opportunity laws), employee relations (hour and wage legislation), occupational safety, product design, and pricing. Governments can impose other responsibilities on businesses, such as requiring them to provide health insurance to their employees.

Businesses sometimes want government regulation in order to enhance their competitive position. During an economic downturn, businesses are more likely to accept regulation in exchange for government assistance. At other times, firms within regulated industries may work with government bureaucrats and legislators to fix prices or eliminate competitors. These "IRON TRIANGLES"—made up of business managers, regulators, and politicians—protect established firms at the expense of the consumer and any potential competitors.

Deregulation. Although government regulation of business increased dramatically in the twentieth century, there have been instances when governments have deregulated industry.

Beginning in the 1970's, when economic growth slowed down in most industrialized nations, governments of the United States, Great Britain, and elsewhere removed restrictions on business activity. Governments also privatized some of their state-owned industries. Supporters of deregulation and privatization hoped that, once freed from governmental restrictions, businesses would become more efficient and productive.

Business attitudes toward government reflect the diversity of the business community. Large corporations are more likely to accept regulation because they can spread its costs over wider bases. Small-business owners, on the other hand, frequently complain that regulation imposes a disproportionate burden on them. The members of some industries seek government regulation, while others oppose government interference. Similarly, the business community has split over the merits of deregulation.

Annual stockholder meetings, such as this AT&T meeting in 1996, are forums in which business management must answer to its shareholders. (AP/Wide World Photos)

Business Ethics Issues and Corresponding U.S. Legislation

Issue	Date	Laws Affecting
Discrimination in employment	1963	Equal Pay Act of 1963
	1964	Civil Rights Act of 1964; Title VII
Employee privacy	1988	Polygraph tests: Federal legislation banning polygraphs for screening applicants and random testing of employees except in certain security situations
		Drug testing: Various state and city laws prohibiting or limiting random testing
Sexual harassment		EEOC guidelines interpreting Title VII
Employee safety and health	1970	Occupational Safety and Health Act
Consumer product safety	1938	Food, Drug, and Cosmetic Act
	1958	Delaney Clause
	1966	Hazardous Substances Labeling Act
	1969	Child Protection and Toy Safety Act
	1972	Consumer Product Safety Act
	1976	Magnuson-Moss Warranty Act
Truth in advertising	1968	Consumer Credit Protection Act; Title I; Truth in Lending Act
	1993	New labeling requirements from the FDA for all processed foods
Environmental protection	1969	National Environmental Protection Act
	1971 1991	Clean Air Act
	1972	Clean Water Act
	1976	Toxic Substances Control Act
	1976	Resource Conservation and Recovery Act
	1980	CERCLA (Superfund)
Bribery of foreign officials	1977	Foreign Corrupt Practices Act
South Africa: trade and investment	1986	Comprehensive Anti-Apartheid Act
Plant closings	1988	Worker Adjustment and Retraining Act
	1988	Economic Dislocation and Worker Adjustment Assistance Act

President Bill Clinton confers with North Carolina representative Eva Clayton (left), who presented him with a letter signed by fellow new members of Congress supporting his economic plans after he met with business leaders in early 1993. (AP/Wide World Photos)

Most businesspeople recognize how important it is to reach public officials who make decisions affecting business. In order to influence regulators and legislators, businesses often form trade associations to lobby the government on their behalf.

Debate over the deregulation of U.S. industry in the late 1970's and early 1980's highlights the complexity of the business-government relationship. The circumstances favoring deregulation varied by industry. Economic or technological change led some industries to support deregulation. In other cases, deregulators gathered political support to overcome strong industry opposition. Finally, some industries were able to totally defeat deregulation.

Special Interest Groups. Social scientists have produced a vast literature discussing the relationship between interest groups and the state. Marxists believe that business interests dominate the governments of all capitalist societies. They point out that, in many authoritarian societies, business and government are closely intertwined. Although democracies appear to be more pluralistic, Marxists contend that government actions are nearly always motivated by a desire to promote or protect business. Marxists have documented that many government officials have backgrounds in business (either as owners, managers, or lawyers serving corporate interests). They also cite iron triangles as examples of the cozy relationship which exists between business and government. Other interest groups might achieve minor victories, but only if they do not challenge the dominance of business. In short, Marxists assert that the government reflects the interests of the business (or capitalist) class.

Opponents of this viewpoint maintain that the pluralism evident in modern democratic societies is genuine. They argue that other interest groups (such as labor unions, consumer advocates, and environmentalists) do exert considerable influence on government policy making, and in many instances these groups are at odds with business. For example, labor unions have secured legislation requiring businesses to accept collective bargaining over wages and working conditions, while consumer advocates have convinced governments to regulate how businesses design their products.

Iron Triangles. Government officials are not merely the pawns of special interests. In fact, businesses that operate within iron triangles are just as dependent on regulators as the regulators are dependent on them. Political scientists speak of a "bureaucratic imperative" that motivates government officials to place the interests of their agency above those of the constituency the agency is designed to serve. Furthermore, in many cases, government agencies serve several constituencies; thus, officials can play one interest off against another. The existence of competing INTEREST GROUPS also allows politicians to act on their own conception of the public interest.

Social scientists have long debated the merits of interest-group politics. Some believe that a balance has been reached between business and other interest groups, thus ensuring the stability and legitimacy of democratic governments. These people consider the presence of many organized interest groups a reflection of a healthy state of democracy; the more interests, the better. Others fear that self-serving interest groups have created, piecemeal, large, unwieldy governments. The legitimacy of democratic governments is threatened when politics is viewed as no more than the interplay of interest groups, with no regard for the general welfare.

Bibliography
Mack, Charles S. *Business, Politics, and the Practice of Government Relations.* Westport, Conn.: Quorum, 1997.
McQuaid, Kim. *Uneasy Partners: Big Business in American Politics, 1945-1990.* Baltimore: Johns Hopkins University Press, 1994.
Steiner, George A., and John F. Steiner. *Business, Government, and Society: A Managerial Perspective.* 6th ed. New York: McGraw-Hill, 1991.
Wilson, James Q. *Bureaucracy: What Government Agencies Do and Why They Do It.* New York: Basic Books, 1989.

Jonathan J. Bean

Busing

As a tool for desegregating public schools, busing has been controversial, and both Congress and the U.S. Supreme Court have struggled to deal with the issue.

School desegregation has been perhaps the most controversial American educational issue of the twentieth century. Busing, one of the more feasible strategies for achieving school desegregation, generated great controversy as desegregation plans were implemented between the late 1960's and 1980's.

Ending School Segregation. Until the U.S. Supreme Court's *Brown v. Board of Education* decision in 1954, segregated schools were legal in the South. The *Brown* decision was supposed to bring an end to legal (de jure) segregation, the practice of state-imposed segregation. A Supreme Court decision in 1955 addressed the issue of remediation and ordered that the elimination of segregated dual school systems proceed "with all deliberate speed." However, thirteen years passed before the Supreme Court became disillusioned with the delay tactics and obstructions employed by

many southern school districts and began enforcement of its desegregation decree.

Busing to Facilitate Integration. In *Swann v. Charlotte-Mecklenburg Board of Education* (1971), the Supreme Court established that busing was an acceptable strategy for desegregating school systems. In upholding busing, the Supreme Court was aware that it might impose a degree of hardship on some districts. While busing was sanctioned in the *Swann* decision, it was done so only in regard to de jure segregation.

In *Keyes v. Denver School District No. 1* (1973), the Supreme Court ordered busing for the first time outside the South. In this case the Court also ruled for the first time on the issue of de facto SEGREGATION, that is, segregation "in fact," which generally arises from discrimi-

Because of the strong opposition of some members of the community to court-ordered busing in Boston in 1974, police cars had to escort many buses to protect them from protesters hurling stones. (AP/Wide World Photos)

natory residential patterns. In evaluating the Denver school system, the Court concluded that when segregative intent existed in a substantial portion of the school system, then a systemwide remedy to assure nondiscrimination was acceptable. A systemwide remedy necessitated reassignment of large numbers of students, which typically required at least some busing. In some desegregation cases, the federal courts used busing when forced to develop their own desegregation plans.

Some southern school districts built desegregation plans on voluntary integration strategies, such as freedom-of-choice plans, voluntary transfer plans, and magnet schools. A federal circuit court argued that the only acceptable desegregation plans would be those

that actually worked and that actually accomplished desegregation.

In 1968, in *Green v. County School Board of New Kent County*, the Supreme Court rejected a freedom-of-choice plan. It concluded that such plans neither demonstrate significant levels of desegregation nor remove the racial identification attached to specific schools. While freedom of choice was rejected as the primary strategy in desegregation plans, however, it was not precluded from being used as a supplemental component in a more comprehensive desegregation plan.

The federal courts came to a similar conclusion regarding voluntary transfer plans. White parents saw no benefit in having their children attend traditionally black schools that were

Children boarding a school bus in Cleveland, Ohio, on the first day of court-ordered busing in September, 1979. (AP/Wide World Photos)

perceived to be educationally inferior. On the other hand, many ᴀғʀɪᴄᴀɴ ᴀᴍᴇʀɪᴄᴀɴ parents did not see the value in having their children attend mostly white schools where they were unwelcome.

Unquestionably the most successful of the voluntary desegregation plans, magnet schools have grown greatly since their inception in 1972. Generally, these are racially integrated public schools that have innovative programs and activities that attract students from throughout a school district. Freedom-of-choice, voluntary transfer, and magnet programs all require some degree of busing if they are to be properly executed. In some instances voluntary desegregation plans have involved more busing than mandatory pupil reassignment plans initiated by federal courts. Voluntary plans permit parents and children to remain outside the process while remaining within the public schools. Many such plans, however, have proved unacceptable to the courts.

Resistance to Busing. Busing to achieve integration met with considerable opposition at the local, state, and federal levels. Although busing was merely a strategy to facilitate meaningful integration, it eventually became symbolic of all that some people found distasteful about the desegregation process. Opponents of desegregation characterized it as "forced busing." The issue of forced busing, for many, was associated with the reluctance of white parents to send their children to what had previously been inferior all-black schools. Actually, considerably more minority students than white students were bused for desegregation purposes.

Although the legitimacy of busing was upheld in the *Keyes* decision, the parameters for its use were questioned the following year in *Milliken v. Bradley* (1974). The Supreme Court failed to support metropolitan busing in Michigan that would have involved the city of Detroit and fifty-three surrounding suburban school districts. Detroit schools had more than 63 percent African American enrollment, while neighboring suburban districts were almost exclusively white. The Supreme Court reasoned that the plaintiffs did not demonstrate constitutional violations on the part of the suburban communities. The plaintiffs' request to include the suburban school districts in the desegregation effort was denied.

During this same period, Congress passed legislation that placed restrictions on the use of busing for desegregation beyond the next-nearest school. This permitted many students to remain at their neighborhood schools, and since many neighborhoods were racially segregated, the legislation actually contributed to school segregation.

Despite the guidelines established in the *Milliken* decision regarding metropolitan busing, the restrictive busing legislation passed by Congress, and other precedent-setting decisions in the federal courts, school desegregation continued to move forward. The responsibility of proof had changed, however—from demonstrating the mere existence of segregation in a school system to the more difficult task of proving segregative intent on the part of school officials.

Much concern surfaced in Congress and in the federal courts about the movement of white families to areas outside racially mixed school districts and the tendency of white parents to place their children in private schools. While part of the decline in the number of white students can be attributed to desegregation and busing, white enrollment had actually begun to decline almost a decade before integration began. This decrease was a function of the declining white birthrate, departures to private schools, and departures to the suburbs.

Reduced Opposition to Busing. Opposition to busing appeared to diminish in the 1980's. The Reagan administration tended to focus on other domestic and foreign issues. Nevertheless, the Reagan administration was firmly opposed to busing. It even threatened to re-open desegregation cases already settled through extensive busing if it believed that the remedy was too drastic. The administration argued that desegregation should occur on a voluntary basis. Consequently, it supported voluntary desegregation plans such as magnet schools, tuition tax credits, and school "choice" programs. Busing became a side issue as debates focused on the impact that tuition tax credits and choice programs would have on public schools.

Bibliography

Bell, Derrick A., Jr. *Race, Racism, and American Law*. 2d ed. Boston: Little, Brown, 1980.

Douglas, Davison M. *School Busing: Constitutional and Political Developments*. New York: Garland, 1994.

Rippa, S. Alexander. *Education in a Free Society: An American History*. 7th ed. New York: Longman, 1992.

Sitkoff, Harvard. *The Struggle for Black Equality: 1954-1992*. New York: Hill and Wang, 1993.

Charles C. Jackson

C

Capital Punishment

The United States is one of the world's few democracies that maintains the death penalty. Whether it should maintain capital punishment has been a matter of practical, moral, and constitutional debate.

Execution of murderers, rapists, and blasphemers was practiced on a moderate scale during the seventeenth and eighteenth centuries throughout Britain's North American colonies. During the nineteenth century about 5,400 convicted criminals were executed throughout the United States.

As executions increased, so did interest in reforming capital punishment laws. Reformers of the 1800's succeeded in reducing dramatically the number of capital crimes, establishing capital punishment under centralized state rather than local control, and conducting executions privately rather than publicly.

Between 1900 and 1929, more than 3,600 individuals suffered the death penalty. From 1930 to 1967, there were 3,859 executions in the United States, with 1935 the peak year. Most executions were for murder, but many were for rape. The South had the highest number of executions, with a disproportionate number of African Americans executed. After 1967 executions dropped dramatically because of organized opposition to the death penalty and the CIVIL RIGHTS MOVEMENT.

Banning and Reinstatement. In 1972 the U.S. Supreme Court declared existing death penalty laws unconstitutional as part of its deliberations in the case of *Furman v. Georgia.* The Court believed that death sentences were applied inconsistently and unfairly, especially against the poor and minorities. These sentences, according to the Court, violated both the Eighth Amendment's section on "cruel and unusual punishment" and the Fourteenth Amendment, which guarantees "equal protection of the law." The Court's decision effectively banned executions from 1972 to 1976.

Because the Court did not ban capital punishment outright, various state legislatures enacted death penalty statutes in attempts to satisfy the Court's ruling. Some legislatures attempted to develop "mandatory death sentences," whereby the death penalty was imposed on *all* persons guilty of certain crimes. The Supreme Court rejected this approach, however, saying that all aggravated murders are not alike. The Court reasoned that juries and judges need to consider "mitigating circumstances" surrounding each crime.

With the mandatory death penalty ruled out, some states, including Georgia, proposed using "guided discretion" statutes. One of the first cases to follow guided discretion was that of *Gregg v. Georgia* (1976). The jury first determined the defendant's guilt for armed robbery and murder. Then the jury was given a checklist of ten "aggravating circumstances." They had to agree on at least one circumstance before recommending capital punishment. Finally, the jury had to consider whether there were mitigating circumstances.

In 1976 the Supreme Court found guided discretion statutes acceptable because the juries and judges had guidelines on how to make their decisions on life-and-death matters. A number of states, among them Florida, Texas, and Ohio, soon had similar models. The innovation of guided discretion, although not exempt from problems of implementation, made the capital punishment process more

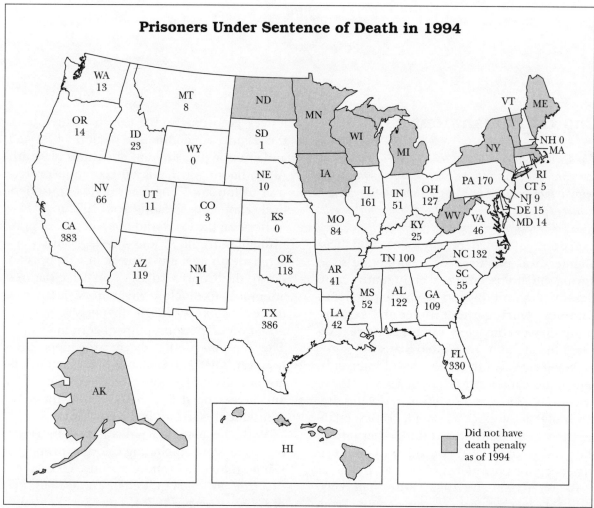

Prisoners Under Sentence of Death in 1994

WA	13
MT	8
ND	
MN	
ME	
VT	
NH	0
MA	
OR	14
ID	23
WY	0
SD	1
WI	
MI	
NY	
PA	170
RI	
CT	5
NV	66
UT	11
CO	3
NE	10
IA	
IL	161
IN	51
OH	127
NJ	9
DE	15
MD	14
CA	383
KS	0
MO	84
KY	25
WV	
VA	46
AZ	119
NM	1
OK	118
AR	41
TN	100
NC	132
SC	55
MS	52
AL	122
GA	109
TX	386
LA	42
FL	330
AK	
HI	

Did not have death penalty as of 1994

Source: Data are from U.S. Department of Justice, Bureau of Justice Statistics, *Sourcebook of Criminal Justice Statistics—1993.* Washington, D.C.: U.S. Government Printing Office, 1994. Primary source, NAACP Legal Defense and Educational Fund.

Note: Thirty-seven states had the death penalty in 1994; 13 states and the District of Columbia did not. In addition to those individuals under state death sentences, 5 people were under federal death sentences and 8 were under U.S. military death sentences. U.S. total was 2,848.

fair by narrowing the class of people subject to the death penalty.

Once capital punishment was reinstated in 1976, sentencing people to death row increased rapidly. By 1993 the number of inmates on death row had reached 2,716. Nevertheless, actual executions remained infrequent, primarily because of the lengthy appeals process. Critics of the system began to argue that the ratio of inmates awaiting execution to those actually executed was grotesque and inhumane. Public concern about violent CRIME during the 1990's led politicians to increase the number of capital crimes, thereby worsening the situation.

The 1990's also saw the Supreme Court tighten the appeals process for the condemned. In 1993 the Court decreed that unless so-called new evidence in cases was incontrovertible, executions were to proceed.

Justifications for Capital Punishment. Advocates of capital punishment believe that executions protect the public by removing any chance of the killers going free. They cite examples of murder-for-hire criminals and serial killers as types of criminals who should be destroyed for the public good. Opponents counter that most condemned prisoners are of a different sort—people caught up in the passion of their crimes or people entangled in situations leading unexpectedly to lethal violence.

Supporters avow that capital punishment strikes fear in the hearts of potential killers. Logically, harsh punishment should be a strong deterrent in keeping people from carrying out heinous schemes. However, studies have shown that capital punishment has little deterrent effect.

Some on both sides of the argument about capital punishment favor a return to public executions, via television. Supporters of capital punishment argue that looking at executions directly on television would deter potential criminals. Others, however, believe that public executions would arouse revulsion against capital punishment.

When outrageous criminals—such as mass poisoners or political assassins—are found guilty, cries for justice and vengeance are almost instinctual in humans. The public looks to government to punish criminals appropriately. This process, one argument goes, acts as a safety valve for discharging instinctual vengeance.

Costs of Capital Punishment. It is commonly believed that it is more expensive to maintain life-sentence prisoners than it is to execute them. Surprisingly, however, studies have demonstrated that executions are significantly more costly than life sentences. To begin with, court trials in capital cases are more expensive than those for noncapital cases.

Prosecution and defense teams must prepare for two separate trials: to determine whether the defendant is guilty and, if guilty, to determine whether capital punishment is warranted. The trial phase also involves selecting a "death qualified" jury (one whose members are not opposed to capital punishment).

The gas chamber in California's San Quentin penitentiary. (AP/Wide World Photos)

The most expensive aspect is the extensive appeals process, which takes an average of eight years. During the 1980's, when the average execution cost about $1.8 million per case, Florida estimated that it spent six times more per person to execute criminals than to maintain them in prison for life without parole.

Ethical and Constitutional Implications. Beyond practical considerations, capital punishment raises moral questions about the sacredness of human life. Its advocates contend that capital punishment affirms human life by exalting the value of innocent victims. Some also argue that it is ethical to execute someone who has committed a particularly heinous crime. Opponents counter that capital punishment cheapens human life and puts government on the same low moral level as criminals.

Opponents of capital punishment object on moral grounds to sentencing mentally impaired individuals to the death penalty because these people often do not understand their crimes. The courts have upheld the constitutionality of executing mentally retarded persons but have suggested that "diminished mental capacity" be considered as a mitigating factor. Those challenging the death penalty on

The Fifth Amendment

No person shall be held to answer for a capital, or otherwise infamous crime, unless on a presentment or indictment of a Grand Jury, except in cases arising in the land or naval forces, or in the Militia, when in actual service in time of War or public danger; nor shall any person be subject for the same offence to be twice put in jeopardy of life or limb, nor shall be compelled in any criminal case to be a witness against himself, nor be deprived of life, liberty, or property, without due process of law; nor shall private property be taken for public use without just compensation.

The Eighth Amendment

Excessive bail shall not be required, nor excessive fines imposed, nor cruel and unusual punishments inflicted.

moral grounds also object to the execution of juvenile murderers. The courts have upheld the constitutionality of capital punishment for youthful offenders, leaving the minimum age requirement for execution to the discretion of state legislatures.

Some controversy over capital punishment stems from interpretations of the U.S. CONSTITUTION and its first ten amendments, the BILL OF RIGHTS. The Fifth Amendment explicitly refers to capital crimes twice, thereby rendering capital punishment constitutional. The Eighth Amendment, however, can be argued to restrict capital punishment by authorizing the courts to decide whether punishments rendered are "cruel and unusual." During the early 1970's, the U.S. Supreme Court interpreted this to mean that the Court could determine "evolving standards of decency," implying that punishments tolerated in 1800 might not be acceptable in modern society.

Opponents of capital punishment have seized on the phrase "cruel and unusual" as a rallying cry to protest the lack of uniform standards of courts in handing down death sentences. They have also used the phrase to question the treatment of inmates on death row, who alternate between fear and hope during the lengthy appeals process. Moreover, opponents of capital punishment have used the phrase "cruel and unusual punishment" to challenge the methods of execution (most commonly electrocution or lethal injection) as inhumane. Nevertheless, since 1976, when executions resumed, the Supreme Court has usually rejected the moral grounds of "cruel and unusual punishment" as espoused by opponents of capital punishment.

Fairness in the System. It has been argued that capital punishment is most often applied to indigents, minorities, the mentally retarded, and violent youths. Defenders of capital punishment contend that the death penalty itself is not biased against these groups; the fact that disproportionate numbers of them have been sentenced to death, they say, has to do with the aberrant behaviors exhibited by these groups. Opponents, however, offer statistical data demonstrating that most death row inmates are poor and cannot afford top-level lawyers to defend them. A 1987 study found that clients of court-appointed lawyers

Executions in the United States, 1930-1995

Year or Period	Total	White	Black
1930 to 1939	1,667	827	816
1940 to 1949	1,284	490	781
1950 to 1959	717	336	376
1960 to 1967	191	98	93
1968 to 1976	0	0	0
1977 to 1982	6	5	1
1983	5	4	1
1984	21	13	8
1985	18	11	7
1986	18	11	7
1987	25	13	12
1988	11	6	5
1989	16	8	8
1990	23	16	7
1991	14	7	7
1992	31	19	11
1993	38	23	14
1994	31	20	11
1995	56	33	22
All years	**4,172**	**1,940**	**2,187**

Source: U.S. Bureau of the Census, *Statistical Abstract of the United States: 1997*. 117th ed. Washington, D.C.: U.S. Government Printing Office, 1997.

Note: Excludes executions by military authorities. Figures in "total" column include races other than white and black.

in Texas were more than twice as likely to receive the death penalty as those who hired their own lawyers.

The Civil Rights movement of the 1950's and 1960's was instrumental in the Supreme Court's ordering a moratorium on death sentences in 1972 until fair and equitable procedures were established for all races. The Court was influenced by studies showing that African American males suffered a disproportionate number of the executions carried out. Once the Court revamped sentencing procedures and allowed for the resumption of executions, the proportion of African American executions dropped.

Some critics complain that racial bias still exists in the sentencing of black criminals to death. A 1990 study showed that African Americans who killed whites were more likely to receive the death penalty than those who killed African Americans. Moreover, during the five years following the 1988 enactment of the federal "drug kingpin law," which permitted applying the death penalty to persons convicted of drug-related killings, federal prosecutors sought the death penalty against thirty-seven individuals, twenty-nine of whom were black.

Political Ramifications. In 1966 public approval of capital punishment reached a historic low of 42 percent but rose steadily thereafter. By 1993 it reached 72 percent. Much of the shift can be attributed to rising crime rates.

Political leaders often take their cues from PUBLIC OPINION POLLS and media representations of public opinion, ranging from talk shows to editorials. During the 1990's successful politicians supported crime bills, tougher sentencing practices, a reduced number of appeals, and capital punishment. Even governors seldom granted executive clemency for fear of appearing "soft on crime."

Despite the large amounts of money, time, and effort expended in the United States on capital punishment, it represents a minor aspect of the CRIMINAL JUSTICE SYSTEM. Only a small percentage of murderers receive the death penalty, and an even smaller percentage are actually executed. Nevertheless, because of the finality of execution and the difficult moral issues presented by capital punishment, it has received much attention and will continue to engender considerable controversy.

Bibliography

Bedau, Hugo A. *The Death Penalty in America: Current Controversies.* New York: Oxford University Press, 1997.

Costanzo, Mark. *Just Revenge: Costs and Consequences of the Death Penalty.* New York: St. Martin's Press, 1997.

Haines, Herbert H. *Against Capital Punishment: The Anti-death Penalty Movement in America, 1972-1994.* New York: Oxford University Press, 1996.

Koosed, Margery B. *Capital Punishment.* New York: Garland, 1996.

Megivern, James J. *The Death Penalty: A Historical and Theological Survey.* New York: Paulist Press, 1997.

Randa, Laura E. *Society's Final Solution: A History and Discussion of the Death Penalty.* Lanham, Md.: University Press of America, 1997.

Richard Whitworth

Capitalism

An economic system based on a free market and private ownership of property and industry, with the goal of making profits, the capitalistic U.S. system depends on the safeguarding of private property and on the use of the marketplace to promote economic efficiency.

Capitalism rests on private ownership of property and promotes economic efficiency through the market. The market is any location in which an exchange takes place between a willing buyer and willing seller of land, commodities, or labor. Capitalists believe that a "fair market price" is possible for everything that is traded and that optimum prices and allocation of resources will take place with everyone seeking to buy low and sell high.

The pursuit of individual gain or profit is said to be the motivating force of the system. The most successful operation of the entire system is said to result if the market is allowed to function without undue government interference. Capitalists tend to lament excessive government interference in business, but not even the staunchest capitalists believe that private property or the market can exist without government or a framework of laws. Government may be a necessary evil, but it is necessary. If government is necessary, what are the particular laws that capitalism needs? Capitalism certainly appears to require order and stability in which AGRICULTURE, industry, and commerce can take place, but it requires more than that.

Capitalism and the Law. Capitalism needs special laws protecting private property so that the fruits of agricultural, industrial, and commercial activity can be protected from those who would steal it. Such prohibitions also rest on the notion that anyone able to steal money would also probably be able to kill or otherwise assault or harm their victims.

Capitalism also requires laws that protect the market, starting with the protection of contracts between buyers and sellers. The influence of capitalism on the American judicial system is demonstrated in the U.S. CONSTITUTION, which forbids state governments from passing laws "impairing the obligation of contracts." The Framers inserted this language not only to protect commerce but also to stop violence that was arising as a result of interference with interstate commerce.

Capitalism also requires laws against fraud. The most basic fraud laws are those specifying and insisting on accurate weights and measures, widely recognized as a governmental duty. From this necessity it is comparatively easy to find reasons for laws against fraud, forgery, and embezzlement, which also impair contracts. By the late twentieth century, capitalism relied on an array of electronic and computerized capabilities that also required regulatory measures. In addition, modern technology has created new foods and drugs, the quality and safety of which consumers have difficulty evaluating. These also require regulation.

Laws Creating Specific Market Conditions. Operating without regulation, capitalism tends to produce very wealthy holders of private property who may be able to purchase market positions in which they—solely or in the company of a few others—control certain property so that monopolies and oligopolies are created. Monopolies and oligopolies have developed enough times that most business and government leaders believe government should prevent monopolies and other restraints to trade. The U.S. government uses various antimonopoly, antirestraint of trade, and ANTITRUST LAWS to preserve the competitive system. Such laws are also connected with fraud statutes in the area of securities.

Currency. A key relationship between capitalism and the legal system is the regula-

A director of the Better Business Bureau poses with documents relating to a widespread banking fraud scheme. Sophisticated Nigerian con artists bilked an estimated $200 million from businesses and churches around the world by getting them to pay large sums of money for information on nonexistent funds said to belong to them. (AP/Wide World Photos)

The head of a California savings and loan institution, Charles H. Keating, Jr., was arrested in 1990 for security fraud on charges of selling worthless "junk" bonds to keep his corporation afloat. (AP/Wide World Photos)

tion of the amount and kind of legal tender or currency the government permits. In ancient times, legal tender was nearly always a durable good, such as a precious metal. The government's job was basically to set accurate standards of weight and quality for such metals. Some economists argue that governments should avoid regulating currency altogether by returning to the gold standard as a measure of all currencies, since that would avoid the dangers of inflation that result from substituting paper currency for gold. Other economists, probably a majority, believe that governments can take prudent actions to regulate currency through systems such as the U.S. Federal Reserve banking system. From either perspective, the government is responsible for establishing the rules for the legal tender, currency, or money supply.

Taxation. Every government needs revenue, derived from taxes, to pay for even minimal police, firefighting, and military services. This fact leads to the question of how taxes should be raised. Capitalists, who wish for the maximum amount of private ownership, usually argue for minimal TAXATION. Arguments abound in economics over what types of taxes are most intrusive on the marketplace. Most capitalists favor taxes on consumption rather than on wealth (for example, property taxes) or income. If more than one kind of taxation is deemed necessary, capitalist economists favor consumption taxes first, income taxes second, and property taxes third. Almost without exception, capitalist economists oppose so-called business or privilege taxes. They also typically note that business taxes usually generate the least revenue. Capitalists do not object to user taxes, which shift the burden of taxation to those persons who can be clearly identified as the beneficiaries of governmental services.

Additional Regulation of the Economy. Capitalist economists have a strong tendency to oppose REGULATORY AGENCIES, which have become increasingly common in the United States. One key problem with regulatory agencies is that they are often established by vague legislation that creates the agency and then directs it to write such additional rules and regulations as it deems necessary. Decisions by regulatory agencies represent a delegation of power in which the arena of legislation shifts from the legislative branch to the executive branch.

Bibliography
Bell, Daniel. *The Cultural Contradictions of Capitalism.* 20th anniversary ed. with a new afterword by the author. New York: Basic Books, 1996.
Nelson, Joel I. *Post-industrial Capitalism: Exploring Economic Inequality in America.* Newbury Park, Calif.: Sage Publications, 1995.
Thurow, Lester C. *The Future of Capitalism: How Today's Economic Forces Shape Tomorrow's World.* New York: Penguin Books, 1996.

Richard L. Wilson

Censorship

By examining material in advance of its publication, performance, or broadcast, government censorship aims to prevent "objectionable" materials from being distributed. Modern democracies such as the United States abhor censorship of nearly all expression except obscenity.

Repressive governments have given censorship, or "prior restraint," a bad name. If dictators wait until after something to which they object is published, the dangerous ideas are already widespread. Extreme penalties may not deter some critics from voicing their opposition to a regime. In modern democracies, on the other hand, censorship is generally shunned. In the United States, censorship is allowed by the federal or state governments only if such prior restraint can be made compatible with the free expression portions of the First Amendment to the U.S. CONSTITUTION. It reads: "Congress shall make no law . . . abridging the freedom of speech, or of the press; or the right of the people peaceably to assemble."

The First Amendment. The U.S. Constitution's First Amendment divides the free expression of ideas into two major categories: freedom of speech and the press, and freedom of peaceable assembly. Neither speech nor press is to be restrained, but the presence of the word "peaceably" in connection with assemblies indicates that assemblies can be, and routinely are, subject to prior restraint or censorship. However, even in the case of assembly, prior restraints are allowed only for reasons such as allowing free movement of traffic in public areas. They must not be used to block the presentation of ideas simply because they are objectionable to the authorities.

Freedom of speech and the press is different from freedom of assembly because of its more passive character, although the U.S. Supreme Court has not always consistently and officially said so. The press, in particular, is regarded as a less dangerous medium for the expression of ideas, since reading is a far more passive activity than speaking to an audience. Someone making a speech might incite a riot, but it is difficult to imagine a crowd reading a newspaper and then rioting. Because speech is frequently given before an assembly, it falls partially under the First Amendment's requirement that assembly must be peaceable to avoid being restrained.

The essence of freedom of speech and the press is that there shall be no prior restraint—no censorship of any material in advance of its distribution. This requirement clearly implies that there may be punishments or restraints applied afterward. In an age when censorship laws were focused against "blasphemy," John Milton argued in his *Areopagitica* (1644)

against such laws. By the eighteenth century, the battle against censorship had been sufficiently successful that the great jurist William Blackstone could write that "liberty of the press is indeed essential to the nature of a free state; but this consists of laying no *previous* restraints upon publications."

This tradition carried over into the American colonies and led to the adoption of the First Amendment to the U.S. Constitution in 1791. Freedom of the press became an issue only a few years after the passage of the BILL OF RIGHTS when the Federalists passed the Alien and Sedition Acts in 1798 to punish political opponents. They justified the acts by saying they did not impose a prior restraint. The political outcry was so great that Federalist John Adams lost the 1800 election to Thomas Jefferson, who pardoned all who had been convicted under the acts. The Alien and Sedition Acts came to be considered such a black mark that no attempt was made to pass anything like them for more than a hundred years.

Throughout the 1800's, the common understanding of the First Amendment was that the federal government could not pass a law that restricted freedom of the press. Since the Bill of Rights was interpreted as applying only to the national government, however, sedition laws existed in various states. After the Fourteenth Amendment was passed in 1868, a basis for applying the principles of the Bill of Rights to the states was established. During World War I, Congress passed the Sedition Act and the ESPIONAGE Act, which produced the first "free speech" cases, but no restraints on the press in advance of publication were enacted.

Prior Restraint Cases. The first U.S. Supreme Court decision on prior restraint was *Near v. Minnesota* (1931). A man named Near published an anti-Semitic newsletter in Minneapolis, Minnesota, which charged that local government officials were Jewish-influenced and corrupt. Authorities sought to use a state statute to prevent Near from publishing, but the U.S. Supreme Court held that this was an impermissible prior restraint. Also, for the first time, it applied the free press portion of the First Amendment to state governments, utilizing the due process clause of the Fourteenth Amendment selectively incorporating part of the Bill of Rights.

The second Supreme Court prior restraint case, *New York Times Co. v. United States* (1971), the "Pentagon papers" case, involved hundreds of top-secret government documents photocopied by Daniel Ellsberg, who violated security clearance laws. The documents were printed by *The New York Times* and other newspapers. They disclosed U.S. violations of international law and other matters damaging to the government. The Pentagon papers were clearly stolen government property, but the legal question was whether the newspapers could be restrained in advance from publishing them. The Supreme Court ruled against the government.

Given the Court's disregard of the U.S. government's opposition to publication of the Pentagon papers, it is hard to imagine other circumstances which would justify prior restraint. The Court has never found a case that justified prior restraint. Since 1931 it has not allowed any state or local government to exercise prior restraint, even when expression of ideas embarrasses government.

Obscenity. The Supreme Court has found it necessary to confront obscenity and pornography, particularly when applying the First Amendment

to the states, many of which long had restrictive statutes on such subjects. Despite the clear language of the First Amendment that "Congress shall make no law" abridging freedom of the press or speech, there have long been other rights which the Court has counterbalanced against the right of free expression. For example, there is a right of the adult population to avoid being assaulted in public by widespread display of materials they might regard as offensive. There is an even more important need to protect children from pornographic materials. Prior restraint is allowable for any pornography involving sexual acts by children.

Regarding the publication of pornographic

A tireless nineteenth century crusader against pornography, Anthony Comstock lobbied Congress to pass legislation against sending pornographic materials through the mails. In 1873 Congress passed a restrictive law known as the "Comstock Law" in his honor. (Library of Congress)

materials depicting adults for the use of other adults in the privacy of their own homes, the Supreme Court has found grounds to provide prior restraint of some materials. It has had difficulty in doing so in practice, however, principally because of the strong constitutional opposition to prior restraint. Also, although the Supreme Court has consistently held that obscene materials are not protected under the First Amendment, it has had problems defining obscenity.

Roth v. United States. In *Roth v. United States* (1957) the Supreme Court attempted to define obscenity for the first time in the modern era. The first premise of the Court's decision was that "all ideas having even the slightest redeeming social importance—unorthodox ideas, controversial ideas, even ideas hateful to the prevailing climate of opinion—have the full protection of the [First Amendment] guarantees." Because the First Amendment has been interpreted to protect virtually all ideas against prior restraint except obscene ones, the definition of obscenity was crucial. Chief Justice Earl Warren once said that defining obscenity presented the Court with its "most difficult" area of adjudication. In *Roth*, the Court said that to be obscene, expression had to be "utterly without redeeming social importance." Obscenity was fully defined by the following phrase: "Whether to the average person applying modern community standards, the dominant theme of the material taken as a whole appeals to prurient interests."

Self-styled champions of "Christian values," Mel Gabler (pictured speaking in 1986) and his wife, Norma Gabler, began crusading against what they regarded as objectionable textbooks in 1961 and became a powerful censorship force in education. (AP/Wide World Photos)

When this Florida student prepared an anatomically correct sculpture of a nude man for display at her high school, she was ordered to cover it. (AP/Wide World Photos)

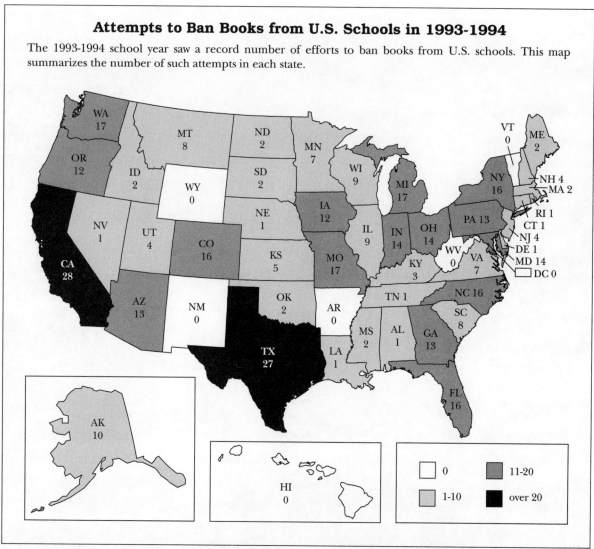

Attempts to Ban Books from U.S. Schools in 1993-1994

The 1993-1994 school year saw a record number of efforts to ban books from U.S. schools. This map summarizes the number of such attempts in each state.

Legend:
- 0
- 1-10
- 11-20
- over 20

Source: Parenting (February, 1995), based on information from People for the American Way.

"Prurient" was defined as "material having a tendency to excite lustful thoughts." The Court asserted that "sex and obscenity are not synonymous," however, because equating sex and obscenity might legitimize banning a wide range of artistic, medical, and scientific materials. The *Roth* decision itself involves a number of words not easy to define, such as "lustful" and "prurient." Moreover, how can one decide that something is "utterly without redeeming social importance"? What "community standards" should be followed? Who is

an "average person"? Lower courts quickly found that ruling on whether particular works fit within a definition that includes such vague words was daunting.

The Supreme Court does not provide clear definitions that can serve as workable guidelines for legislators, courts, and attorneys. It invites a flood of litigation, because only it can determine what its own vague guidelines mean. Since it did not do so in *Roth*, many more obscenity cases came before it. Furthermore, the Court's own agreement on the *Roth* definition was short-lived.

From 1967 until 1973, the Court reversed convictions for the dissemination of obscene materials when at least five justices deemed them not obscene. At one point in the struggle to define hard-core pornography, Justice Potter Stewart, with evident frustration, said of obscenity, "I can't define it, but I know it when I see it." The Court then decided obscenity cases on an individual and retroactive basis, which was unsatisfactory for lower courts, prosecuting attorneys, police officers, defense attorneys, the producers of the materials, and the public.

Miller v. California. In 1973 the Supreme Court offered a new definition of obscenity in *Miller v. California* and the companion case *Paris Adult Theatre v. Slaton.* It became the new leading case on the subject but proved little better than its predecessor. The *Miller* definition specifically rejected the standard "utterly without redeeming social value" in favor of a broader standard. The obscenity label could be applied only to a work which, "taken as a whole, appeals to the prurient interest," which depicts or describes sexual conduct in a "patently offensive way," and which, "taken as a whole, lacks serious literary, artistic, political, or scientific value." Second, the Court rejected

An Alabama high school administrator with history textbooks banned in 1981 because advocates of censorship claimed that the books espoused "godless humanism." (AP/Wide World Photos)

the notion of national community standards in favor of local community standards.

Some communities promptly began defining obscenity restrictively. After one Georgia community banned the 1971 film *Carnal Knowledge*, the case reached the Supreme Court. Once again, in *Jenkins v. Georgia* (1974), the Court faced making a decision on a case-by-case basis. The Court held that the film could not be found to appeal to the prurient interest or be found patently offensive under Georgia community standards, thus setting a guideline for the limits of allowable differences in local community standards.

Censorship and prior restraint are so alien to the American system that the Supreme Court has found it virtually impossible to apply censorship in any area. On one hand, the Court acknowledges that adults have a right to be protected from unwanted public obscenity and that children must be protected. On the other, the Court is uncomfortable with any form of prior restraint. Its failure to provide clear standards has led to considerable litigation.

The Broadcast Media. The issue of obscenity becomes still more complicated in electronic broadcasting. While the freedom to express political ideas is well protected, this protection is not as great for the broadcast media as it is for print media. The reason is that radio and television must use broadcast or microwave frequencies which are considered public property. Therefore the owners of radio and television stations must receive a license from the Federal Communications Commission (FCC). The licensing requirement can be viewed as a form of prior restraint. The government does not seek to control news broadcasts or individual broadcasts of artistic, scientific, or medical materials.

Nevertheless, broadcasters, knowing that their lucrative licenses may be revoked or denied renewal, engage in considerable self-censorship, which also occurs in the film industry. Generally, self-censorship has been sufficiently effective that only a few cases of license nonrenewal exist. Some conservative commentators and politicians have argued that this self-censorship does not go far enough. In fact, a sizable minority of citizens are concerned by what they describe as a climate of permissiveness with regard to sex and violence, particularly on television.

Public Live Presentations. Public live presentations fall into the category of assemblies and are therefore subject to the restriction that they must be "peaceable." Since the question of riots or violent behavior is not often at stake, an issue more often debated is the extent to which governments can restrain public live presentations of a sexual nature. Public displays in areas of public traffic, where such presentations might assault the sensibilities of some adults or be viewed by children, are widely prohibited by indecent exposure laws.

The problem is more complex for public live presentations in private businesses or in publicly or privately owned and operated theaters. Those who favor censorship have been most successful in restricting sexually explicit presentations in establishments that sell alcoholic beverages or those in which activities that come close to prostitution can be documented. For other privately owned establishments open exclusively to adults, local governments have generally found it difficult to write statutes or ordinances specific enough to avoid being declared unconstitutionally vague without at the same time being declared unconstitutional for restraining freedom of expression. Even publicly owned and operated theaters have been forced to permit their use by productions that include nudity.

Bibliography

Amey, Lawrence, et al., eds. *Censorship.* 3 vols. Pasadena, Calif.: Salem Press, 1997.

Foerstel, Herbert N. *Banned in the U.S.A.: A Reference Guide to Book Censorship in Schools and Public Libraries.* Westport, Conn.: Greenwood Press, 1994.

————. *Free Expression and Censorship in America: An Encyclopedia.* Westport, Conn.: Greenwood Press, 1997.

Jensen, Carl, and Project Censored. *Twenty Years of Censored News.* New York: Seven Stories Press, 1997.

Stay, Byron L., ed. *Censorship: Opposing Viewpoints.* San Diego, Calif.: Greenhaven Press, 1997.

White, Harry. *Anatomy of Censorship: Why the Censors Have It Wrong.* Lanham, Md.: University Press of America, 1997.

Richard L. Wilson

Checks and Balances

Checks and balances are the principal means by which the U.S. Constitution prevents any one branch of the government from dominating the others. The Constitution divides power in such a way as to require at least two, and occasionally all three, branches of the government to act before anything can be accomplished.

The Framers of the U.S. CONSTITUTION devised a system of SEPARATION OF POWERS in which each form of governmental power is exercised by a separate branch of government. The branches are not fully independent of one another, however. Each has constitutional powers with which it can check and regulate the actions of the others to some extent, thereby helping to balance the overall powers of each branch. Moreover, the members of each branch are selected by different means or constituencies and tend to represent different factions, INTEREST GROUPS, or political ideas.

The Presidency. CONGRESS can be limited by the PRESIDENCY in several ways. Every federal bill or measure passed by Congress that is to have the force of LAW must be presented to the president for consideration. Presidents who do not approve of measures may use their VETO POWER by returning them unsigned to Congress, along with their objections. Presidential vetoes, however, are not final. Congress may still force bills into law by passing them again with two-thirds majorities in each house. This is usually difficult, as presidents have considerable political influence.

A president's ability to make a veto "stick" is one of the indicators used by press and public to judge the presidential administration's political strength. Presidents also have other influential legislative functions. Under the Constitution, they may make formal recommendations to Congress for action; such programs normally have great political weight. Presidents submit NATIONAL BUDGETS to Congress every year, setting legislative agendas for government FUNDING and TAXATION.

Key Terms

EXECUTIVE BRANCH: the presidency and the major departments of the government such as state, defense, treasury, and justice

EXECUTIVE POWER: power to execute or administer the laws passed by the legislature

JUDICIAL BRANCH: federal judiciary, headed by the U.S. Supreme Court, and including courts of appeals, district courts, and a few specialized courts

JUDICIAL POWER: court's power to interpret the law by deciding individual cases

JUDICIAL REVIEW: power of courts to decide whether a statute or executive act is in accordance with the Constitution

LEGISLATIVE BRANCH: the U.S. Congress, which consists of the Senate and House of Representatives

LEGISLATIVE POWER: power to make laws

VETO POWER: president's authority to prevent bills passed by Congress from becoming law unless overridden by a two-thirds vote in each house

President Bill Clinton signs a crime bill in September, 1994, as Vice President Al Gore (behind Clinton), members of Congress, and relatives of crime victims watch. (AP/Wide World Photos)

The president's executive powers also help check the legislative branch. The president may be able to decide how much administrative weight to give to enforcing a law. A program that is not enforced has little influence. Moreover, to the extent that a statute is ambiguous, the president's interpretation of it controls its execution and its meaning in practice. The president can also call Congress into special or emergency session. However, today this constitutional power is little used, because Congress is in session most of the year.

The Supreme Court. The U.S. SUPREME COURT also has significant power over Congress. Lawsuits sometimes raise issues of whether particular laws are constitutional or how they should be interpreted. When such cases arise within the Supreme Court's juris-

diction, the Court has the power to decide on the meaning of the law or to declare it unconstitutional. Although it is not found explicitly in the Constitution, this power—often called the power of JUDICIAL REVIEW—has existed since the Court's decision in *Marbury v. Madison* in 1803. In this landmark case, the Court held that the Constitution is superior to laws made by Congress.

The Supreme Court exercises the same power of judicial review over administrative acts, including some acts of the president. For example, the Court might rule a particular executive action unlawful because it is not authorized by legislation.

Congress and the President. Congress may also limit the president. First, Congress makes the laws and can override the president's veto.

Bound by the laws, the president is charged by the Constitution to "take care that the laws be faithfully executed." Although the president is empowered to execute the laws, the president must also obey them. Thus by making law, Congress can tie the president's hands. A president who violates a statute can be subjected to IMPEACHMENT by the House of Representatives and removed from office if convicted by the Senate. Moreover, the Senate must approve most executive appointments and all treaties. By enacting the budget, Congress controls the expenditure of all government monies and thus may prevent the president from executing particular programs.

Congress and the Courts. Congress has a number of checks against the judiciary, which has been called the weakest, or least dangerous, branch of the government. Persons nominated to be federal judges must be confirmed by Congress. The power to reject judicial nominees was exercised frequently by the Senate during the second half of the twentieth century, often to prevent too sharp a shift in judicial ideology. If Congress dislikes the Court's interpretation of a law, it may alter or clarify the statute. Congress may also initiate constitutional amendments. Congress has power to set the size of the federal court system, including the size of the Supreme Court

Before Republican president Ronald Reagan's nomination of Associate Justice William H. Rehnquist as chief justice could be confirmed, Rehnquist had to go before the Senate Judiciary Committee to answer questions in 1986. Although powerful Democratic members of the committee, such as Edward Kennedy—seen here shaking hands with Rehnquist (right)—opposed Rehnquist's nomination, he was confirmed. (AP/Wide World Photos)

itself. The appellate jurisdiction of the Supreme Court is also subject to Congress's control to some extent. Congress removed certain cases from the Court's jurisdiction for a time after the Civil War. Federal judges, like the president, are subject to impeachment and removal from office.

Presidents also have some powers over the courts. They nominate all federal judges and can attempt to shape future decisions through appointment power. Presidents may pardon people who have been convicted of criminal offenses. Court decisions that interpret statutes may require execution by presidents, and their decisions can affect implementation of the decisions.

The National and State Governments. In a federal system, such as that of the United States, governmental power is divided between the central and STATE GOVERNMENTS.

James Madison wrote that a federal system is a superior form of limited government because power is divided between two governments, each of which has its separate branches. For example, in the United States, state governments have the greatest role in CRIME control, education, and general traffic and safety regulations. Many decisions are made locally, which helps prevent any branch of the federal government from becoming oppressive or tyrannical. The division of powers between the federal and state governments is, therefore, a further implementation of checks and balances.

The Ideal of Limited Government. The roots of the idea of checks and balances lie in the admiration of early American political thinkers for limited government. They had observed European nations in which the divine right of kings was accepted and in which

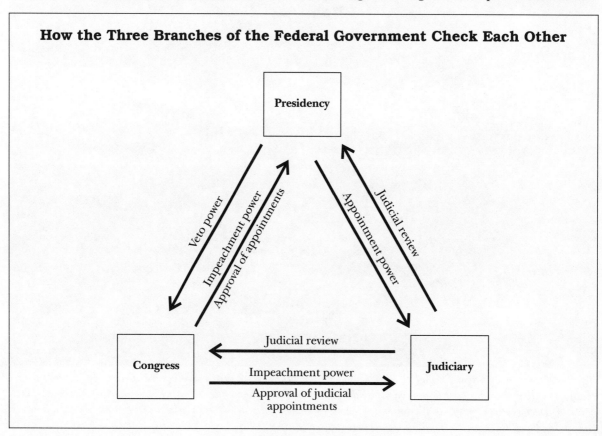

How the Three Branches of the Federal Government Check Each Other

Presidency

Veto power

Impeachment power

Approval of appointments

Judicial review

Appointment power

Judicial review

Impeachment power

Approval of judicial appointments

Congress

Judiciary

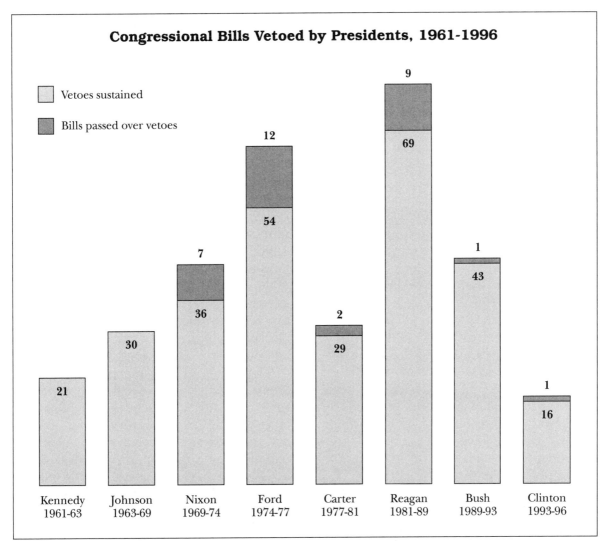

Congressional Bills Vetoed by Presidents, 1961-1996

Vetoes sustained

Bills passed over vetoes

President	Vetoes sustained	Bills passed over vetoes
Kennedy 1961-63	21	
Johnson 1963-69	30	
Nixon 1969-74	36	7
Ford 1974-77	54	12
Carter 1977-81	29	2
Reagan 1981-89	69	9
Bush 1989-93	43	1
Clinton 1993-96	16	1

Source: U.S. Bureau of the Census, *Statistical Abstract of the United States: 1997.* 117th ed. Washington, D.C.: U.S. Government Printing Office, 1997.

subjects had little liberty. Their own heritage was English, but in England a system of rights had developed as well as a partial system of separation of powers. The English tradition of limited government was reflected in the form and powers of many of the colonial governments.

Therefore, even before the AMERICAN REVOLUTION created a new nation needing a new government, the ideal of limited government had taken firm hold in the United States. The theory of individual natural rights and limited government propounded by John Locke inspired the generation of American revolutionary leaders. The Framers of the Constitution sought to limit government, both textually and structurally. The structure they devised incorporated separate governmental branches sharing power by means of the elaborate system of checks and balances set out above. James Madison argued that "unless these departments be so far connected and blended as to give each a constitutional control over the others, the degree of separation which the maxim requires, as essential to a free government, can never in practice be duly maintained."

The limited government established by the Constitution has not always operated to protect minorities or minority opinions; even the Supreme Court acquiesced in state-mandated discrimination in *Plessy v. Ferguson* (1896) and in the internment during World War II of U.S. citizens of Japanese ancestry. Still, in contrast to countries in which brutality and mass murder by government are common, the United States has been successful in restraining political power. Periods of severe repression have been rare and short-lived for the most part. In the United States, most people live out their lives without the fear that the government will unjustly imprison, torture, or kill them.

The great challenge to the political institutions of the United States in the twenty-first century will be to make sure that the system of checks and balances does not paralyze government entirely. There are many veto points or checks within the structure. As public opinion has become more diverse and as special interests have proliferated, positive political action has become harder to achieve.

Bibliography

Edwards, George C., III, and Stephen J. Wayne. *Presidential Leadership: Politics and Policy Making.* 3d ed. New York: St. Martin's Press, 1994.

Lowi, Theodore. *The Personal President: Power Invested, Promise Unfulfilled.* Ithaca, N.Y.: Cornell University Press, 1985.

Panagopoulos, Epaminondas P. *Essays on the History and Meaning of Checks and Balances.* Lanham, Md.: University Press of America, 1985.

Spitzer, Robert J. *The Presidential Veto: Touchstone of the American Presidency.* Albany: State University of New York Press, 1988.

Robert Jacobs

Citizen Movements

Citizen movements are organized efforts by people sharing common goals and values who engage in collective political action to change, or to resist change in, some aspect of society.

Citizen movements form among people dissatisfied with things as they are who want to reform political processes. Such movements appeal to political outsiders. These may include citizens whom the political system has disadvantaged or disenfranchised, or groups whose interests and needs have been neglected. Such movements combine conventional forms of political participation such as voting, INTEREST GROUP pressure, and LOBBYING of elected officials with unconventional political activities such as protests, sit-ins, demonstrations, and rallies.

The Nature of Movements. Citizen movements attract people deeply committed to causes and willing to spend considerable time and resources to try to bring about political and social change. They have been an important means of participation by political outsiders and have had a dramatic impact on politics, particularly in the United States, where they have attracted more followers than in any other democracy. Important movements in American history include the abolitionist movement, the temperance and prohibition movements, the labor movement, the WOMAN SUFFRAGE movement, the CIVIL RIGHTS MOVEMENT, and the Christian Right movement.

Shared values provide the basis for the formation of a movement. People join movements to defend or promote values threatened or ignored by public policy makers. Not every political grievance, however, leads to the formation of a citizen movement. There are always more people upset with conventional politics than movements to represent them. Successful movements are those with enough money, leaders, and organizations to create and sustain them.

Leadership. Citizen movements need effective leaders to persuade people to act on the social and political problems that they perceive. Among the most important leadership qualities are charisma to inspire citizen participation, communication skills to publicize the cause, and organizational ability to raise money. Citizen movements are often associated with the work of dynamic leaders. For example, Martin Luther King, Jr., led the Civil Rights movement; Pat Robertson and Jerry Falwell helped organize the Christian Right movement; and H. Ross Perot founded United We Stand.

Charismatic leaders at the top are important, but movements need hundreds of leaders at local, state, and national levels to keep people involved and convince them that collective action can bring about political change. Leaders often take advantage of existing organizations within the community to mobilize citizen ACTIVISM.

Tactics and Strategies. A citizen movement is a GRASSROOTS phenomenon. Its power comes from the number, commitment, and energy of the people who join the movement. Citizen movements often use unconventional strategies to attract attention to their cause because the changes they desire may be hard to achieve through voting and interest group activity. Until the ratification of the Nineteenth Amendment in 1920, for example, women could not vote, so it was impossible for them to effect change through voting. The woman suffrage movement used rallies and political protests to attract attention. The Civil Rights movement of the 1950's and 1960's used boycotts, sit-ins, and nonviolent CIVIL DISOBEDIENCE to make itself heard.

Conventional political leaders often complain that movements' goals are too uncompromising and their tactics too confrontational. To members of movements, that is precisely the point: They want to draw attention to issues about which they feel strongly. Unconventional tactics are not always popular, but they draw media attention.

During the early 1920's, Jamaican immigrant Marcus Garvey (in plumed hat) organized the first large-scale mass movement of African Americans, the Universal Negro Improvement Association. (AP/Wide World Photos)

Citizen movements rarely rely on unconventional tactics alone. There often are different factions of a movement that advocate different kinds of political action. These factions can threaten a movement's vitality as adherents clash over the issue of strategy. The Civil Rights movement, for example, became fragmented between radical and moderate factions on whether the movement should remain committed to the strategy of nonviolence. The radicals renounced nonviolence while the moderates retained it. Successful movements strike a balance between conventional and unconventional strategies.

Disappearance of Movements. It is hard to sustain the high levels of commitment necessary for effective movements. Members tire of the time and financial dedication that move-

ments demand. Political failure or success can also undermine movements. The Populist movement of the late 1800's, for example, faded away because farmers were unable to win political concessions on the issues they cared most about: changing the monetary standard from gold to silver and getting greater public control over the railroads and banks. Farmers lost enthusiasm for a movement that seemed unable to have a direct impact on politics. The abolitionist movement, by contrast, disappeared with the ratification of the Thirteenth Amendment outlawing slavery in 1865.

Other successful citizen movements are eventually transformed from political outsiders to political insiders. The labor movement changed from a politically militant organization in the 1930's to a moderate and bureau-

Texas senator and balanced-budget advocate Phil Gramm addressing the Christian Coalition in 1995. (AP/Wide World Photos)

In October, 1995, hundreds of thousands of African Americans converged on Washington, D.C., heeding the call of Nation of Islam leader Louis Farrakhan (visible on television screen) for a million men to demonstrate the commitment of black men to building strong families and communities. (AP/Wide World Photos)

cratic group of labor unions by the 1950's. Politically liberal civil rights organizations of the 1970's and 1980's replaced the grassroots insurgency of the movement in the 1950's. This transition from social movement to interest group is on one hand a sign that the movement has gained political status. Civil Rights organizations and labor unions became important factions within the DEMOCRATIC PARTY.

On the other hand, the price of political access for a citizen movement is a loss of urgency and a dampening of the enthusiasm that originally propelled the movement. In the American political system, insiders learn the importance of political compromise, consensus, and moderation—values that the citizen movement originally derided. To get things accomplished, interest groups must moderate

long-term goals in exchange for short-term victories. Citizen movements may endure and continue to have an impact, but in a different political form and using different strategies.

Movements in Democracies. Citizen movements are important for a democracy because they get people involved in politics, raise issues formerly excluded from the policy process, and help make fundamental and dramatic political changes. They are one of the most effective means for political outsiders to enter American politics. These movements encourage meaningful citizen participation and allow people to see the reward for and the value of the U.S. democratic system.

Citizen movements also shake up political institutions. This is important because the checks and balances of the U.S. political system can make it difficult to get anything done at all. Movements bring public attention to issues that policymakers have ignored but that are important to a large number of people. Some of the most significant social and political reforms in America's history—the ending of slavery, citizenship rights for blacks, the right of women to vote, and raising the moral issues of abortion and family values—would not have been possible without citizen movements.

Because citizen movements use unconventional tactics and are politically immoderate, they invite conflict and disrupt American politics and society. Citizen movements have helped to fuel the most divisive crises in American history—the Civil War, the struggle for civil rights, and the battle over abortion. People usually have strong feelings for or against a citizen movement, and it is only natural to question if they do more harm than good for democracy and social order.

Bibliography

Gamson, William. *The Strategy of Social Protest.* 2d ed. Belmont, Calif.: Wadsworth, 1990.

Rochon, Thomas R., and David S. Meyer, eds. *Coalitions and Political Movements: The Lessons of the Nuclear Freeze.* Boulder, Colo.: L. Rienner, 1997.

Stacewicz, Richard. *Winter Soldiers: An Oral History of the Vietnam Veterans Against the War.* New York: Twayne, 1997.

Weil, Frederick D. *Extremism, Protest, Social Movements, and Democracy.* Greenwich, Conn.: JAI, 1996.

J. Christopher Soper

Citizenship

Membership in a political state, citizenship gives persons in representative democracies both rights and responsibilities as active participants within the civil community.

Citizenship is defined as recognition that individual persons are legal members of a state. Thus, national citizenship can be narrowly construed as membership in a country. For example, anyone who is born in the United States is a natural-born citizen with all the privileges of that position. People of foreign birth and citizenship (aliens) may become U.S. citizens by the process of naturalization. Rules for naturalization are spelled out in the U.S. CONSTITUTION. Although rights and responsibilities are implicit in the acceptance or recognition of citizenship, this narrow usage of the term ignores more philosophically significant understandings of the ideal of citizenship.

Ideological Origins. The ideal notion of citizenship extends beyond simple state membership. For centuries, human societies have imbued the concept of citizenship with special meaning: an identity as a part of a group that shares a common heritage, destiny, and country. States and societies are reflections of the people, and the citizen has a special place in the social relationships that integrate the community. For example, recognition as a citizen of ancient Athens gave a person an exclusive place within that society. Citizenship was so important in the ancient Roman state that it was granted as a reward throughout its dominions.

Citizenship grants rights and privileges, but also implies that the state has a right to make certain demands upon the individual. Citizens are tightly controlled in modern authoritarian or autocratic systems. Citizens in those systems are bound to perform duties and provide services, and the real authority in the system comes from the top down. Individual citizens have relatively little control over the demands their rulers make, and citizenship is often restricted to a very few. Only in the evolution of representative and participatory democracies did citizenship develop greater significance and power, especially in the context of twentieth century nationalism.

The examples of ancient Athens and the Roman Republic are instructive because modern society has inherited many of its citizenship ideals from those civilizations. Even so, the ideals were not fully achieved in practice in those societies. Athenian democracy was a form of direct democracy; common citizens participated in active governance and were allowed to participate in the assembly, and many public offices of importance were chosen by lot.

Twentieth century Americans have inherited an ideal concept of citizenship from Rome and Athens, emphasizing empowerment, participation, and selfless obligation to the community, and live in societies where the reality has the potential to approximate more closely the ideal. Citizenship is more significant in representative democracies, because of their inclusive character. Citizenship in twentieth century democracies is based on ancient ideals set in new contexts.

Citizenship gained its full democratic significance as the idea of nationalism grew. Twentieth century nationalism requires that citizens embrace a political identity, based on common ideals, culture, and history, that personally identifies the individual with the state and its society. To be a citizen of a country substantially defines who people are in a personal way, and what they believe about the world around them. Modern democracies expanded on the idea of "rule of the people" in the modern nation-state.

Citizenship in the Modern World. Twentieth century states are complex organizations,

Japanese Americans taking the oath of citizenship in San Francisco in 1954, two years after the federal McCarran-Walter Act lifted restrictions on Asians becoming U.S. citizens. (Pacific Citizen)

with many institutions of government and society that integrate nations over large territories and populations. These complex institutional structures—which usually include standing armies, highly developed police and judicial structures, and many public agencies that manage political, social, and economic affairs—require the participation of the masses of people to work properly. Nation-states have become more expansive because society—including industry, science, education, transportation, and communications—integrates the contributions of millions of people. Representative democracies, such as that of the United States, have had the greatest impact in expanding the idea of citizenship.

In a representative democracy like that of the United States, citizens choose representatives to act as their agents in government. Voters may select individuals to represent them in legislatures, in local governments, or as chief executives. Representative government is necessary because direct democracy would be impossible in large nations with millions of people. Representative democracy is based on rules and laws that allow citizens freely to elect and replace their rulers. Thus, representative democracy has allowed society to expand democratic participation to more people.

Citizenship Rights. CIVIL RIGHTS and CIVIL LIBERTIES are important, but often overlooked, aspects of citizenship. Civil rights and liberties form the basis for the powers of citizenship but are meaningless unless people actively work to make them effective. Although democracy does not force citizens to participate, citizenship in a democracy be-

Nearly ten thousand immigrants were sworn in as U.S. citizens at a mass ceremony attended by Vice President George Bush in Miami, Florida, in 1984. (AP/Wide World Photos)

comes useless unless the citizens are educated and aware of their political world, understand the rules of the system, and take an active part in political life. Thus, citizenship is directly linked to participation. Civil rights—positive acts of government to defend against violation of liberty—will be maintained only when citizens actively exercise their civil liberties.

Citizenship in a representative democracy is empowering and liberating but carries significant responsibilities with it. Citizen participation must go beyond occasional visits to the ballot box to include public service, volunteer activity, involvement in campaigns, and active membership in political groups, associations, and lobbies.

Citizenship Responsibilities. The ideal of the modern citizen has been pivotal in the philosophy behind establishing modern democracies. Leaders of the American Revolution, such as James Madison and Thomas Jefferson, emphasized that public spiritedness and social responsibility were required if democracy were to work. Public service and political education are necessary to develop a responsible citizenry that engages in political affairs and is even willing to die for its country in a national cause.

No modern state can survive for long unless the masses of people are committed to and identify with the common enterprise. Modern states integrate their citizens into their projects either by force or by choice. Representative democracies offer the opportunity for citizenship to be empowering and liberating, and grant the ability for citizenship to be creative and dignifying.

A great danger to democracy emerges when people ignore their responsibilities as citizens. When the public is uninterested in elections and political affairs and is preoccupied with the business of survival or narrow self-interest, citizens in a political democracy are in danger of losing their power. Citizens must empower themselves, and civil rights and liberties will lose their significance if not given constant attention by the people.

A key to the success of democracy is in the education of its citizens. In an age of high-speed information through electronic media, it becomes easy for citizens to believe they are well informed when they may have only the most superficial understanding of their political world from the media. Modern citizens must try to learn about politics and the world, cultivate understanding and tolerance, and analyze events and information critically. Intelligent, well-educated citizens are then responsible to step forward and make themselves heard in the public arena.

Bibliography

Bouvier, Leon F. *Embracing America: A Look at Which Immigrants Become Citizens.* Washington, D.C.: Center for Immigration Studies, 1996.

Center for Civic Education. *We the People: The Citizen and the Constitution.* Calabasas, Calif.: Author, 1995.

Nie, Norman H., Jane Junn, and Kenneth Stehlik-Barry. *Education and Democratic Citizenship in America.* Chicago: University of Chicago Press, 1996.

Rimmerman, Craig A. *The New Citizenship: Unconventional Politics, Activism, and Service.* Boulder, Colo.: Westview Press, 1997.

Smith, Rogers M. *Civic Ideals: Conflicting Visions of Citizenship in U.S. History.* New Haven, Conn.: Yale University Press, 1997.

Anthony R. Brunello

City Government

Municipalities are political subdivisions created by states. Twentieth century U.S. cities are governed by elected mayors and councils, elected commissioners, or elected councils and appointed city managers.

Willie L. Brown, Jr., a former speaker of the California State Assembly, campaigning for mayor of San Francisco in 1995. (Reuters/Lou Dematteis/Archive Photos)

During the American colonial era, municipal (city) governments generally followed the British model of a common council consisting of a mayor, a recorder, and aldermen. In New England, town meetings were widely used in local communities. However, the colonies were primarily rural and agriculture-based. After the Revolutionary War, many cities were governed through a borough system, in which unelected town leaders volunteered to make decisions for the community.

Nineteenth Century City Government. In the 1820's and 1830's, the reforms of Jacksonian democracy led to more nearly universal male suffrage and mass-based political activity, and a new generation of municipal leaders emerged. More formal governmental systems were also created, most notably the mayor-council arrangements. Until the middle of the nineteenth century, councils were dominant and mayors played secondary roles. In the mid-nineteenth century, some cities created independent boards and commissions to perform ADMINISTRATIVE PROCEDURES. These governing structures were dominated by the business interests in the community.

After the Civil War, new factory districts developed in cities, whose populations grew rapidly as immigrants from Europe and migrants from rural areas arrived seeking employment. Cities began to be controlled by politicians who used the political system for personal advancement. In the last quarter of the nineteenth century, political machines evolved in most large cities in the United States. Machine politicians relied on two constituencies, voters and business, to maintain their power. They traded jobs and business contracts for electoral and financial support. Opposition to the corruption and excesses of the machines resulted in a reform movement at the turn of the century.

Twentieth Century Reforms. In 1894 the National Municipal League was organized to reform the corrupt practices of the cities. By the early twentieth century, all large cities were members of the organization. Reforms advocated by this organization included at-large elections (in which all voters vote on all council seats), nonpartisan elections, one-chamber city councils, strong mayoral systems, CIVIL SERVICE appointments for most administrative positions, and home rule (locally written) charters. New forms of urban government began to appear, including the commission system and the city-manager system.

By the 1990's the mayor-council system was the most common form of city government in the United States. Mayor-council systems have independently elected mayors. Their primary responsibility is to implement ordinances passed by councils. Composed of council members or aldermen, councils can range from less than ten to more than forty members.

Types of City Governments. In strong-mayor systems, mayors generally serve four-year terms, prepare city budgets to submit to councils, appoint and remove agency heads, define administrative duties, transfer monies without council approval, and possess a veto power. In weak-mayor systems, mayors have few duties other than presiding over council meetings and attending ceremonial functions.

Council or public boards appoint and supervise department heads. In most mayor-council systems, the distribution of power falls somewhere between these two illustrations. In general, larger cities have stronger mayors.

In the commission form of government the only elected city officials are commissioners. They are normally elected at large on a nonpartisan ballot. Collectively, they perform both policy and legislative functions, including enacting laws and approving budgets. Each commissioner also heads an administrative department. Assignment of departments may be by election or by commission appointment. One of the commissioners serves as mayor. The mayor may be chosen by the people or by the commission; however, the functions of this position are ceremonial. The mayor presides over commission meetings and represents the city at official functions.

Council-manager city governments have elected city councils and mayors. The councils act as the cities' legislatures and appoint professional city managers. Mayors may be elected by the people or selected by councils from their own memberships. Their duties, however, are largely ceremonial. Such mayors have neither veto nor appointment power. City executive functions are performed by the managers, who propose budgets, appoint department heads, and supervise their activities. In theory, councils make policy and city managers execute it. In practice, city managers frequently make policy recommendations to councils. However, they serve at the pleasure of councils.

Systems used by municipalities to elect city council members vary. In the 1990's approximately 13 percent of U.S. cities used a ward system, in which each council member is elected from a geographical subdivision of the municipality. Sixty percent used an at-large system, in which each council member is elected by all the voters in the city and represents the entire city. Approximately 27 per-

How U.S. City Councils Are Elected

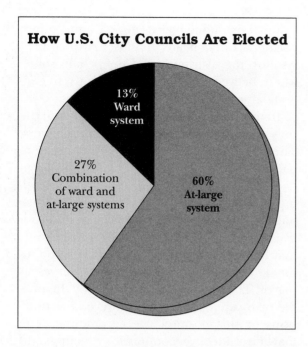

13%
Ward
system

27%
Combination
of ward and
at-large systems

60%
At-large
system

cent of council elections used a combination of ward and at-large systems. Almost three-quarters of municipal elections were nonpartisan; that is, only the candidate's name appeared on the ballot, without party affiliation being identified.

Growth of Urban Populations. When the U.S. CONSTITUTION was adopted in 1789, only 5 percent of Americans lived in urban centers with populations of at least 2,500 residents. Throughout the United States there were only twenty-four such communities at that time. Only New York, Philadelphia, Baltimore, Boston, and Charleston, South Carolina, had populations of more than ten thousand. During the nineteenth century, the growth of urban areas was steady. Between 1820 and 1860, as Europeans came to the United States, city populations rose three times faster than the population as a whole. By 1860 one hundred cities had populations of more than 10,000, and nine had more than 100,000. By the twentieth century, 40 percent of all Americans lived in cities with populations of more than 2,500. By the end of the century, more than 75 percent of Americans lived in urban areas.

City-State Relations. Despite the growing importance of the city in American life, urban areas were limited in their decision-making authority and influence. Cities, generally governed by a business elite, were ignored by rural-dominated state legislatures in the nineteenth century. As immigrants flocked to the cities in the last half of the nineteenth century, restrictions on the city's authority became the rule. Courts have ruled consistently that cities were creations of the states and, as such, have limited authority beyond that granted by the state.

Cities operate under charters granted by their states. Charters define the cities' boundaries, structures, functions, methods of finance, and powers of election and appointment. In general, the larger the city, the greater the discretionary authority. Legally, cities have a status inferior to that of the states that issue their charters. As early as 1819, the U.S. Supreme Court held that states could amend or rescind city charters at will.

Cities also faced obstacles in dealing with rural-dominated state legislatures from the nineteenth century until the mid-1960's. During that era of great urban growth, the heavily populated urban areas were grossly underrepresented in most state legislatures. Many major city problems—from traffic congestion to

Dillon's Rule

In an 1868 court case, the chief justice of Iowa's state supreme court, John F. Dillon, offered what became the definitive interpretation of the relationship between American cities and states. In his decision he described cities as mere tenants at the will of state legislatures. His 1872 treatise on this subject became the defining edict on municipal law in the United States. "Dillon's Rule," as it has since been called, says that any conflicts concerning the powers of the city are to be resolved in favor of the state.

San Francisco's city hall undergoing earthquake repair in late 1997. San Francisco is unusual in having a single government for both city and county functions—a situation partly due to the fact that it occupies the tip of a peninsula and thus borders few other municipalities. (AP/Wide World Photos)

slums—were largely ignored by state legislatures. In 1964 the U.S. Supreme Court ruled that all state legislative houses must be apportioned based on the principle of one person-one vote. Afterward, state legislatures became more responsive to urban needs. In the 1990's cities performed a variety of services including public safety, public works, and parks and recreation. With more than 75 percent of the population of the United States living in cities, they have become central to U.S. political, social, and economic life.

Bibliography

Goldfield, David, and Blaine Brownell. *Urban America: A History*. 2d ed. Boston: Houghton Mifflin, 1990.

Judd, Dennis R., and Todd Swanstrom. *City Politics: Private Power and Public Policy*. New York: HarperCollins, 1994.

Peterson, George E. *Big-City Politics, Governance, and Fiscal Constraints*. Washington, D.C.: Urban Institute Press, 1994.

Pohlmann, Marcus D. *Governing the Postindustrial City*. New York: Longman, 1993.

Shumsky, Neil L. *American Cities: A Collection of Essays*. New York: Garland, 1996.

William V. Moore

Civil Disobedience

Civil disobedience is a form of political activism characterized by intentional violation of the law. Nonviolent disruptive actions, usually based on moral principles, are used to emphasize presumptive injustices.

The fundamental tenet of civil disobedience is purposeful, nonviolent opposition to laws or policies enacted by the state. In the United States, civil disobedience is associated with the intentional disregard for laws or policies enacted by the federal government, individual states, or local municipalities that individuals, groups, or specific populations find objectionable on moral or ethical grounds. Opposition to such laws is demonstrated in a variety of ways—from mainly verbal antagonism to outright disobedience.

Some argue that civil disobedience must involve the willful resistance to laws, statutes, or social norms that are perceived to violate the ethical or moral ideals of certain segments of society. Others perceive civil disobedience to be the right of the individual or group to oppose the authority of the state when the state infringes upon CIVIL LIBERTIES. Still others view civil disobedience and other forms of resistance merely as unlawful activity.

Elements of "Civil Disobedience." By most definitions, civil disobedience fulfills five specific conditions: the action taken by the protagonist is clearly illegal; it is done openly, rather than secretly; it is intended to call attention to a law, policy, or social condition; its intent is to improve the condition or change the law or policy; and the protagonists are willing to suffer the consequences for their acts of defiance. Much attention has been given to the last condition.

For some, civil disobedience requires the protagonist's willingness to endure whatever sanctions are forthcoming from the state for violating the law. Any attempt on the part of the protagonist to avoid sanctions changes the violation from civil disobedience to merely breaking the law. Many people believe that if individuals or groups are found guilty of violating the law, they should suffer the consequences, regardless of their belief that the law is unfair. These people argue that illegal acts perpetrated during student rebellions, civil rights demonstrations, war protests, or anti-abortion activities should culminate in the protagonists being prosecuted despite their claims that the law they broke or social policy they were protesting was unjust.

In some circumstances, the protagonist has

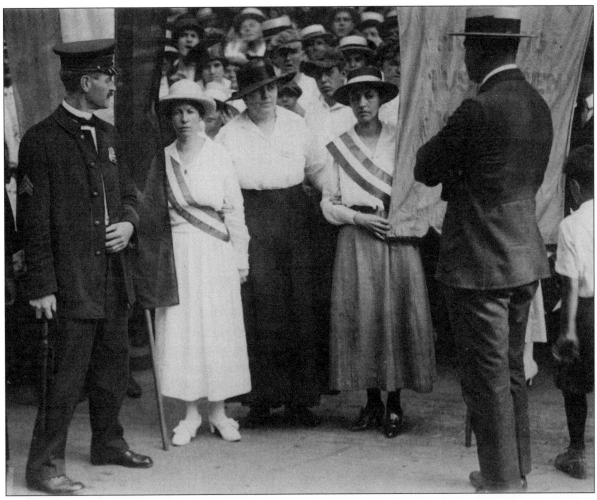

Woman suffragists often defied the law to advance their cause, as when Alice Paul (center) and others were arrested for picketing the White House in 1917. (Library of Congress)

no intention of avoiding the penalty for disobedience. In such instances, civil disobedience may be in consonance with nonviolent resistance and nonviolent direct action. In such cases, the goal may be to raise the level of consciousness regarding what the protagonist believes to be an immoral or unethical law. In other cases, the protagonist's intention is to fight the penalties for disobeying the law in the court system, with the aim of tying up the courts and judicial system, further dramatizing the initial concern. This strategy may be accompanied by the protagonist's insisting on a trial by jury, entailing lengthy litigation.

Civil Disobedience and Nonviolence. Civil disobedience also has been closely tied to the idea of nonviolence. While it has not been exclusively identified with nonviolent resistance, it has come to be seen as a nonviolent mode of protest. Many citizens believe that reform would be beneficial in areas such as social welfare, health care, or the way political campaigns are financed. Many would insist, however, that reforms be pursued without violating the law, and particularly without the use of violence.

Proponents of the view that citizens have the right to disobey unjust laws or policies

Major Events in the History of Civil Disobedience

1849	Henry David Thoreau publishes "Resistance to Civil Government" (later known as "Civil Disobedience").
1906	Mohandas K. Gandhi urges Indians in South Africa to go to jail rather than accept racist policies. This is the beginning of the *satyagraha* strategy.
1919	Gandhi leads nationwide closing of businesses in India to protest discriminatory legislation.
1920-1922	Gandhi leads boycott of courts and councils in India and develops noncooperation strategies.
1928	Gandhi organizes on behalf of indigo workers in Bihar, India, and initiates fasting as a form of *satyagraha*.
1932-1933	Gandhi engages in fasts to protest untouchability.
1942	Gandhi arrested for *satyagraha* activities.
1955	Martin Luther King, Jr., leads boycott of transit company in Montgomery, Alabama.
1956-1960	King leads protest demonstrations throughout the South.
1963	King leads the March on Washington for civil rights.
1965	King leads the "Freedom March" from Selma to Montgomery and organizes voter registration drive.
1968	King initiates a "Poor People's Campaign" but is assassinated before it can be carried out.

argue that it is good to disobey any law that encroaches upon human rights. In such instances, civil disobedience is the organized expression of opposition to an existing evil (the law). Civil disobedience did not create the evil, but directs resistance in a rationalized manner. Accordingly, civil disobedience may provide an organized outlet for opposition that is more acceptable than outright rebellion or some other form of unrestrained resistance.

Civil disobedience has been an invaluable tool for oppressed groups around the world. In most instances, the oppressed group or marginalized population does not have the political power to bring about social change. Violence or physical confrontation would merely legitimize the existing power structure's use of force to eliminate any opposition to the status quo. Civil disobedience through nonviolent direct action—disobeying unjust laws, refusing to carry out some perceived unjust function, or otherwise protesting some policy or law—has in many instances forced the power structure to use alternative methods for dealing with the perceived threat. Civil disobedience draws attention not only to the action itself but also to the reason for disobedience. It is conceivable that the continued existence of a policy or law perceived as unjust or immoral is the result of a lack of awareness or understanding regarding its impact on the powerless or oppressed group.

The Influence of Thoreau. Civil disobedience has a long and storied history in the development of American society. Credit for the birth of civil disobedience in the United States is often given to Henry David Thoreau, the nineteenth century American writer who wrote the essay "Civil Disobedience" in 1846 after being jailed for refusing to pay a Massachusetts poll tax.

Civil disobedience and other forms of nonviolent resistance have proved to be effective tools for effecting social change. It is particularly critical when the protagonists are politically powerless and seek to bring about profound and systemic change. Regardless of the social arrangement in a society, whether the situation involves the suppression of a numerical minority, the suppression of a numerical majority, or the marginalization of an ethnic or religious population, any attempt to effect change through force or physical violence typically results in the oppressed group's being

Mohandas Gandhi

The struggles of India's nationalist leader Mohandas Gandhi (1869-1948) against British colonial regimes in South Africa and India illustrate the potential power of civil disobedience.

While studying law in England, Gandhi became familiar with Henry David Thoreau's views, on which he later built his own nonviolent strategies. From 1893 to 1914, Gandhi fought against discriminatory legislation and mistreatment of Indians in South Africa's Natal Colony. While helping to improve the political, social, and economic conditions of Indians, he developed his moral doctrine of *Satyagraha* and the nonviolent techniques he later used on a vastly larger scale in India.

After World War I, Gandhi returned to India, where he joined the nationalist movement seeking independence from British rule. Using civil disobedience as a nonviolent political tactic to challenge the legitimacy of British sovereignty, he led strikes, boycotts, and nonviolent direct-action strategies. He encouraged fellow Indians to discard foreign clothing in favor of Indian-made garments. Frequently jailed because of his actions, he quietly fasted and repeatedly forced the British to capitulate to many of his demands. More important, he forced the British to respond to Indian nationalist protests nonviolently. After India won its independence in 1947, much of the credit went to Gandhi's insistence on nonviolent civil disobedience.

further oppressed. Civil disobedience allows the protagonist to challenge unjust laws or social conditions without experiencing the full might of the state. Public opinion serves to restrain the state from using undue physical force to terminate nonviolent opposition.

Bibliography
Sharp, Gene. *The Politics of Nonviolent Action.* Boston: Porter Sargent, 1973.
Smith, Michael P., and Kenneth L. Deutsch, eds. *Political Obligation and Civil Disobedience: Readings.* New York: Thomas Y. Crowell, 1972.
Zinn, Howard. *Disobedience and Democracy: Nine Fallacies on Law and Order.* New York: Random House, 1968.
Zwiebach, Burton. *Civility and Disobedience.* Cambridge, England: Cambridge University Press, 1975.

Charles C. Jackson

Civil Law

The division of law, sometimes called "private law," which applies to the rights governing conduct between individuals who use courts for redress is known as civil law. Its goals are compensation in the form of money damages or equitable relief and the restoration of injured parties to their former status.

The major subdivisions of American law are criminal law and civil law. Because CRIME is considered an offense against society, the government initiates criminal actions through the offices of public prosecutors or district attorneys. Criminal law seeks to punish wrongdoers for violating societal rules, generally through imposition of fines or imprisonment. Criminal law also aims to serve as a deterrent to other citizens in society. A premise of the criminal law concerns the presumption of innocence of the accused until proved guilty beyond a reasonable doubt. If that burden is not met, then the accused is released.

Definitions. Civil cases, on the other hand, are primarily brought by private individuals or organizations against persons or entities who have allegedly injured or wronged them. Civil law seeks to compensate the persons initiating lawsuits (plaintiffs) for wrongs through awards of monetary damages or other remedies. In most civil cases, plaintiffs must prove their cases by the preponderance or weight of the evidence—which essentially means merely tipping the scales slightly in the plaintiff's direction. Other civil cases sometimes require proof by clear and convincing evidence, a standard more demanding than preponderance of the evidence but below the burden of proof required in criminal cases. Certain cases (such as battery) are actionable in independent criminal and civil proceedings.

Damages. Civil law awards money damages to right wrongs done to plaintiffs, assuming that the plaintiffs prevail at trial. Damages awardable in a civil case are of four types: compensatory, punitive, nominal, and liquidated. Compensatory damages attempt to compensate the plaintiff for any past, present, or future losses resulting from the defendants' wrongful conduct. In awarding compensatory damages, courts try to put plaintiffs in the same financial position they were in before they were wronged.

Punitive or exemplary damages punish wrongdoers for unconscionable, willful, or wanton conduct. They also are awarded to deter others from similar conduct. Punitive damages are awarded to the plaintiff over and above the compensatory amount. They are additional damages for a civil wrong and are not a substitute for criminal punishment. In order to receive punitive damages, therefore, the plaintiff must prevail at trial.

Nominal damages, generally token sums (such as one dollar), are awarded to vindicate a plaintiff's claim or establish a legal right in cases where no evidence of specific harm exists. Liquidated damages are stipulated in a contract by the parties as the amount to be paid as compensation for loss in the event of a breach.

Equity. Civil law may be subdivided into law and equity. Law, referring to the original COMMON-LAW courts that developed in medieval England, granted money damages according to rigid and strict rules and procedures. Grievances where money was not the remedy sought were brought before a British religious and political leader called a chancellor, sometimes referred to as the "king's conscience." Attempting to mitigate the harshness of strict rules and statutes, equity courts applied flexible principles of fairness and discretion in individual cases. Instead of relying on rules of law to reach decisions, courts of equity use as guidelines in the decision-making process equitable maxims, or short statements containing the gist of equity law.

The dual system of law and equity became part of the American legal system. In fact, until they were merged and integrated in 1938, law and equity courts were completely divided, each having a separate administrative system. Distinctions between the two still exist in principle. The threshold requirement for entering equity is the existence of an incomplete or inadequate remedy at law. Because jury trials are unavailable in equity, a judge acting as chancellor can fashion an appropriate remedy in the case. Among equitable remedies are injunctions, or judicial orders directing another to act or refrain from acting in a certain manner; reformation, used to rectify or reform an agreement to reflect the true intention of the parties; rescission, or cancellation of an agreement because of mistake, duress, fraud, or undue influence; and specific performance, requiring the defendant to fulfill contractual obligations. Mixed actions seeking both common-law and equitable remedies may be brought in one lawsuit, with the legal issues decided by a jury and the equitable issues by a judge/chancellor.

Bibliography

Apple, James G. *A Primer on the Civil-Law System.* Washington, D.C.: Federal Judicial Center, 1995.

Grilliot, Harold J., and Frank A. Schubert. *Introduction to Law and the Legal System.* 5th ed. Boston: Houghton Mifflin, 1992

Kreml, William P. *The Constitutional Divide: The Private and Public Sectors in American Law.* Columbia: University of South Carolina Press, 1997.

Walston-Dunham, Beth. *Introduction to Law.* 2d ed. St. Paul, Minn.: West, 1994.

Marcia J. Weiss

Civil Liberties

Civil liberties are personal freedoms possessed by individuals, such as freedom of speech, protections against arbitrary criminal punishments, and opportunities to own and sell property.

Civil liberties are the personal freedoms that protect members of a state from having their words and actions controlled by their government. The ability of people to speak freely and criticize their own governments depends on the existence of laws and government structures that protect the exercise of such freedoms. The same is also true of people's abilities to practice their religious beliefs freely. Similarly, freedom from arbitrary criminal prosecution and government control over people's property and economic decisions requires mechanisms to prevent governments from having complete control over individuals.

Although citizens of the United States, Canada, and other Western democracies take for granted their entitlement to protected civil liberties, the exercise of individual freedoms depends on two critical factors. First, the historical traditions and political values of a society must favor individualism and the existence of protected liberties. Second, the governing system of a society must contain mechanisms that limit the power of government to interfere in individuals' lives.

Traditional Societies. Not all societies have favored individualism and the existence of protected liberties. In many traditional societies, for example, people had to obey their kings, chiefs, religious leaders, or other authority figures. Such leaders were often presumed to possess divine authority to control the lives of their subjects and to determine what rules were best for the community or nation. Instead of being free to think and speak as they wished, people in such societies risked punishment if they criticized leaders.

Ownership of property and decisions about matters such as appropriate AGRICULTURAL MANAGEMENT activities and commercial transactions are determined by the leaders' rules. In addition, CRIME and punishments might have been defined by the leaders or by religious or other historical traditions. These traditions typically did not include protections for persons accused of crimes against arbitrary prosecutions or excessive punishments.

Modern Societies. Although citizens of modern democracies may view the aforementioned conditions as describing feudal societies, many modern countries embody aspects of these characteristics. In countries in which a single religion is dominant, for example, the people's shared beliefs may place significant authority in the hands of religious leaders who may also control the country's civil government. Religiously based societal values may include the belief that certain behaviors merit punishment by the government. In some societies, definitions of personal freedoms may reflect societal values about the roles of men and women in society, or about the ENTITLEMENTS of certain ethnic or social class groups.

During the 1920's two Italian immigrants, Nicola Sacco and Bartolomeo Vanzetti, became national celebrities when they were convicted of killing guards in a payroll robbery, although evidence against them was weak. Many believed they were prosecuted because of their unpopular anarchistic beliefs, and their trial occurred at a time when civil liberties were not strongly supported by the courts. (AP/Wide World Photos)

For example, men have more freedom than women in some societies. Whether or not based on religion, widely shared beliefs in a society can define which civil liberties, if any, are expected to exist and remain free from interference by authorities.

Communism and Civil Liberties. Alternatively, a dominant political ideology that is accepted by most people within a society can also shape expectations about civil liberties. In formerly communist countries, for example, people were taught to believe that they should act for the benefit of the entire society. Many people in such societies accepted government control over their property and the punishment of persons who criticized government.

Citizens of the United States, Canada, and other Western democracies are taught to value individualism. Individualism, personal autonomy, and freedom to make decisions are at the heart of the political and economic systems in such countries. In the United States, these beliefs were originally shaped by a vision of NATURAL LAW articulated by philosophers whose works influenced the country's Founders. Under their conception of natural law, every human being automatically possesses certain freedoms. Thomas Jefferson enunciated this principle in the DECLARATION OF INDEPENDENCE, which states

> We hold these truths to be self-evident, that all men are created equal, that they are endowed by their Creator with certain unalienable rights, that among these are Life, Liberty, and the pursuit of Happiness.

This characterization of individual freedoms differs greatly from those dominating communist countries and some religiously dominated societies, such as Iran.

Protections of Liberties. Strong values favoring individual liberty are not sufficient by themselves. There must also be mechanisms to protect that liberty. A country may make formal statements about the freedoms its citizens possess, but if no mechanism actually protects those freedoms, they remain merely words on paper.

Countries that seek to define and protect civil liberties confront a difficult paradox: They want to protect individual freedoms from infringement by government, yet government itself is the only entity with sufficient power and authority to protect those freedoms. For example, citizens of a country may desire freedom of speech, rights for accused defendants, and freedom to own and sell property. If a dictator, however, controls their government and uses military force to restrict civil liberties, how will the people's values and expectations be fulfilled? Tolerance of dissent is a key attribute that indicates whether a society's government will accept and support civil liberties. Dictatorial governments based on military power rarely permit opposing viewpoints to be expressed. They limit the exercise of personal liberty by jailing political opponents, usually without the benefit of fair and open trials.

Constitutionalism. The constitutional design and operation of a governing system is an essential element for the existence and protection of civil liberties. Countries can most readily protect civil liberties through a constitutional democracy. Constitutions are fundamental documents that are written to define a government's structure and powers. They can also describe the civil liberties protections to which citizens are entitled. A constitution can both define civil liberties and authorize the governmental powers to limit the opportunities for government to infringe upon the freedoms enjoyed by the citizens. Democracy provides the means to enforce compliance with the constitution. For example, if a democratically elected government violates its fundamental document by limiting freedom of speech that is guaranteed in its constitution, its citizens can vote in new leaders likely to be more responsive to their values.

Constitutional democracy creates favorable conditions for protection of civil liberties but does not automatically ensure them. Significant problems can exist in ensuring the protection of civil liberties for individuals whose views and behavior differ from those of most citizens. Members of minority groups—religious, political, ethnic, or racial—may find it more difficult than other people to speak freely, practice their religions, or receive fair trials if a government directs its policies against them. If most citizens support government repres-

sion of the civil liberties of selected groups, the mechanisms of democracy and citizen voting may fail to bring the government into line with its constitution's principles. For example, AFRICAN AMERICANS long did not receive fair treatment by police and prosecutors, yet the white majority in many states supported this denial of civil liberties.

An additional governmental mechanism that can help to protect civil liberties is separation of powers. If the judicial branch of government is empowered to overrule actions taken by the executive and legislative branches, then at least one governmental voice may exist

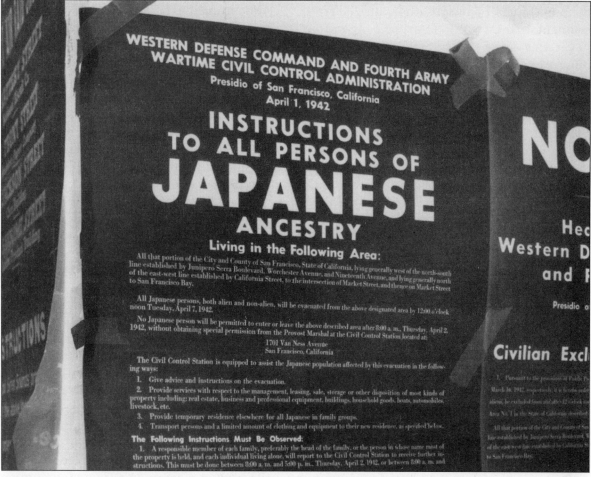

The wartime hysteria following Japan's sudden attack on Pearl Harbor at the end of 1941 left few Americans willing to protest publicly when the federal government suspended the civil liberties of Japanese Americans living along the West Coast by rounding them up and sending them to internment camps for the duration of the war. (National Archives)

First Amendment Controversies

Issue	Reasons to Limit	Reasons Not to Limit
Does the First Amendment protect the right of members of the Native American Church to smoke peyote as part of their religious rituals?	Peyote is a controlled substance. To permit its use might endanger the lives of the user and others.	The free exercise of religion by the Native American Church requires the use of peyote. Freedom of religion should not be infringed.
Does the First Amendment protect the right of art galleries to display publicly artworks that may be considered obscene or offensive?	The First Amendment does not protect pornography or obscenity. If a work is considered offensive by people in the community, it should not be displayed.	Freedom of speech and freedom of the press imply free expression. Art is in the eye of the beholder.
Does the First Amendment protect those who burn the American flag in violation of state laws?	The flag is the country's most important symbol. State governments ought to be allowed to protect it.	Burning the flag is as legitimate an act of protest as speaking out against a government policy. Preventing flag-burning would be banning a form of political expression.
Should schools and public libraries ban books that contain racially offensive terms?	Use of some racial terms is offensive and may lower the self-esteem of minority students.	Censorship restricts the flow of ideas. Students would be prevented from reading literature that was written in a time when such terms were considered more acceptable.
Should the press be allowed to print any government documents?	The press's freedom should be restricted to ensure national security.	Government decisions should be exposed to the will of the people.
Should newspapers and the media be allowed access to participants in a trial before a verdict has been delivered?	Unlimited discussion of trial-related matters in a public forum may infringe upon Fifth Amendment rights to due process.	Matters of public concern should be open for discussion.

to make sure that the other components of government do not unlawfully deprive people of their freedom.

Comparison of the constitutions of the United States and the former Soviet Union shows that a written constitution by itself does not guarantee protection of civil liberties. Basic civil liberties protections for freedom of speech and free exercise of religion were written into both constitutions. Opponents of the Communist Party that governed the Soviet Union, however, were frequently imprisoned

George Orwell's 1949 novel Nineteen Eighty-Four *depicted a grim future world in which civil liberties do not exist.* (Museum of Modern Art, Film Stills Archive)

for criticizing the government, and the government sought to prevent Jews, Christians, Muslims, and others from freely practicing their religious beliefs. The Soviet Constitution contained words that guaranteed civil liberties, but there was no governmental mechanism to enforce these guarantees. Governmental power was consolidated in the hands of the leaders of the dominant political party and no other executive, legislative, or judicial officials could overrule their decisions. Civil liberties existed only as words on paper, and the government did not fulfill its function of upholding all the provisions of its own constitution.

The U.S. Constitution. By contrast, the U.S. CONSTITUTION gives federal judges life tenure and the power to review actions by other branches of government. The justices on the U.S. Supreme Court have used their protected status and genuine power to ensure that Americans enjoy equal opportunities to speak freely, practice their religions, control private property, and receive fair trials without undue interference from government. Historically, however, the judicial branch did not always protect free speech for communists, ensure fair trials for members of racial minority groups, or protect certain other freedoms.

The Supreme Court began regularly to prevent government infringement of various civil liberties during the 1950's. For example, in 1989 the Court clashed with the viewpoints held by most Americans in declaring that political radicals could burn American flags as a means of expressing their political beliefs. Because the justices possessed actual power and secure tenure, they could act to protect the freedom of an unpopular political minority in the face of opposition from the other branches of government and even most citizens.

Protecting Civil Liberties. Governmental protection of civil liberties is regarded as an important priority by citizens and governments in the Western world. Because many of these countries are the dominant economic and military powers of the world, they can assert their desires to protect civil liberties when they interact with other countries. As dominant actors in the United Nations, these countries can have their conceptions of civil liberties and human rights placed in declarations made by the United Nations, the world's largest forum for international interaction and discussion. U.S. declarations often advocate freedom of speech and press, religious liberties, and protections for those accused of crime.

Democratic countries can also make their foreign aid and trade activities contingent on other governments' protection of civil liberties. This pressure is frequently focused specifically on civil liberties issues; however, it carries with it the suggestion that civil liberties could be better protected through the adoption of democratic governing structures and free enterprise economic systems. The United States, for example, regularly pressures other countries to permit freedom of the press and to stop the use of child and prison labor under conditions that are akin to slavery.

Although the values of these powerful democracies have made the protection of civil liberties an issue of international scope, these countries are selective in applying pressure to advance this goal. Countries that have strategic military importance or economic importance, such as oil-producing states, can often maintain beneficial interactions with Western democracies whether or not they share the values and governmental structures that foster protection of individual freedoms. Much to the disappointment of political pressure groups, such as Amnesty International, which advocate the expansion of civil liberties protections throughout the world, governmental commitments to civil liberties are rarely top priorities, even among the constitutional democracies that encourage other countries to follow their example.

Bibliography

Abraham, Henry J., and Barbara A. Perry. *Freedom and the Court: Civil Rights and Liberties in the United States.* 7th ed. New York: Oxford University Press, 1998.

Center for Civic Education. *We the People: The Citizen and the Constitution.* Calabasas, Calif.: Author, 1995.

Cohen, William, and David J. Danelski. *Constitutional Law: Civil Liberty and Individual Rights.* 3d ed. Westbury, N.Y.: Foundation Press, 1994.

Mendelson, Wallace. *The American Constitution and Civil Liberties.* Homewood, Ill.: Dorsey Press, 1981.

Smith, F. LaGard. *ACLU: The Devil's Advocate: The Seduction of Civil Liberties in America.* Colorado Springs, Colo.: Marcon, 1996.

Christopher E. Smith

Civil Procedure

Rules relating to the practice of civil, rather than criminal, law are known as civil procedure. Civil law and civil procedure are intended to ensure that persons involved in lawsuits (litigants) have opportunities to present their claims and defenses before an impartial judicial tribunal and to ensure that such claims and defenses receive fair treatment.

The rules and practices regulating conduct of "civil" (that is, noncriminal) litigation before judicial tribunals form the basis of civil procedure. While many of these rules and practices are codified, some are temporary and informal understandings driven by immediate needs and circumstances.

The Structure of Civil Procedure. Each American state adopts its own unique rules and practices regarding litigation within its courts. Nevertheless, there is great uniformity in the schemes they have adopted. These systems generally parallel the federal scheme contained in the rules of civil procedure that prescribe the rules for the conduct of civil trials in federal district courts. Any discussion of federal procedure thus generally applies to the states as well.

The predominant characteristic of civil litigation is the intervention of the state in resolving what are viewed essentially as private disputes. In Anglo-American practice, the mechanism for doing this is the adversarial method. Under it, parties to litigation have primary responsibility for preparing and presenting their cases to judges and juries. Procedural rules are constructed to facilitate the active role of the parties and to maintain the neutrality of the state.

The central and organizing event in civil litigation is the trial. This is true even though fewer than 6 percent of all cases filed in courts in the United States ever reach the trial stage. The trial is central because it brings all the participants face to face with one another and with the issues at stake.

Pretrial Procedure. Litigation typically begins when the plaintiffs file claims for relief after claiming to have been injured by the unlawful acts of others (the defendants). Court summonses order the defendants to appear and respond to the complaints. Defendants may contest the accuracy of the plaintiffs' stories. Alternatively, they may concede their accuracy, while asserting that the plaintiffs should not obtain relief. Finally, defendants may take no position on the correctness of the plaintiffs' versions of events, while arguing that their cases should not go on because the courts lack the power to hear them. The first position ordinarily is conveyed through an "answer," the second and third through written arguments to the court known as motions.

If the defendants file answers, the parties immediately begin "discovery"—gathering facts. Discovery involves direct communication between the parties (usually through their lawyers) in which they seek documents and take written and oral answers to specific questions that they pose to each other. The court remains in the background, stepping in only when one party asserts that the other is uncooperative and asks it to resolve a dispute.

Much of the high cost of litigation in the United States is associated with the discovery stage. That cost is primarily the result of the long hours spent by lawyers examining documents and taking lengthy depositions to develop the evidence they present at trial. Most defendants prefer to avoid discovery to minimize costs and limit the invasion of their privacy or disclosure of trade or business secrets.

Preliminary motions may raise a variety of procedural defenses to the complaint. In essence, defendants assert that plaintiffs are not entitled to continue with their lawsuits. Defendants may argue that the plaintiffs, although feeling injured, have no legally recognized right, that their claims have not been properly stated, that the courts lack power over them or the subject matter of the lawsuit, or that they have not been properly notified of the suits. Such defenses may raise constitutional questions related to the DUE PROCESS clause of the Fourteenth Amendment or the structure of the judicial power between the federal and state governments.

When preliminary motions are made, judges must resolve the issues raised by the motions. Rulings are always on matters of law and do not involve the truthfulness or untruthfulness of plaintiff assertions.

Trial Procedure. In the American adversarial system, modern trials have been called ritualized combat. The underlying philosophy is that truth emerges when the parties confront each other and parry each other's blows. Plaintiffs begin by calling favorable witnesses and introducing supportive evidence, seeking to prove the defendants' unlawful acts and their own injuries. The defendants seek to undermine the plaintiffs' cases.

Finally, both sides summarize the evidence from their different vantage points and urge the judges and juries to decide in their favor. Juries then deliberate and render verdicts—which usually end the litigation process.

Juries. To reach verdicts, juries weigh evidence and apply the law to the facts. When testimony conflicts, juries must decide whom to believe. Unlike criminal cases, civil cases do not require juries to find guilt beyond a "reasonable doubt" before reaching verdicts.

Judges then enter judgments on the verdicts, unless there is a mistake of law affecting the outcome or a jury makes an obvious mistake. When this happens, judges determine whether to grant new trials or judgments for the opposing sides.

Many people have argued that juries have outlived their usefulness because too many trial outcomes depend on persuading laypersons to reach simple verdicts on sets of highly complex and technical issues. Indeed, the United States is virtually alone in the use of juries in civil trials.

Post-Trial Procedure. Once judgments are entered, losing parties may appeal if they have objected to judicial rulings during, before, or after a trial. If the issue has not been "preserved," it is not subject to appellate review. One exception is where a trial court does not have subject-matter jurisdiction over the case. This exception is important because it goes to the very structure of the United States as a federal union in which the central government has only those powers delegated to it under the Constitution.

Questions of law ordinarily are reviewed *de novo*—that is, on the assumption that the court of appeals is as competent to decide them as was the trial court. There are, however, instances where the applicable law grants the trial court discretion as to what choices it can make under specified situations. In such cases, the review is for "abuse of discretion," which means that the trial court's rulings are given deference and will be overruled only if they

The central goal of civil procedure is to provide a forum in which the cases of competing litigants can be presented fairly and judged by wholly impartial judges or juries. (AP/Wide World Photos)

fall outside the zone of permissible choices available to the trial court. Finally, appellate courts are reluctant to overrule factual findings of a jury or a trial court. Such findings are overruled only where they are "clearly erroneous."

Within the federal system and most states, there is a second tier of appellate review, a "supreme court." No parties have an automatic right to have their civil cases reviewed at this second tier. Typically, the loser in the first tier of appellate review seeks *certiorari* (a request for discretionary review) from the court. The likelihood of obtaining a grant of *certiorari* is generally small. The U.S. Supreme Court grants fewer than one such request in twenty. It generally grants petitions only in cases of exceptional importance to society or if it wishes to provide uniform guidelines or statements of the law where there has been significant disagreement among the lower courts on the interpretation of the law.

Fairness, Justice, and Systemic Values. The main purpose of civil procedure is generally framed in terms of resolving private disputes and of doing justice among the parties. Civil

procedure also involves significant societal interests. These interests range from substantive social norms and values regarding what constitutes justice and fairness to issues of ADMINISTRATIVE PROCEDURES and economic efficiency. They also include the nature of the relationships among the various levels of government in the federal union, as well as relationships among the legislative, executive, and judicial arms of those governments.

The primary role of civil procedure in modern society has been debated. If its purpose is to assure fairness and justice, is the adversarial system the fairest means of reaching that result? Some contend that the purpose of civil procedure has never been to discover the truth of past events, but only to resolve disputes and allow disputants to get on with their lives. Many who hold this view maintain that alternative dispute resolution (ADR) mechanisms, such as professional counseling, formalized negotiation processes, and mediation and conciliation practices, are fairer means of resolving disputes. They further argue, even if one assumes that justice lies in discovering the truth or falseness of a plaintiff's claim and in providing the appropriate relief, the modern adversarial system is an unfair method for doing so. Such persons generally concede that the current system is an improvement over previous ones in that there is less emphasis on lawyers' skills. Nevertheless, procedural rules continue to be complicated and well beyond the mastery of laypersons. Litigants are often forced to settle for unsatisfactory results rather than proceed to trial.

Alternative Dispute Resolution (ADR) Approaches. In response to these criticisms, there has been a movement toward using arbitration, mediation, and conciliation, as well as an encouragement of privately crafted rules and increased experimentation within the courts with simplified rules of procedure.

Some of the most profound changes in civil procedure in recent years have come from the use of the courts by disadvantaged members of society to protect their collective rights. Thus, victims of school segregation, asbestos pollution, securities fraud, and sexual harassment have all employed the "class action" device to obtain collective relief. Rules originally adopted to deal with individualized claims have had to be modified to take these types of claims into account.

Class-action suits may promote administrative efficiency but also raise the issue of the roughness of the justice being done. Are the members of the class receiving fair and adequate representation? Are the individual defendant's procedural protections eroded? Should judges involved in collectivized suits remain passive or become active case managers? There are no simple answers to these questions, and the answers that have been proposed raise additional issues about the nature of the relationship of the state and the court system to individuals and to groups within society.

These issues are further complicated by the fact that much modern litigation is instituted by or against the government, throwing into doubt the capacity of the judicial system to act as an impartial arbiter between similarly placed litigants. In other words, there is a serious question as to whether the same rules can be meaningfully applied both to the private individual or corporation and to the government.

Federalism. Civil procedure has direct implications for the structure and functioning of the federal union. Substantial concerns include such issues as when a state or federal court can assert "personal jurisdiction" over an out-of-state defendant; the distribution of cases between federal and state courts; whose law—federal or state (and if state, which state)—governs actions brought in federal and state courts; and what effect a state or federal court should give to the decisions of another state or federal court. Another issue is the question of when practices within a state court can be said to violate the United States Constitution. The answers to these questions under American civil procedure directly affect the structure, relationship, and character of the federal union, and they remain areas of inquiry, divergent views, and societal manipulation.

Bibliography

Glannon, Joseph W. *Civil Procedure: Examples and Explanations.* 3d ed. New York: Aspen Law & Business, 1997.

Hazard, Geoffrey C., and Michele Taruffo. *American Civil Procedure: An Introduction.* New Haven, Conn.: Yale University Press, 1993.

Kane, Mary K. *Civil Procedure in a Nutshell.* 4th ed. St. Paul, Minn.: West, 1996.

Marcus, Richard L., Martin H. Redish, and Edward F. Sherman. *Civil Procedure: A Modern Approach.* 2d ed. St. Paul, Minn.: West, 1995.

Yeazell, Stephen C. *Civil Procedure.* 4th ed. Boston: Little, Brown, 1996.

Maxwell O. Chibundu

Civil Rights

Narrowly defined, civil rights are affirmative government promises to protect the rights of members of certain groups, such as minorities.

Civil rights and CIVIL LIBERTIES constitute the realm of human individual rights. The terms "civil rights" and "civil liberties" are often used interchangeably; however, civil liberties are usually defined as *negative limits* on government's treatment of private citizens. By contrast, civil rights are usually seen in the United States to be *affirmative obligations* that various levels of government have to protect citizens from discrimination by the government or private citizens. Both are important parts of human rights, particularly for democratic governments, since how well a regime protects its citizens individually is of paramount concern.

Civil Rights in Constitutional History. Civil liberties have a longer and clearer relationship to American government than civil rights. From the nation's founding in 1787 to the Civil War of the early 1860's, constitutional theory protected state governments (and only indirectly their citizens) from federal government power. During this period, the provision considered to be the most important of the BILL OF RIGHTS was the Tenth Amendment: "The powers not delegated to the United States by the constitution, nor prohibited by it to the states are reserved for the states respectively, or to the people."

The argument that the Bill of Rights restrained only the federal government stemmed from the wording of the First Amendment, which begins: "Congress shall make no law." While this phrase was omitted from the other nine amendments, the unwritten assumption was that the word "Congress" should be applied to all ten. It was natural for this assumption to be tested, as it was in *Barron v. Baltimore* (1833). Barron's livelihood came from a wharf that was rendered useless when the city of Baltimore dumped paving debris in the water, raising the bottom of the bay too high near the wharf. To compensate for his losses, Barron sued the city.

Baltimore was a subunit under Maryland State, whose constitution did not provide for the guarantee against such losses as the federal constitution's Fifth Amendment did. Thus, aware that he could not succeed in the Maryland courts, Barron turned to the federal COURTS, only to discover upon reaching the U.S. SUPREME COURT that it regarded the Fifth Amendment as applying only to the federal government. In effect, Barron was told, if the Maryland constitution did not offer him protection, he could not receive it from the federal government. With this decision, the Supreme Court made clear that the first ten amendments to the U.S. Constitution applied only to the federal government and not to the states.

Pre-Civil War views of civil rights showed clearly in the case of *Dred Scott v. Sandford* (1857). Scott was an African American slave sold to a new owner, who took him to a free state and a free territory and then back to a slave state. Since the Constitution's language did not include the word "slavery," it was not clear whether Scott's time in free areas meant that he had become free.

In the highly politically charged pre-Civil War atmosphere, the Supreme Court might well have found that Scott was still a slave on technical grounds. However, it went far beyond that by declaring unconstitutional the Missouri Compromise—an 1820 law that dictated which new states could have slavery. This was the first congressional enactment to be invalidated since 1803. Since the 1820 compromise had prevented a clash between North and South over slavery, the decision had explosive consequences leading to the Civil War. Another critical effect of the *Dred Scott* decision was to reinforce the notion that one had citizenship in one's home state as well as another

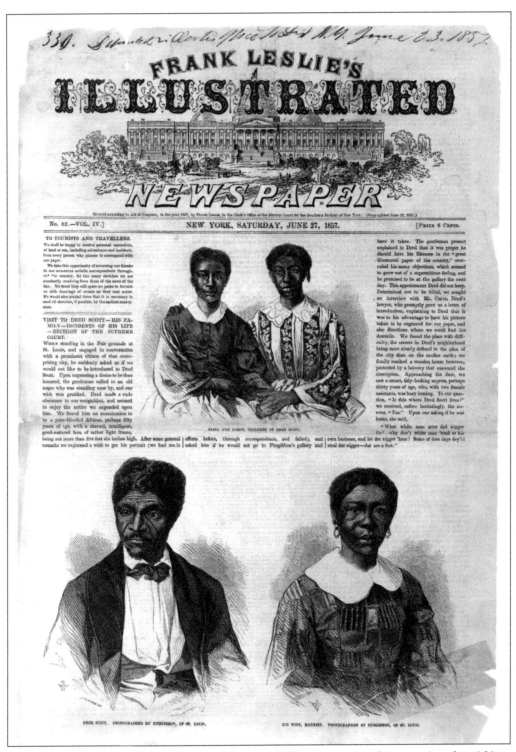

The Supreme Court's ruling against Dred Scott in 1857 was interpreted as meaning that African Americans could not be citizens of the United States—a view later decisively overturned by the Fourteenth Amendment to the U.S. Constitution. (Library of Congress)

set of rights acquired only through that state in the federal government, and that the limits on the federal government did not necessarily apply to the state government.

The Fourteenth Amendment. After the Civil War, Congress sought to insert language into the Constitution that would at least potentially reverse both *Barron* and *Scott.* The Fourteenth Amendment's first section has four parts, the first of which reads, "All persons born or naturalized in the United States, and subject to the jurisdiction thereof, are citizens of the United States and of the State wherein they reside." This first statement sought to undo the notion of citizenship established in *Barron*, whereby persons are primarily considered citizens of the states in which they reside and only secondarily citizens of the United States. The Fourteenth Amendment's language appeared to mean that *all* persons, black and white, were citizens of both the United States and the states in which they lived, and that AFRICAN AMERICANS could not be denied citizenship as they had in southern states. This allowed the

Because of growing public awareness of the importance of civil rights, Americans as far from Southern California as these demonstrators in Seattle, Washington, protested the beating of undocumented Mexican immigrants by police officers in Riverside County, California, in early 1996. (AP/Wide World Photos)

U.S. Constitution to reach through the boundaries of the state to each individual citizen.

The Fourteenth Amendment then stated: "No State shall make or enforce any law which shall abridge the privileges or immunities of citizens of the United States; nor shall any State deprive any person of life, liberty, or property, without DUE PROCESS OF LAW, nor deny to any person within its jurisdiction the equal protection of the laws." From a reading of the "plain meaning of the text," these words would seem to reverse the Court's decision in *Barron* by insisting that in subsequent comparable cases, those who found themselves in situations like Barron's could not be denied their property without due process of law. Once the Fourteenth Amendment had been ratified, it would appear that *Barron* had been overturned by an act of the American people.

The Supreme Court's Response. The Supreme Court, however, did not initially respond as if such were the case. Instead, the court seemed to resurrect the pre-Fourteenth Amendment constitutional understanding. In one important case, hundreds of butchers operating small individual businesses in New Orleans were thrown out of business after a corrupt Louisiana law granted a state monopoly to one butchering company. The small butchers sued, arguing that they had been deprived of their livelihoods by the state without due process of law. In what later seemed a curious decision, the Supreme Court ruled, in what are known as the Slaughterhouse cases (1873) that the Fourteenth Amendment sought only to make African American citizens equal with white citizens and did not affect relationships among white citizens.

A few years later, in the Civil Rights cases (1883), the Supreme Court invalidated the CIVIL RIGHTS ACT of 1875. This law had made it a federal CRIME for public conveyances, hotels, restaurants, or amusement halls to refuse admission to anyone because of race, color, or previous condition of servitude, but the Court found that the Fourteenth Amendment stopped only government discrimination, not that of individuals or businesses.

Separate-but-Equal Doctrine. The Court's outlook was even more damaging to civil rights when it confronted a case of governmental discrimination in *Plessy v. Ferguson* (1896). Homer Plessy, only one-eighth African American in descent, was classified as an African American and was denied the opportunity to ride in the segregated first-class sections of public transportation in Louisiana. He sued on grounds that segregation in public transportation denied him EQUAL PROTECTION OF THE LAWS under the Fourteenth Amendment. The Court ruled, however, that Plessy was provided "equal protection" as long as the state provided him with "equal" facilities, even if the facilities were separate. By this means, the doctrine of "separate but equal" came to be the binding interpretation of the equal protection clause.

The result of these cases was that the late nineteenth century Supreme Court treated the Fourteenth Amendment as if it did not exist for ordinary citizens. If one were a white butcher in New Orleans, one was not covered by the Fourteenth Amendment, because the Court said that the "original intent" of those who proposed the amendment was merely to bring blacks to the level of whites. If one were an African American citizen, one could claim no protection from the amendment if a state provided any kind of remotely comparable separated facilities, even if they were quite unequal in fact. From a current perspective, the Fourteenth Amendment seems not to have provided much protection for U.S. citizens.

Applying the Equal Protection Clause. For nearly sixty years, the Supreme Court did not significantly reverse its opinion; however, it did chip away at *Plessy* around the edges. It had still not gone very far when Earl Warren was named chief justice of the United States in 1953. His leadership enabled the Court to move toward protecting civil rights by applying the equal protection clause. The first decision in this direction was the famous *Brown v. Board of Education* case (1954), which overturned the *Plessy* case by deciding that "separate but equal" was an impossibility because segregated schools were inherently unequal.

In overturning *Plessy*, the Court announced a new JURISPRUDENCE with revolutionary implications. Some legal scholars wrote searching challenges to *Brown*. However, the Court

When the Supreme Court ruled in Brown v. Board of Education *it observed that racially segregated schools were inherently unequal.* (Library of Congress)

won—not simply because it was the highest court in the land but because its interpretation of the Fourteenth Amendment rang truer to the amendment's original language than did earlier views. In fact, segregated schools had not been equal to integrated schools, and the "separate but equal" doctrine had been used fundamentally to discriminate against African Americans by maintaining grossly unequal facilities.

State action was the principal focus toward which *Brown* was directed. Southern states had been taxing all of their citizens, black and white, but had been using that tax revenue to benefit whites far more than blacks. Since African American citizens had no effective way to vote in most southern states, they had no political remedy against discrimination. The states' abusive use of coercive power gave the

Supreme Court its greatest moral justification for ending segregation in schools and other facilities.

Limitations on Court Power. The Supreme Court, the least powerful of American national institutions, must lead largely by persuading citizens that its decisions are correct. American COURTS do have sufficient legitimate strength so that the federal and state executive branches respond to court orders, and individuals who defy the courts find themselves in great difficulty. In *Brown*, however, the Court was seeking not to influence an individual but to persuade large masses of people who had the force of the state on which to counterpoise their power against the courts. Many southern states responded to *Brown* by erecting legal and constitutional barriers against the decision, continuing to use their coercive power to

Signs such as this in a segregated restaurant were common, particularly in the South, before the federal civil rights legislation of the 1960's. (National Archives)

deny African Americans "equal protection." At the same time, they failed to protect African Americans from private racist groups such as the Ku Klux Klan.

Lacking support from the U.S. government's executive and legislative branches, the Court was unable on its own power to achieve the end of segregation. In the decade between the 1954 *Brown* decision and the passage of the Civil Rights Act of 1964, the courts decided case after case striking down discriminatory laws in southern states, a process that was so slow and tedious that only 1 percent of southern students were attending integrated schools by 1964. Only with the passage of the Civil Rights Acts of 1964 and 1965 did all three branches of the federal government begin to act in concert for equal protection. Only when these acts were enforced by a sympathetic presidential administration in the 1960's did the country begin to make real progress toward eliminating the improper use of southern state governmental power.

The problem was big. It was a question of striking down not only a handful of specific laws giving preference to whites over African Americans but also a whole fabric of law that protected privileges acquired over years of discrimination. The U.S. Constitution is designed to protect minorities that already have legal protections. Within the nation as a whole, white southerners became a minority who used the legal system to maintain their previous benefits. While legislation should not be retroactive, the legal system should also benefit citizens equally, or the system's legal legitimacy will erode.

The attempt to redress all the problems caused by segregation was yet more difficult because many discriminatory acts were in the domain of activities long regarded as private and beyond the legitimate scope of government activity. Given their past benefits, citizens could rely on the constitutional and legal structure to resist integration. The Supreme Court could strike down statutes and state constitutional provisions one after the other, but once it had rendered the legal system presumably neutral, schools would still be largely segregated because of private decisions made by citizens without any overt governmental support. This became especially clear in the pattern of segregation in northern schools, which proved to be based on residential housing patterns.

Importance of Government Action. When the Supreme Court found deliberate decisions made by local authorities to maintain school segregation, it struck them down. It could do far less, however, when discrimination was not the result of deliberate governmental action. This, in fact, is what the notion of civil rights entails: affirmative guarantees that the government acts to provide fairness for all individuals. Moreover, other groups besides African Americans claim to have suffered discrimination in the past (no group more obviously so than women) and were not granted equal protection of the laws in the late 1800's, despite their pressing claims at that time. For some groups, such as homosexuals, the case for relief from past discrimination is not so clear. They must advance their claims carefully and persuasively if they are to win the support of a broad segment of fellow Americans.

Bibliography

Ashmore, Harry S. *Civil Rights and Wrongs: A Memoir of Race and Politics, 1944-1996.* Rev. ed. Columbia: University of South Carolina Press, 1997.

Bradley, David, and Shelley Fisher Fishkin, eds. *The Encyclopedia of Civil Rights in America.* 3 vols. Armonk, N.Y.: Sharpe Reference, 1998.

Graham, Hugh D., ed. *Civil Rights in the United States.* University Park: Pennsylvania State University Press, 1994.

Richard L. Wilson

Passage of effective federal civil rights legislation was retarded by the strong opposition of conservative southern politicians, such as South Carolina's Strom Thurmond and Georgia's Norman Talmadge, seen here immediately after both spoke against a civil rights law on the Senate floor in 1957. (AP/Wide World Photos)

Civil Rights Acts

During the years immediately following the Civil War and after a nearly century-long hiatus, the federal government enacted sweeping legislation designed to guarantee equal civil rights to all Americans, and particularly African Americans.

After the Thirteenth Amendment abolished SLAVERY throughout the United States in 1865, most newly free AFRICAN AMERICANS were without property or education, and most white southerners bitterly opposed any fundamental improvement in their CIVIL RIGHTS. Southern state governments responded to their emancipation by passing repressive legislation, known as "black laws," that severely restricted the rights of African Americans. Outraged northern Republicans called for federal intervention to protect African American rights and to assert the northern control over the South they believed their victory in the Civil War had won them.

Civil Rights Act of 1866. In April, 1866, the Republican-dominated Congress overrode President Andrew Johnson's VETO to pass the first federal civil rights act. This law conferred CITIZENSHIP on African Americans. The law enumerated specific rights that were to be guaranteed to African Americans. These included FREEDOM OF CONTRACT, the right to sue and give evidence in court, and full PROPERTY RIGHTS. The law's constitutionality was questionable because it was not clear that Congress

African Americans gathered in the District of Columbia in early 1866 to celebrate the abolition of slavery. (Library of Congress)

was empowered to pass legislation on issues such as citizenship. To ensure that the Civil Rights Act's major provisions would stand up to legal challenges, Congress included them in the Fourteenth Amendment, which was ratified two years later.

Civil Rights Act of 1875. Neither the Civil Rights Act of 1866 nor the CIVIL WAR AMENDMENTS protected African Americans from white southern discrimination and abuse as northern Republicans had hoped. When the white supremacist Ku Klux Klan conducted a wave of terrorism against African Americans and Republicans in the South, Congress responded with the Ku Klux Klan Acts of 1870 and 1871. These laws provided police protection to enforce the rights guaranteed in the Fourteenth and Fifteenth Amendments. In several decisions the U.S. Supreme Court ruled that key parts of the statutes exceeded Congress's constitutional powers.

Congress responded with stronger legislation. In March, 1875, President Ulysses S. Grant signed into law the Civil Rights Act of 1875. This far-reaching act outlawed racial SEGREGATION in public accommodations and made it illegal to exclude African Americans from jury trials. In the Civil Rights cases (1883), however, the Supreme Court struck down most of the 1875 law, holding that the Fourteenth Amendment did not authorize Congress to prohibit dis-

Although President Ulysses S. Grant's administration has generally been considered a failure, he worked to enforce Reconstruction legislation assisting African Americans and signed the Civil Rights Act of 1875. (Library of Congress)

crimination by private individuals. This Court decision virtually ended federal government attempts to protect African Americans from private discrimination for another seven decades.

The Fifteenth Amendment guaranteed the right to vote to all citizens, but its guarantees meant little to African Americans in the South until the passage of federal civil rights laws a century later. (Associated Publishers)

Civil Rights Act of 1957. During the mid-1950's the Civil Rights movement challenged racial segregation and discrimination in many areas of southern life. One area where progress proved slow was voting rights. White intimidation and irregular registration procedures limited electoral participation by African Americans. By 1957 support for voting rights legislation was growing among members of Congress. However, there was strong southern opposition to changing the status quo. It was a Texas senator, however, Lyndon B. Johnson, the Senate majority leader, who took the lead. Using his considerable legislative abilities, Johnson shepherded a new civil rights bill through Congress.

The resulting Civil Rights Act of 1957 created the U.S. Commission on Civil Rights, to investigate civil rights violations. The law raised the Justice Department's Civil Rights Section to the status of a division, headed by an assistant attorney general. It also made it a federal crime to harass those attempting to vote and allowed the ATTORNEY GENERAL OF THE UNITED STATES to initiate proceedings against those violating the law.

The 1957 law's short-term effects were modest. Although the number of African American voters in the South did grow, many impediments to voting remained, especially in the rural South. Many criticized the act's weak enforcement procedures: The Commission on Civil Rights could gather information but could not take action against voting rights violations.

During the early 1960's President John F.

President Dwight D. Eisenhower oversees the swearing in of the first members of the U.S. Commission on Civil Rights in 1958. (Library of Congress)

Kennedy's administration used the law against some of the worst cases of harassment. More important, passage of the act renewed the principle of federal government responsibility for civil rights and called attention to the importance of voting rights in the Civil Rights movement.

Civil Rights Act of 1960. The federal civil rights commission made its first report in 1959. It documented massive denial of African American voting rights in the South and recommended that the president appoint federal voting registrars. This time the administration and Congress responded by enacting a law to have federal courts appoint "referees" to answer voting rights complaints. It was a weak law, which brought about no major changes. It did not challenge discriminatory voting requirements, such as unfairly administered literacy tests. Other provisions of the Civil Rights

Act of 1960 empowered the federal civil rights commission to administer oaths and permit U.S. government property to be used for desegregated schools when facilities for locally desegregated schools are unavailable.

Passage of the Civil Rights Act of 1964. The next major civil rights legislation was proposed by President John F. Kennedy after he confronted Alabama governor George Wallace over the admission of black students to the University of Alabama in June, 1963. Kennedy declared that the bill should be passed "not merely for reasons of economic efficiency, world diplomacy and domestic tranquility— but above all because it is right."

After Kennedy's assassination in late 1963, the new civil rights bill was forcefully advocated by his successor, Lyndon B. Johnson. Its passage was also facilitated by pressure from the growing Civil Rights movement. Passage

The large crowd assembled to watch President Lyndon B. Johnson sign the Civil Rights Act of 1964 included the Reverend Martin Luther King, Jr., who can be seen directly above the president. (National Archives)

finally came after senators voted to end a fili-buster on June 19, 1964—exactly one year after Kennedy had proposed the bill. President Johnson and Senate minority leader Everett M. Dirksen shared credit for its passage. Though long opposed to civil rights legislation, Dirksen implored fellow Republicans to support the bill as "an idea whose time has come."

Provisions of the Civil Rights Act of 1964. In contrast to the civil rights acts that preceded it, the 1964 law attacked segregation on a broad front. Its main provisions appeared in the first seven of its ten titles. Title I, concerned with voting, was intended to create more effective enforcement of the right to vote in federal elections without consideration of color or race. It expedited procedures for settling voting rights suits and mandated that uniform standards be applied to all persons registering to vote. To combat discriminatory use of literacy tests, it defined "literacy" as equivalent to completion of the sixth grade. Finally, it empowered the U.S. attorney general to bring suit if there was a "pattern or practice" of voting discrimination.

Title II forbade discrimination on the basis of race, color, religion, or national origin in places of public accommodation. Privately owned or operated facilities, such as country clubs, were exempted. Title III dealt with public facilities such as municipally owned or state-owned or operated hospitals, libraries, and parks. It authorized the attorney general to bring civil suits to order desegregation of facilities violating the law.

Title IV concerned public education. It authorized the U.S. Office of Education to organize training institutes to prepare school personnel to deal with desegregation; to assist school districts, states, and other political subdivisions in implementing school desegregation plans; and to offer financial assistance to school boards to facilitate their hiring of specialists for in-service training.

Title V reauthorized the U.S. Commission on Civil Rights for four years and gave it additional powers to investigate voting fraud. Title VI required federal agencies offering contracts, grants, or loans to bar discrimination on the grounds of race, color, or national origin from programs they supported financially.

Title VII established a federal right to equal opportunity in employment and created the Equal Employment Opportunity Commission (EEOC) to assist in implementing this right. Employers, employment agencies, and labor unions were required to treat all persons equally, without regard to color, race, religion, sex, or national origin. Equality or nondiscrimination was mandated in all phases of employment, including hiring, firing, promotion, job assignments, and apprenticeship and training.

Civil Rights Act of 1968. Also known as the Fair Housing Act, this law banned racial discrimination in the sale or rental of most types of housing. It also extended most of the protections of the BILL OF RIGHTS to Native Americans

After 1965 the Civil Rights movement turned increasing attention to the North, where it found extensive segregation rooted in residential patterns. The prevalence of segregated housing determined the composition of schools and other aspects of urban life. In 1966 Martin Luther King, Jr.'s Chicago campaign focused national attention on the housing issue. His lack of success there showed that northern resistance to desegregating white neighborhoods would be difficult to overcome. Urban riots in northern and western cities provoked a "white backlash." Many northern whites stopped supporting civil rights reform. In 1966 and 1967 President Lyndon B. Johnson tried and failed to persuade Congress to pass civil rights bills outlawing discrimination in housing.

In 1968 liberal Senate Democrats drafted a new civil rights bill containing a fair housing

President Harry S Truman's meeting with representatives of the National Congress of American Indians in 1946 was a distant prelude to the Indian Bill of Rights contained in the Civil Rights Act of 1968. (Library of Congress)

provision. Heavy lobbying by Clarence Mitchell, of the National Association for the Advancement of Colored People (NAACP), helped to marshal a majority of senators in support of the bill. As with earlier civil rights measures, southern senators attempted to talk the bill to death with a FILIBUSTER.

Provisions of the 1968 Act. The main thrust of the Civil Rights Act of 1968 was to outlaw discrimination on the basis of race, religion, or national origin in the sale and rental of most forms of housing, as well as in the advertising, listing, and financing of housing. Exempted from the act's coverage were single-family houses not listed with realtors and small apartment buildings lived in by the owner. However, shortly after the act became law, the

Supreme Court ruled that the Civil Rights Act of 1866 prohibited racial discrimination in housing and other property transactions.

Two other provisions of the 1968 act also grew out of the racial turmoil of the 1960's. One enumerated specific civil rights whose violations were punishable under federal law. Another sought to make the act more acceptable to the growing number of Americans concerned about urban riots by specifying stiff penalties for inciting or engaging in riots.

As an open-housing measure, the 1968 act proved disappointing. Its enforcement provisions were weak. Those with complaints of discrimination were directed to file them with the Department of Housing and Urban Development (HUD), which was to negotiate voluntary settlements. The federal government was to intervene only in cases displaying clear patterns of past discrimination. Meanwhile, white resentment against attempts to integrate their neighborhoods remained high. Banks often found ways to avoid the law's provisions, making it difficult for African Americans to secure loans.

The Indian Bill of Rights. The Civil Rights Act of 1968 contained another provision unrelated to concerns over fair housing: the Indian Bill of Rights. This was grounded in the fact that Indians on reservations, as members of tribal communities, were not considered to be covered by the Bill of Rights.

The 1968 law extended a variety of constitutional protections to Native Americans concerning the authority of their tribal governments. Among these were freedom of speech and religion, as well as protections for those suspected or accused of crimes. In fact, all or part of the First, Fourth, Fifth, Six, and Eighth Amendments were held to apply to reservation Indians, as was the Fourteenth Amendment's guarantee of due process.

Civil Rights Act of 1991. To many supporters of the Civil Rights movement, the 1980's was a period of disappointment, when earlier gains were threatened by a more conservative political atmosphere. Especially troubling from this viewpoint was the direction taken by the U.S. Supreme Court. In 1989 the Court issued a number of decisions that seemed to endanger past protections against employment discrimination by making the position of voluntary AFFIRMATIVE ACTION programs less secure. Reaction against these decisions made it easier for liberal Democrats to create a bipartisan coalition in Congress to pass a new civil rights bill. Though the administration of President George Bush did not initially support the bill, he did sign it after two years of congressional debate.

The Civil Rights Act of 1991 comprised a series of amendments to Title VII of the Civil Rights Act of 1964. Among its many sections were three important provisions. One sought to overturn the 1989 Supreme Court decision on employment discrimination. The act make it easier for employees to bring discrimination suits. Another provision extended the 1875 Civil Rights Act's ban on racial discrimination in contracts to cover protection from harassment on the job. Finally, the act allowed victims of discrimination to sue for larger monetary damages in cases brought under the 1964 Civil Rights Act and the 1990 Americans with Disabilities Act.

Though rather technical and legalistic in character, the 1991 Civil Rights Act did make it easier for those who considered themselves victims of various types of discrimination to bring their cases to court.

Bibliography

Loevy, Robert D. *The Civil Rights Act of 1964: The Passage of the Law That Ended Racial Segregation.* Albany: State University of New York Press, 1997.

Nieman, Donald G. *Promises to Keep: African Americans and the Constitutional Order, 1776 to the Present.* New York: Oxford University Press, 1991.

Weisbrot, Robert. *Freedom Bound: A History of America's Civil Rights Movement.* New York: Plume, 1991.

Wunder, John R. *"Retained by the People": A History of the American Indians and the Bill of Rights.* New York: Oxford University Press, 1994.

Christopher E. Kent

Civil Rights Movement

This movement sought to bring equality under the law to African Americans. The quest for political equality in the second half of the twentieth century transformed the face of American politics; the pursuit of economic equality has met with greater opposition and had less success.

The modern Civil Rights movement is generally regarded as having begun with a bus boycott in Alabama in 1955. However, the AFRICAN AMERICAN struggle for civil rights has much deeper roots. The founding of the National Association for the Advancement of Colored People (NAACP) in 1909, for example, was an early attempt to organize in the pursuit of civil rights. However, with the exception of a few court victories won by NAACP attorneys, little progress was made in black civil rights after World War II.

Rise of the Civil Rights Movement. On December 1, 1955, a seemingly minor incident in Montgomery, Alabama, transformed the face of the Civil Rights movement. On that day, Rosa Parks, a black seamstress, refused to give up her seat on a Montgomery bus to a white passenger. Her arrest ushered in the modern Civil Rights movement. Led by a newly arrived Baptist minister, the Reverend Martin Luther King, Jr., local African Americans organized one of the most effective boycotts in U.S. history, a boycott of the city's bus system. Almost a year after the boycott began, Montgomery officials reluctantly desegregated the bus system after a decision from the Supreme Court.

King emerged from the bus boycott as a national political figure. In 1957 he and his supporters established the Southern Christian Leadership Conference (SCLC). Combining

Martin Luther King, Jr. (in dark glasses), Stokely Carmichael (center right foreground), and other civil rights protesters link arms as police try to arrest them at a demonstration in Mississippi during the early 1960's. (Schomburg Center for Research in Black Culture, New York Public Library)

James Meredith entering University of Mississippi after winning his legal battle against segregation in 1962. (Library of Congress)

his Christian beliefs with the precepts of non-violent resistance, he led several PROTEST MOVEMENTS against what he called the moral injustices of a segregated society. In 1963 he outlined his views in his famous "Letter from a Birmingham Jail," in which he explained why some laws are inherently unjust. That same year he also led more than 250,000 marchers on Washington, D.C. In 1965 he led one of the last major protests of the Civil Rights movement when he and his supporters marched from Selma to Montgomery, Alabama, to pressure Congress to pass a voting rights bill.

Another significant phase of the Civil Rights movement involved the "sit-ins." Triggered by four black college students seeking service at the "white" lunch counter of the local Woolworth in Greensboro, North Caro-

lina, sit-ins eventually were organized in more than sixty communities. Two months after the sit-in started in Greensboro, the lunch counters were integrated.

Many of the student leaders in the sit-in movement came together in 1960 and established the Student Nonviolent Coordinating Committee (SNCC). SNCC played a major role in voter registration drives throughout the South. By the mid-1960's, tired of the violence against them and the slow pace of change, SNCC became one of the most militant of the civil rights organizations and a key exponent of "black power."

In 1960 the older Congress of Racial Equality (CORE) initiated "Freedom Rides." Thirteen riders—some white, some black—boarded buses in Washington, D.C., on a trip through

A defining moment in the Civil Rights movement occurred when more than a quarter million demonstrators marched on Washington, D.C., and gathered at the Lincoln Memorial on August 28, 1963. (AP/Wide World Photos)

the heart of the deep South. Attacked and viciously beaten by white mobs outside Anniston, Alabama, and in Birmingham, the Freedom Riders focused the attention of the nation on the failure of southern states to protect passengers in interstate travel.

Realizing the difficulties blacks experienced in seeking service in public accommodations such as hotels, restaurants, and theaters, Congress passed the landmark Civil Rights Act of 1964, which made it illegal to discriminate in public accommodations on grounds of "race, color, religion or national origin." Another section of the law banned discrimination in employment and established the Equal Employment Opportunity Commission (EEOC) to enforce the law. The section on employment discrimination established AFFIRMATIVE ACTION, an approach that has been blamed by some for eroding white support for the Civil Rights movement.

The Decline of the Movement. After 1965 the Civil Rights movement declined as its broad base of public support eroded. Many Americans believed that Congress had passed enough CIVIL RIGHTS ACTS to deal with discrimination and it was time to let them work. Another factor was the nationalization of the push for civil rights. Until the mid-1960's the civil rights issue was widely viewed as a southern problem. When the movement moved northward, some white northerners abandoned their support. With the institution of busing for school desegregation and the attempt to integrate housing, many white Americans felt threatened.

Controversy over affirmative action policies also divided support for the movement. To many Americans, affirmative action meant quotas and programs that unfairly threatened their own job security. Another factor was the diffusion of the movement as it was broadened to include discrimination based on age, gender, physical disability, and sexual orientation. Fewer Americans were willing to support what they viewed as special privileges for women, persons with disabilities, and homosexuals than to support civil rights, particularly voting rights, for African Americans.

Widespread urban riots of the late 1960's shattered white support for civil rights. White voters and politicians—President Lyndon B. Johnson among them—felt betrayed by the riots. They thought that the nation was trying to deal with the problems of racism and discrimination. Congress had passed three civil rights laws and one voting rights law within an eight-year period. When the Watts riot in Los Angeles broke out within a week after passage of the Voting Rights Act of 1965, "white backlash" against civil rights essentially brought the movement to a halt.

The riots represented the chasm that still existed between black and white, and they frightened many whites into thinking of "law and order" first and civil rights gains second. On the national scene, the escalating war in Vietnam drew attention away from the Civil Rights movement. When Martin Luther King, Jr., openly opposed the war, he was widely criticized by many civil rights leaders, as well as by President Johnson. In the late 1960's opposition to the Vietnam War displaced the issue of civil rights.

Ideological disputes among black leaders of the movement also led to its collapse. Major disputes arose among civil rights organizations such as the NAACP, SCLC, CORE, and SNCC with respect to tactics and objectives. Younger African Americans, particularly those in SNCC, were dismayed by the slow pace of change and, as a result, favored more militant tactics. The emergence of the Black Power movement in 1966, led by young leaders such as Stokely Carmichael of SNCC, was a direct assault on the approach of King and other moderates.

Accomplishments. The Civil Rights movement forever altered the political landscape of the United States. Perhaps its greatest accomplishment can be seen in the thousands of African Americans who came to hold elective office. The number of black members of Congress was at a record high in the mid-1990's. African Americans have been elected to almost every political office in all areas of the country. The Civil Rights movement also ended the humiliating practice of segregation and abolished the laws which attempted to create two classes of citizens. Finally, the Civil Rights movement created a sense of pride and self-esteem among those who participated in the movement.

Bibliography
Branch, Taylor. *Parting the Waters: America in the King Years, 1954-63.* New York: Simon & Schuster, 1988.
_____. *Pillar of Fire: America in the King Years, 1963-65.* New York: Simon & Schuster, 1998.
Davis, Townsend. *Weary Feet, Rested Souls: A Guided History of the Civil Rights Movement.* New York: W. W. Norton, 1998.
Dent, Thomas C. *Southern Journey: A Return to the Civil Rights Movement.* New York: Willam Morrow, 1997.
Luker, Ralph. *Historical Dictionary of the Civil Rights Movement.* Lanham, Md.: Scarecrow Press, 1997.
Young, Andrew. *An Easy Burden: The Civil Rights Movement and the Transformation of America.* New York: HarperCollins, 1996.

Darryl Paulson

Civil Service

Civil service is government's civilian personnel system. American civil service systems are governed by regulations encouraging personnel decisions to be made on the basis of merit principles, protecting public employees from abuses of political and administrative power, and encouraging fairness and equality of opportunity.

Government civilian workforces are organized in many different ways. Variations generally reflect the cultures and politics of communities or interests of dominant political elites. In most nations, governments are among the largest employers. Government employment is generally based on rules and regulations, but personal or class biases often influence who is hired, what they are paid, and how they rise in the government bureaucracy. Hiring may be based upon social class, wealth, or merit criteria, such as education and job experience.

In less-developed nations, and even in poorer regions of the United States, positions in government agencies are often highly prized because they offer stable employment in unstable economies. Government jobs can offer an opportunity for personal power or influence.

History of Civil Service in the United States. During the early years of the republic, the federal civil service system based hiring decisions on "fitness of character." Government officials were frequently chosen because of their service during the AMERICAN REVOLUTION. Recruiting former military officers with proven loyalty assured support for the new government and its leaders during a time when many in the new nation were not supporters. It also increased the likelihood of recruiting educated persons.

By the early 1800's, as factionalism and partisan competition in national politics increased, a "spoils system" developed: Government jobs were distributed as rewards to friends and political supporters. The administration of President Andrew Jackson is generally identified with the birth of the spoils system, in which competence was less valued than partisan loyalties.

The Reconstruction period following the Civil War saw major national scandals involving elected and appointed officials, a series of economic recessions, and mounting public

A Central American refugee seeking asylum in the United States takes an oath, swearing that the information he has provided is true. Like average American citizens, almost all of his direct dealings with government are with members of the civil service. (United Nations Human Rights Commission)

dissatisfaction with the poor quality of government services. That dissatisfaction, along with the assassination of President James Garfield by an angry job-seeker in 1882 and the fear among Republican officials that their supporters would be forced out of federal jobs after the next election, encouraged passage of the Pendleton Civil Service Act of 1883.

The Pendleton Act created the Civil Service Commission to oversee a federal personnel system based on merit. Initially only a small percentage of federal jobs were covered under civil service regulations, but that percentage expanded in later years, and adoption of merit principles was encouraged in state and local personnel systems. Vestiges of the spoils system still remain in the United States, where new presidents appoint between 2,500 and 5,000

federal officials. State governors, mayors, and other officials make thousands more political appointments. Nevertheless, the vast majority of civil service systems in the United States are merit-based.

Federal Reforms. Because of abuses of power during the Nixon administration and widespread sentiment that the civil service system had become inflexible and unresponsive to executive direction, Congress passed the Civil Service Reform Act of 1978. This act created the Senior Executive Service, the Merit Systems Protection Board, and the Office of Personnel Management. The Senior Executive Service permits presidents greater flexibility to move executive-level administrators from one agency to another and to provide monetary rewards based on perfor-

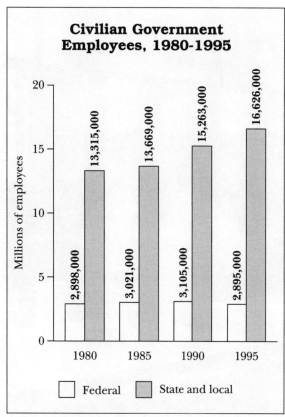

Civilian Government Employees, 1980-1995

Millions of employees

1980: 2,898,000 (Federal), 13,315,000 (State and local)
1985: 3,021,000 (Federal), 13,669,000 (State and local)
1990: 3,105,000 (Federal), 15,263,000 (State and local)
1995: 2,895,000 (Federal), 16,626,000 (State and local)

☐ Federal ■ State and local

Source: U.S. Bureau of the Census, *Statistical Abstract of the United States: 1997.* 117th ed. Washington, D.C.: U.S. Government Printing Office, 1997.

mance. The Merit Systems Protection Board oversees the application of merit principles, and the Office of Personnel Management acts as the executive personnel office in administering the civil service.

Functions of Merit-Based Personnel Systems. Most American civil service systems are based on merit principles. Hiring is based on competitive examinations, with some requiring demonstrations of job-related skills and others consisting primarily of graded application forms with points given for educational attainment, experience, and other qualifications. The names of the applicants demonstrating the necessary skills and competencies are placed on a register or list based on the examination scores. Agency managers are given the names of the top applicants on the register and make their selections after interviewing approved candidates. Promotions and other personnel actions are based upon the same merit principles.

Equity Issues. Civil service systems also are expected to reflect other important social and political values. Equal opportunity regulations help assure that the system represents the population as a whole in terms of the number of women and minorities hired and does not discriminate against those groups or others, such as older workers and workers with disabilities. Equal employment opportunity guidelines assure that recruitment, selection or hiring, promotion, and other personnel actions do not discriminate against persons because of their race, ethnic background, gender, age, or religion.

Civil service systems also typically give special preference to military veterans by adding extra points to their examination scores during hiring and promotion processes and giving them preference during reductions-in-force. Veterans' preference has often been criticized because it tends to give advantage to men in public employment and may be contrary to merit principles. In some civil service systems, veterans' preference is limited to the initial employment or a fixed period of time after leaving military service.

Separate civilian personnel systems are operated by the Federal Bureau of Investigation, the Central Intelligence Agency, and other national security agencies, the Foreign Service in the State Department, and the Foreign Commercial Service in the U.S. Department of Commerce. Typically, state and local governments have separate personnel systems for law enforcement and corrections personnel, health workers, and teachers.

Bibliography

Kettl, Donald F. *Civil Service Reform: Building a Government That Works.* Washington, D.C.: Brookings Institution, 1996.

Maranto, Robert., and David Schultz. *A Short History of the United States Civil Service.* Lanham, Md.: University Press of America, 1991.

United States. Congressional Budget Office. *Reducing the Size of the Federal Civilian Work Force.* Washington, D.C.: Congress of the U.S., 1993.

William L. Waugh, Jr.

Civil War Amendments

Collectively known as the Civil War Amendments, the Thirteenth, Fourteenth, and Fifteenth Amendments to the U.S. Constitution ended slavery, established the principle of equality before the law for American citizens, defined citizenship for all persons born in the United States, and prohibited racial discrimination in voting.

The Civil War (1861-1865) and its aftermath made up one of the greatest periods of change in American history. The end of SLAVERY and the need to define the legal position of former slaves led to three constitutional amendments that introduced the concept of equality to the Constitution and permanently altered the face of American justice and the constitutional order.

Thirteenth Amendment. During the Civil War, the abolition of slavery became a war aim of the U.S. government. President Abraham Lincoln's Emancipation Proclamation (1863) declared slaves in areas still in rebellion against the United States to be free and signaled that a Union victory would mean the end of slavery. As the war ended, concern grew over the proclamation's constitutionality and the continued existence of slavery in areas it did not cover. Congressional Republicans determined to seek a constitutional amendment

---

The Thirteenth Amendment

Section 1. Neither slavery nor involuntary servitude, except as a punishment for crime whereof the party shall have been duly convicted, shall exist within the United States, or any place subject to their jurisdiction.... (*Ratified 1865*)

The Fourteenth Amendment

Section 1. All persons born or naturalized in the United States and subject to the jurisdiction thereof, are citizens of the United States and of the State wherein they reside. No State shall make or enforce any law which shall abridge the privileges or immunities of citizens of the United States; nor shall any State deprive any person of life, liberty, or property, without due process of law; nor deny to any person within its jurisdiction the equal protection of the laws.

Section 2. Representatives shall be apportioned among the several States according to their respective numbers, counting the whole number of persons in each State, excluding

Indians not taxed. But when the right to vote at any election for the choice of electors for President and Vice President of the United States, Representatives in Congress, the Executive and Judicial officers of a State, or the members of the Legislature thereof, is denied to any of the male inhabitants of such State, being twenty-one years of age, and citizens of the United States, or in any way abridged, except for participation in rebellion, or other crime, the basis of representation therein shall be reduced in the proportion which the number of such male citizens shall bear to the whole number of male citizens twenty-one years of age in such State.... (*Ratified 1868*)

The Fifteenth Amendment

Section 1. The right of citizens of the United States to vote shall not be denied or abridged by the United States or by any State on account of race, color, or previous condition of servitude.... (*Ratified 1870*)

Abraham Lincoln's issuance of the Emancipation Proclamation in early 1863 began the process of ending slavery within the United States that was completed with passage of the Thirteenth Amendment in 1865. (Library of Congress)

Many African Americans used the freedom given to them by the Thirteenth Amendment to emigrate out of the South. (Library of Congress)

that would abolish slavery everywhere in the country. The amendment cleared Congress in the spring of 1865 and was ratified at the end of the year. It ended legal American slavery forever.

Fourteenth Amendment. Concern over the status and treatment of former slaves soon led to another amendment. Despite the CIVIL RIGHTS ACT of 1866, many former slaves found their freedom limited by "black codes" passed by southern state legislatures. Republicans of abolitionist background determined to define the status of AFRICAN AMERICANS in terms of legal equality: As they saw it, the Constitution needed to be brought into line with the Declaration of Independence. After a stiff battle in Congress, the Fourteenth Amendment emerged in 1866. Its ratification was made a condition of readmission for for-

mer Confederate states, and it completed the ratification process in 1868.

The Fourteenth Amendment's first section provided the first constitutional definition of American citizenship: all persons born or naturalized in the United States and subject to its jurisdiction. This overturned the Supreme Court decision in *Dred Scott v. Sandford* (1857), which held that African Americans were not citizens even if free.

The Fourteenth Amendment further provided that states might not abridge the "privileges and immunities" of citizens, deprive them of life, liberty, or property without DUE PROCESS OF LAW, or deny them the "equal protection of the laws." The last clause marked the first time that equality before the law was written into the Constitution. Most of the rest of the amendment dealt with post-Civil War concerns that gradually faded in importance. For example, it prohibited government funding of the Confederate war debt.

Interpreting the Fourteenth Amendment. Defining and implementing the amendment's simple language proved a complicated and lengthy process. In the short term, the amendment disappointed those who hoped it would set the rights of African Americans on a firm basis of equality. One reason for this was the Supreme Court's lack of sympathy. In the Slaughterhouse cases of 1873, the Court drastically limited the amendment's scope by ruling that most of the important privileges and immunities were those bestowed by state, rather than federal, citizenship. This opened the door for states and individuals to discriminate against members of minorities. By 1896, when the Court decided the case of *Plessy v. Ferguson*, it found nothing wrong with states requiring the separation of the races, so long as efforts at "equal" treatment were made.

While the Fourteenth Amendment was being limited in its impact on civil rights, the Supreme Court employed it to protect the operations of big business. Corporations were declared "persons" within the meaning of the amendment, and states were increasingly limited as to what steps they might take to regulate them.

It was only in the mid-twentieth century that the Fourteenth Amendment was revived to fulfill something like its original purpose. For decades the National Association for the Advancement of Colored People (NAACP) fought in the courts to challenge racial discrimination and make the Fourteenth Amendment a force in American life. It initially succeeded only in minor improvements in the facilities provided for blacks under the separate-but-equal doctrine.

In 1954 the NAACP finally scored a stunning victory in *Brown v. Board of Education*, when the Supreme Court used the equal protection clause of the Fourteenth Amendment to rule that segregated schools—and by implication other institutions and facilities—were inherently inferior and thus unconstitutional. Similar interpretations of the Fourteenth Amendment would underpin other important civil rights decisions in the second half of the twentieth century.

Incorporation Doctrine. By the time of the *Brown* decision, the Fourteenth Amendment had become vitally important to American justice in another way: as a means of utilizing the BILL OF RIGHTS as a restraint on the states. A major breakthrough came in the 1925 case of *Gitlow v. New York*. Here the Supreme Court decided that the Fourteenth Amendment did "incorporate" the First Amendment's protection of free speech against violation by state government.

Although the Court held back from endorsing the idea that the entire Bill of Rights was incorporated in the Fourteenth Amendment, it did begin the gradual extension of specific rights to the states through the process known as the INCORPORATION DOCTRINE. This process gathered speed under Chief Justice Earl Warren, between 1953 and 1969. Recognition that individual rights were protected against state action by the Fourteenth Amendment began having a major impact on the administration of American justice.

Fifteenth Amendment. The question of whether African Americans should be allowed to vote on the same basis as whites was approached indirectly by the section of the Fourteenth Amendment that provided for a state's congressional representation to be reduced proportionately if it denied the vote to any segment of its adult males. By the late 1860's, many congressional Republicans favored more forceful protection for black voters. While the former Confederate states were required to write black suffrage into their state constitutions as a condition of readmittance to the Union, it was always possible that such provisions could be altered in the future.

There were also pressing political considerations. Democratic Party strength was reviving, and seventeen states still denied African Americans the vote. Enfranchising blacks in the border, midwestern, and western states became a matter of crucial importance to Republicans.

The Fifteenth Amendment was originally proposed as a positive statement of manhood suffrage, with protections against states requiring property qualifications or literacy tests. In order to secure passage by the necessary two-thirds majority in the House of Representatives, however, the amendment's sponsors had to compromise. The amendment emerged with negative wording: States could not *deny* the right to vote based on race. In this form, the amendment was ratified in 1870.

The history of the Fifteenth Amendment ran generally parallel to that of the Fourteenth: short-term disappointment followed by mid-twentieth century revival. By the 1890's southern and border states were finding ways around the amendment. Its wording implied that the right to vote could be denied on a basis other than race, and such pretexts were developed with a decidedly negative effect on black voting rights. Literacy tests, poll taxes, and all-white primary elections were used to deny African Americans the vote.

Not until 1944 did the Supreme Court rule white primaries in violation of the Fifteenth Amendment, in *Smith v. Allwright.* In 1964 the Twenty-fourth Amendment prohibited the poll tax in federal elections. The most effective revitalization of the Fifteenth Amendment's original purpose came with passage of the Voting Rights Act of 1965.

The Civil War Amendments have had a major impact on the Constitution. They offered the possibility of intervention by the federal government to protect citizens from

African Americans march in New York City in early 1870 to celebrate ratification of the Fifteenth Amendment. (Library of Congress)

unconstitutional abuse by a state or even private individuals. Moreover, the Fourteenth Amendment expressly incorporated the concept of equality into the Constitution.

Bibliography

Berger, Raoul. *The Fourteenth Amendment and the Bill of Rights.* Oklahoma City: University of Oklahoma Press, 1989.

Gillette, William. *The Right to Vote: Politics and the Passage of the Fifteenth Amendment.* Baltimore: The Johns Hopkins University Press, 1969.

Maltz, Earl M. *Civil Rights, the Constitution, and Congress, 1863-1869.* Lawrence: University Press of Kansas, 1990.

Nelson, William E. *The Fourteenth Amendment: From Political Principle to Judicial Doctrine.* Cambridge, Mass.: Harvard University Press, 1988.

William C. Lowe

Commerce Regulation

Government regulates commerce to protect consumers against fraud and monopoly, to protect sellers against unfair competition, and to raise revenue for itself.

To a great extent the economic well-being of a society depends on buying and selling goods. Economic productivity in developed economic systems rests on specialization. Business firms focus on certain products and processes, enabling them to develop highly specialized technology and equipment. Specialization is necessary for efficiency, but cannot benefit the public unless there is effective exchange of the resulting goods and services. Government advances favorable environments for commerce by maintaining law and order. Buying and selling operations work best when free from force and fraud.

Commerce is also a vital area from which to collect taxes. The U.S. government levied its earliest taxes on goods imported from overseas (the U.S. Constitution forbids taxing exports), soon following with excise taxes on alcohol and tobacco products. Since taxing items tends to reduce their consumption, there is a regulatory dimension to such taxes.

Governments are likely to impose outright prohibitions against goods and services deemed harmful. Between 1919 and 1933, for example, the federal government attempted to prohibit the production and sale of alcoholic beverages, without notable success. During the early 1990's, the most prominent contraband goods were addictive drugs, such as marijuana and cocaine. Traditional prohibitions against other vices, such as prostitution, pornography, and gambling, were losing much of their vigor and public support.

Governments often regulate commercial activities by requiring licenses, franchises, or permits to engage in them. This is usually defended as a method of quality control. Com-

---

Key Terms

COMMERCE: buying and selling of goods and services, primarily those currently produced

CONTRACT: legally binding agreement to do something, usually in exchange for something of value

EXCISE TAX: tax levied on production or sale of a product

FRANCHISE: grant of permission to enter some activity from which the general public is barred

NATURAL MONOPOLY: type of production for which efficiency seems to be best achieved if there is only one producer

PRICE DISCRIMINATION: charging different prices to different buyers in situations where there is no comparable difference in the cost of supplying the different buyers

Cash seized by federal agents in a 1990 cocaine drug bust. (AP/Wide World Photos)

panies providing electric power, telephone or cable television service, and other public utilities have been franchised because they were thought to be natural monopolies, that is, services for which it is inefficient to have many firms operating in one area. Public utilities have been subjected to direct government control of their rates and service.

Government Agencies. Government often regulates commerce through specialized administrative boards or commissions. Most states have one or more commissions that regulate public utilities and others that regulate banks and financial institutions. An important role for government regulatory agencies is inspection and examination of private firms. Operations involving food sale and preparation, for example, are subject to sanitary inspection. State and local governments commonly have agencies concerned with establishments that sell and serve alcoholic drinks.

Governments also influence commerce through promotional activity. The U.S. Department of Commerce conducts many activities designed to help business firms, in part through collecting and publishing business information. State and local governments have agencies that try to attract businesses to locate within their borders. More generally, governments assist commerce by providing a stable and unified monetary system, a suitable system of weights and measures, and such infrastructure facilities as highways and airports.

History of U.S. Commerce Regulation. The history of American commerce regulation has

In 1991 the Federal Deposit Insurance Corporation (FDIC) closed several Boston banks and seized their assets in order to protect the interests of depositors. (AP/Wide World Photos)

been closely bound up with the U.S. CONSTITUTION. The Constitution directly authorized Congress to regulate commerce with foreign countries, among the states, and with Native American tribes. States were forbidden to regulate interstate commerce, except as needed for their inspection laws. Regulation of intrastate commerce was among the implied powers left to the individual states by the Tenth Amendment. Closely related to commerce were Congress's powers to create money and regulate its value, punish counterfeiting, set rules for bankruptcy, and provide a postal service. State governments were forbidden to take actions that would impair private contracts, issue paper money, or make anything except gold or silver legal tender.

In the early days of the new republic, state and local governments maintained traditional forms of licensing, inspection, and regulation. These faded away as economic growth and free-enterprise ideology became dominant in the nineteenth century. The federal government undertook no significant regulation of interstate buying and selling of goods until after the Civil War ended in 1865.

As the farm sector experienced economic distress in the postwar deflation, a new sentiment for regulation arose. It focused initially on railroads, spread toward trusts and monopolies in general, and took particular aim at public utilities. In each instance, the problem was perceived to be monopoly, leading to high prices and discriminatory treatment of different customers. Individual state governments tried to regulate railroad rates through the Granger laws of the 1870's. In 1886 the U.S. Supreme Court struck down a state regulation involving interstate shipments. The federal government created the federal Interstate Commerce Commission (ICC) the following year. Initially, the ICC was empowered to require railroads to publish their rates and refrain from unfair discrimination. In 1906 the ICC received explicit authority to set rates.

Antitrust Laws. Congress confronted the issue of business monopoly directly when it passed the Sherman Antitrust Act in 1890. This antitrust law outlawed contracts and conspiracies in restraint of trade or commerce as well as actions to monopolize or attempt to monopolize any part of that trade or commerce. An early case against the sugar trust was dismissed by the courts on grounds that it was directed against manufacturing, rather than commerce. This distinction was soon swept away by the doctrine that monopoly in manufacturing would produce monopoly in commerce as well. The Sherman Act did not prevent a wave of corporate mergers and consolidations, including the formation of the world's largest corporation of its time, United States Steel, in 1901.

With the spirit of reform associated with the Progressive movement, federal regulatory programs expanded after 1900. The Pure Food and Drug Act was passed in 1906. In 1914 the Clayton Act attempted to extend the Sherman Antitrust Act by adding restrictions on price discrimination, interlocking directorships, binding and exclusive dealing contracts, and mergers. That same year the Federal Trade Commission (FTC) was created with authority to enforce the Clayton Act and a prohibition against unfair methods of competition.

World War I led to vast temporary extensions of government regulatory authority. The Lever Food Control Act of 1917 was the principal instrument. Government price controls were put into effect, and direct controls were imposed on businesses vital to national defense and economic strength. The federal government took over direct management of the railroads and telegraph system. These programs were rapidly reversed when the war ended in 1918. Efforts to improve labor standards by direct regulation were also removed. The Supreme Court ruled the federal Child Labor Law of 1916 unconstitutional, because it went beyond the bounds of interstate commerce.

The Great Depression of the 1930's radically altered the regulatory atmosphere. When Franklin D. Roosevelt was inaugurated president in 1933, a quarter of the national labor force was unemployed and the nation's banking system was in shambles. Many of Roosevelt's advisers, unlike other contemporaneous thinkers, believed that the Depression resulted from excessive competition. As a result, major New Deal policies attempted to promote recovery by encouraging producers to group together to reduce competition. In 1933 Congress adopted the first Agricultural Adjustment Act, which provided incentives for farmers to reduce output in order to receive higher prices. In 1935 the Supreme Court invalidated the program as going beyond the scope of interstate commerce. This was the last notable example of judicial opposition to an expanded role for federal economic regulation, however. After 1937 court decisions no longer impeded the regulatory trend.

Labor Law. In the National Labor Relations (Wagner) Act of 1935, federal authority was placed squarely behind the promotion and encouragement of labor unions. The law forbade various antiunion activities by employers and created the National Labor Relations Board to conduct elections for workers to decide if they wanted union representation. In 1937 the Supreme Court acquiesced. The Fair Labor Standards Act of 1938 established minimum wage and maximum hours regulations for interstate commerce; the Supreme Court sustained the law in 1941. A new Agricultural Adjustment Act was adopted in 1938. Even though it went so far as to dictate what individual farmers could grow on their own land, it was upheld by the Supreme Court in 1942. By that year the role of regulating commerce had been extended from the buying and selling of goods to all types of production and employment.

World War II brought vastly extended federal regulation. Price and wage controls were imposed. Products such as gasoline and sugar were rationed. Business firms were told what they could or could not produce. As before, these regulations were removed after the war, but some were temporarily restored during the Korean War (1950-1953). The Taft-Hartley Act of 1947 prohibited some unfair labor practices by labor unions. Effective restraint on big-business mergers was enacted in the Celler-Kefauver Anti-Merger Act of 1950.

Commerce in medical goods and services was gradually brought under extensive government regulation after the creation of Medicare and Medicaid in 1965. New domains of regulation came in 1970 with the creation of the federal Environmental Protection Agency (EPA) and Occupational Safety and Health Administration (OSHA). During the presidency of Jimmy Carter deregulation decreased the federal control of prices and entry in such sectors as railroads, natural gas, highway and air transport, and banking.

Bibliography

Hughes, Jonathan. *The Governmental Habit Redux: Economic Controls from Colonial Times to the Present.* 2d ed. Princeton, N. J.: Princeton University Press, 1991.

Nowotny, Kenneth, David B. Smith, and Harry M. Trebing, eds. *Public Utility Regulation: The Economic and Social Control of Industry.* Boston: Kluwer, 1989.

Rockoff, Hugh. *Drastic Measures: A History of Wage and Price Controls in the United States.* New York: Cambridge University Press, 1984.

Rosenberg, Jerry M. *Encyclopedia of the North American Free Trade Agreement, the New American Community, and Latin-American Trade.* Westport, Conn.: Greenwood Press, 1995.

Paul B. Trescott

Common Law

Common law comprises principles of law long established in customary behavior and based on cumulative court decisions. American law, with its roots in English law, is based as much on common-law practice and previous court decisions as on statutory law.

Originating in the ancient unwritten law of England, American common law drew on the case-law backgrounds of both England and the North American colonies before the AMERICAN REVOLUTION. The authority for the common law is the customary and accepted practices of the English courts and political institutions from centuries ago, sometimes referred to as the "English constitution." In other words, the courts, in the Anglo-American political system, have been more significant in establishing law than in countries using the "Roman law" system of completely codified law.

Sources of the Common Law. England's early Anglo-Saxons had a legal system similar to that of ancient Israel. It was decentralized and related to extended families. The legal code of King Alfred the Great was biblical in nature, beginning with the Ten Commandments and other parts of the Mosaic law. The Danes and the Norwegians also held part of England and thus influenced the English common law with Viking law, or "Danelaw" as it was sometimes called. The highly individualistic nature of Danelaw is reflected in the Magna Carta and later in American institutions. In the common law, JUSTICE comes before power. Monarchs had the power to control and rule but not the right to do so without justice. That was the basis of the English common law.

Though even they professed a belief in the English common law, England's Tudor rulers believed in unlimited royal power under the concept of *Rex Lex*, meaning "The King is Law." The Protestant Reformation in seven-

teenth century England changed that concept to *Lex Rex*, meaning "The Law is King." After the English Revolution of 1642, the rulers also had to be subject to, and limited by, statutory law. England's Glorious Revolution of 1688 further limited royal powers by insisting that the king's powers be shared with elected parliaments.

Common Law in the United States. The American Revolution built on this foundation, and the concept of popular-based, shared, representative government was taken a step further in the U.S. CONSTITUTION. The basic ideas of the Constitution are that government is limited in its powers, and authority must be shared among various parts of the political system. In the American system, law consists of constitutional law, statutory law, and the common law based on judicial precedent. It is a shared power system: shared between the states and the national government, shared within each level of government, and even shared within the types of law argued at various levels of the judiciary.

Americans have looked to the common law as well as to the U.S. BILL OF RIGHTS for protection of their basic rights, but they modified tradition for American use. The land laws in England, for example, were feudal in nature and origin. In the United States, land was much more plentiful, and title was made much easier to change. American emphasis was on the freedom to enter contracts and on the

The Continuing Influence of English Common Law

Section 22.2 of the California Civil Code explicitly states that "the common law of England, so far as it is not repugnant to or inconsistent with the Constitution of the United States, or the Constitution or laws of this State, is the rule of decision in all the courts of this State."

sanctity of contracts. The common law was influenced by the Old Testament. Biblical assumptions of individual responsibility for one's own actions were consonant with the individualism of early American life.

Importance of the Common Law. The sense of justice—what is considered right, just, and fair by the ordinary citizens of the land—is reflected in the common law. Sometimes the common law is referred to as "unwritten law" because of its roots in the customs and traditions of the people. In reality, however, it is written in the court records of hundreds of cases. A more accurate name for it, therefore, is "case law."

To rule on a present case, judges must consult the body of established legal precedents that apply to the current case before the court. Often both litigants in a case will cite judicial precedents and earlier cases in order to make a strong case for their client. Lawyers who show more convincingly that precedent and tradition are on their side frequently win their cases. The intent of following precedents, or *stare decisis*, is to assure continuity, or even-handed justice from year to year and century to century. Its authority is reinforced in the popular mind by the perception of fairness that goes with such consistency. Judges are seen in the popular mind, not as arbitrarily governed by their own idiosyncrasies, but as bound by the accumulated experiences of legal custom. Justice is not capricious.

The common law is also distinguished by the use of juries in determining facts of law and judgment. Guilt or innocence is determined in open court by free citizens whose findings cannot be reversed by the judge. Decisions regarding life, liberty, and property are made by unanimous verdicts of one's peers.

The U.S. Bill of Rights is essentially a reassertion of the fundamental liberties of American citizens under the common law, an additional safeguard to long-standing tradition. Individual liberties that American citizens

have long come to expect owe more to the practice of following common-law traditions than many people realize.

Bibliography
Cantor, Norman F. *Imagining the Law: Common Law and the Foundations of the American Legal System.* New York: HarperCollins, 1997.
Cappalli, Richard B. *The American Common Law Method.* Irvington, N.Y.: Transnational, 1997.
Kirk, Russell. *The Roots of American Order.* 3d ed. Washington, D.C.: Regnery Gateway, 1991.
Schwartz, Bernard. *The Law in America: A History.* New York: McGraw-Hill, 1974.

William H. Burnside

Communications Management

Communications management is a universal concern of modern governments, often motivated as much by political considerations involving power and influence as by the need to retain order in a world of rapidly changing communication technologies.

Communications systems provide means of imparting or transmitting information. Systems linking governments with one another and their citizens are of growing importance to modern governments. During the twentieth century, compelling reasons converged to make communications policy and management major concerns of governments: the increasing complexity of the instruments of mass communications, a growing appreciation of the link between communications networks and societal integration, and the apparent relationship between the form and content of communications on one hand and political power and support on the other.

The Rise of Communications Media. The nineteenth century's principal instrument of mass communication was the press. Even when governments sought to censor it, the medium proved difficult to manage because the printing press was already a decentralized, relatively inexpensive, and widely diffused technology. By contrast, the principal vehicles for twentieth century communications increasingly have involved high technology, electronic modes of mass communication such as telephones, radios, televisions, fax machines, and interfacing computers. Individually and as a set, these technologies both have lent themselves to greater government control and have required it.

The development and mass deployment of telephones was long regarded in the United States as requiring a natural monopoly arrangement favoring American Telephone and Telegraph (AT&T). Elsewhere in the world, the telephone industry remains essentially a government-owned or tightly controlled monopoly. Likewise, because radio and television broadcasting can function effectively only when airwaves and wave bands are assigned in such a manner as to avoid interfering signals, these media also came under public management. As the range for broadcasting has increased, the regulating arrangements have often moved beyond national agencies to international meetings and agreements.

An expanding appreciation of the role of communication grids in knitting together the members of a society has given governments a second set of reasons for concerning themselves with the evolving industries of mass communications. The widespread utilization of these technologies has come to be viewed as a barometer of social integration, measured in such terms as the number of telephones, radios, and televisions per thousand people. These measurements consistently have placed the United States at the head of the list.

Finally, the desire to exercise political power more effectively has encouraged countries throughout the twentieth century to attempt to control the complex and rapidly expanding instruments of mass communications. Information is often inseparable from opinion formulation: Efforts to influence the latter have frequently motivated governments to try to control the former.

Government and Communications. Government itself, as an institution exercising control over an extended territory and the people within it, would be impossible without the ability to communicate its rules to the governed. The fostering and management of systems of communications as a means of achieving political control and stability have long been concerns of governments. By the time the U.S. CONSTITUTION was ratified in 1789, the role of government in fostering a system of postal communications was so firmly established that the provisions empowering the new federal government "to establish post-offices and post-roads" were among the least controversial of those enumerating powers given to Congress. Governments' concern with communications policy increased when the age of electronic communications suddenly provided governments with instantaneous, mass access to their citizens.

The United States intrudes very little into the day-to-day operations of the communications media. The generally followed principle has been to regulate the electronic media to the extent necessary in a nation of thousands of radio and television stations and hundreds of millions of telephones, avoiding hindrances to the free flow of information and the public's ability to communicate. The Federal Communication Act of 1934 gave the Federal Communications Commission (FCC) control over the licensing of radio (and later television) stations throughout the country. The FCC's explicit charge was to seek the "public interest" in its activities. Its approach subsequently has been pragmatic, not doctrinaire. Cross-media ownership among newspapers, radio, and television stations has been permitted, but only

A major new challenge facing the United States at the end of the twentieth century was the question of how far government should go in regulating online computer communications. (AP/Wide World Photos)

within the framework of a fairness doctrine. This doctrine requires that the coverage of stories by the electronic media fairly acknowledges the diversity of viewpoints involved in the issues, much as the equal time doctrine has been applied to require radio and television stations airing the views of one candidate running for public office to give equal air time to challengers.

The Role of the Courts. Federal courts have played an important role in encouraging the free flow of the written word in the United States. The U.S. Supreme Court has persistently given a broad, "preferred status" interpretation to the freedoms of speech, press, and assembly guaranteed in the Constitution. It has also explicitly denied the states and the federal government the right to exercise prior restraint against the publication of stories in all except the most obvious instances of national security violations. The federal courts in general have made it so difficult to prove a charge of libel that newspapers rarely have been inhibited by threatened lawsuits from publishing stories. Even in the field of telephone communication, laws consistently have emphasized the public interest. The telephone industry was originally exempted from ANTITRUST LAW regulation as a natural monopoly in order to facilitate the spread of telephones. The courts subsequently ordered the breakup of the AT&T monopoly over interstate and foreign communications in response to changed circumstances of the 1980's.

Politicians and the Media. U.S. politicians are not above attempting to use the media to manipulate public opinion. Political leaders regularly try to influence presentation of messages. Former U.S. president Ronald Reagan's media aides, for example, have been quoted as saying that they spent five hours every day trying to get their "spin" on the ninety seconds of evening television news about the White House. So-called sunshine laws permitting public access to government information consistently have been more important than national secrecy acts in defining the relationship between the written and electronic media and the government. Anchors of the networks' news programs continue to be appointed by network executives based on experience and audience appeal, not by the president of the United States for their personal and partisan loyalty.

The factors that have required or tempted government to become actively concerned with communications management throughout the twentieth century continue to be relevant. The still-unfolding revolutions in modes of communication, combined with the interdependency of the countries in the modern world, their need to communicate instantaneously and effectively with one another, and the globalization of culture via international communicative grids, generate a series of questions involving public administration. Given their importance, should communications industries be public monopolies, regulated private monopolies, or competitive? What are the most efficient means for advancing the new communications technologies and facilitating public access to them? Governments will play roles in the multichannel programming technologies available through cable television, telephones, fax services, and computer-accessed information networks. The question is what those roles will be.

Bibliography

Alexander, Alison, and Jarice Hanson, eds. *Taking Sides: Clashing Views on Controversial Issues in Mass Media and Society.* Guilford, Conn.: Dushkin, 1995.

Maltese, John Anthony. *Spin Control: The White House Office of Communications and the Management of Presidential News.* Chapel Hill: University of North Carolina Press, 1992.

Paletz, David L., and Robert M. Entman. *Media Power Politics.* New York: Free Press, 1981.

Sargent, Lyman Tower. *Contemporary Political Ideologies: A Comparative Analysis.* Homewood, Ill.: Dorsey Press, 1969.

Joseph R. Rudolph, Jr.

Congress

The legislative branch of the U.S. government, Congress enacts laws, represents the interests of citizens in the national government, oversees the operation of the executive branch, conducts public investigations, and performs a variety of other services.

Congress consists of two separate bodies: the Senate and the House of Representatives. The Senate has one hundred members, with two from each of the fifty states, who serve six-year terms. Originally, senators were elected by the individual state legislatures, but since the ratification of the Seventeenth Amendment to the U.S. CONSTITUTION in 1913, they have been elected directly by the people.

The House of Representatives, whose members serve two-year terms, has 435 voting members apportioned among the states according to population, with each state, no matter how small, guaranteed at least one representative. Under the Constitution of 1787, the House began with sixty-five members, but it was allowed to increase in size after each decennial census. After it grew to 435 members at the beginning of the twentieth century, its members passed legislation limiting it to that size. Since then, population shifts within and among the states have required reapportioning congressional seats so that, as much as possible, each member of the House represents the same number of constituents.

Congressional Terms. Although the Constitution places no limit on how long a member of the House and Senate can serve, its Framers expected that the House of Representatives in particular would experience substantial turn-

over. In fact, it was not unusual during Congress's first century for up to half the membership of the House to change after each election. This trend began changing toward the end of the nineteenth century, when congressional membership became more of a full-time job and more members tried to make "careers" out of political service.

By 1990 the average House member had served about twelve years in that body, and the average senator eleven years. Reflecting growing levels of public dissatisfaction with Congress, fifteen states passed laws or state constitutional amendments in 1992 and 1993 limiting congressional terms to twelve years in the Senate and either twelve or six years in the House.

The modern Congress carries out five key functions in the American governmental system: lawmaking, representation of the interests and desires of the American people, oversight of the executive branch (the bureaucracy) to ensure that programs are properly administered, investigations to inform the public about serious national problems or issues, and constituency service of various types (such as intervening on behalf of constituents with the bureaucracy).

Legislative Powers. The Constitution vests seventeen specific legislative powers in Congress. These range from some of the highest powers exercised by government—such as taxation, regulation of commerce, and declarations of war—to others—such as establishing post offices. This list is followed by a clause giving Congress the power to "make all Laws which shall be necessary and proper for carrying into Execution the foregoing Powers." This "necessary and proper" clause suggests that the enumeration of legislative powers was not intended to be a strict limitation on Congress.

In 1791, within only two years of its first assembling, Congress established a national bank, although such a power was not explicitly

Dessiné par le Barbier Peintre du Roi.   *Gravé par Godefroy de l'Academie Imp.le et Royale de Vienne &c.*

PREMIÈRE ASSEMBLÉE DU CONGRÈS.

Before ratification of the U.S. Constitution created the modern Congress, the ruling body of the U.S. government was known as the Continental Congress. (Library of Congress)

In the early days of Congress, disagreements among political opponents occasionally erupted into physical confrontations, as when Mathew Lyon and Roger Griswold fought over the Sedition Act of 1798 on the House floor. (Library of Congress)

included in the constitutional enumeration. Some, such as Thomas Jefferson, opposed the creation of the bank as too loose a construction of the powers accorded to Congress by the Constitution. The bank's supporters, on the other hand, defended it as "necessary and proper" for carrying into effect other explicit legislative powers, such as control of the currency and the regulation of commerce.

Over the years, expansive interpretations of its lawmaking powers by the members of Congress and sympathetic U.S. Supreme Court decisions have effectively transformed Congress's enumeration of powers into a general legislative power. Rarely is it publicly debated whether the constitutional enumeration authorizes the entry of Congress into new policy fields.

House-Senate Division of Powers. The House and Senate possess approximately equal shares of the lawmaking power. To become laws bills must be passed in identical form by both branches, with each branch free to amend proposals from the other. However, all revenue bills (tax measures) must originate in the House. Moreover, the Senate possesses several nonlegislative powers not shared with the House: the confirmation of presidential nominations to high offices and the ratification of treaties.

The Presidency and Congress. In one crucial respect, Congress shares lawmaking power with the president. All bills passed by the House and Senate must be presented to the president for action. If the president signs them, they become law. If the president vetoes them, they are returned with a list of objections to the branches in which they originated; they then must be approved by two-thirds of each legislative house. If the president neither signs nor vetoes a bill, it becomes law after ten days unless Congress has adjourned, in which case the bill dies (a so-called pocket veto).

From 1789 to 1990 presidents formally vetoed 1,431 bills passed by Congress (of which only 103, or 7 percent, were overridden) and pocket-vetoed another 1,054 bills. The Constitution also vests the president with the authority to "recommend to [Congress's] Consideration such Measures as he shall judge necessary and expedient."

Congress and the Supreme Court. To some extent Congress also shares the lawmaking power with the Supreme Court, for since 1803 the Court has asserted the authority to rule acts of Congress unconstitutional. Although this power of "JUDICIAL REVIEW" is not mentioned in the Constitution itself, the Court maintained that it was necessarily implied as part of the constitutional order. It took until 1857 before the Court once again ruled an act of Congress unconstitutional. Indeed, judicial review did not prove a serious impediment to the congressional will until the New Deal dur-

President George Bush delivering his first state of the union address to Congress in early 1990. (AP/Wide World Photos)

ing the 1930's, when the Court overturned key legislation enthusiastically endorsed by the president and Congress. By the end of the decade, however, the Court shifted its position. In recent decades the Court's judicial review power has been exercised much more often against state legislatures than against Congress.

Structure of Congress. The most important organizational features of the House and Senate are their leadership structures, which centralize power and influence, and their committee systems, which decentralize decision making. In each of the branches, the two major political parties—Democrats and Republicans—select their own leaders. In the House, the leader of the majority party becomes Speaker of the House. Next in line is the majority leader and then the majority whip. The whip is responsible for communicating leadership decisions to party members, informing members about forthcoming votes, maximizing party representation during floor votes, and generally promoting party voting on the floor. The minority party has essentially the same leadership structure, with the exception that there is no minority party equivalent to the Speaker: The top minority party officer is simply called the minority leader.

The parties in the Senate have a similar leadership structure. The principal exception is that under the Constitution the vice president of the United States is the president of the Senate, having the right to preside over debates and to cast tie-breaking votes (which rarely occur). The Senate also chooses a "president pro tempore," which is essentially an honorific position usually given to the most senior member of the majority party. In reality, the top officer of the Senate on a day-to-day basis is the majority leader.

Although party leaders in the House and Senate do possess some real influence in the legislative process, their power pales in comparison to their equivalents in parliamentary systems. For example, congressional leaders have almost no control over the election or reelection of their party colleagues in Congress. Because there is almost nothing they can do to keep unresponsive members from being returned to Congress, their influence comes more from persuasion and bargaining than from command.

The Committee System. Counteracting the centralizing influences of the leadership system is the decentralizing effect of the committee and subcommittee system. Both the House and the Senate divide the legislative workload among committees organized according to subject matter. There are twenty-two such "standing committees" in the House and sixteen in the Senate. (There are also "special committees" and "joint committees" in Congress, but these are generally of less importance than the standing committees.) The standing committees are further subdivided into subcommittees, again based on subject matter; these numbered about 220 in 1994. The subcommittees have become increasingly independent of their parent bodies, thereby spreading power to the large percentage of majority party members who serve as subcommittee chairpersons.

Because Congress is discussed first in the U.S. Constitution and because it is the principal lawmaking branch, many have concluded that American government is characterized by congressional supremacy. Adherents of this view often cite the words of Roger Sherman, a delegate to the Constitutional Convention of 1787, who maintained that the executive should be "nothing more than an institution for carrying the will of the Legislature into effect."

Whatever the original intention regarding the role of Congress in the governmental system, for much of the nineteenth century Congress was clearly the dominant branch on matters of domestic legislation, especially in the decades just before and after the Civil War. By

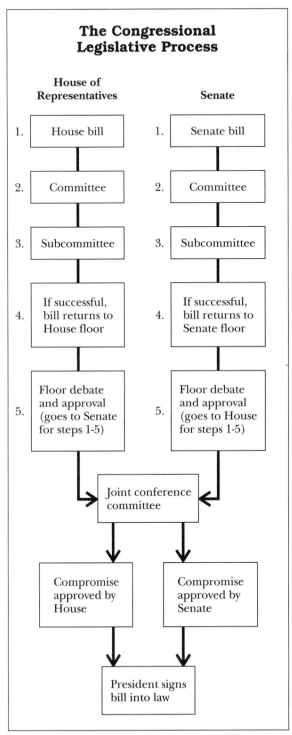

The Congressional Legislative Process

House of Representatives

1. House bill
2. Committee
3. Subcommittee
4. If successful, bill returns to House floor
5. Floor debate and approval (goes to Senate for steps 1-5)

Senate

1. Senate bill
2. Committee
3. Subcommittee
4. If successful, bill returns to Senate floor
5. Floor debate and approval (goes to House for steps 1-5)

Joint conference committee

Compromise approved by House

Compromise approved by Senate

President signs bill into law

Source: Adapted from Jay M. Shafritz, *The Dorsey Dictionary of American Government and Politics.* Chicago: Dorsey Press, 1988. Primary source, Auraria Library, Government Documents Section, Denver, Colo.

the twentieth century, however, political, social, and technological developments had combined to raise the prominence of the presidency in the governmental system. The rise of a more activist national government, the growing importance of foreign affairs, and the development of mass media (especially radio and television) had the effect of making the president, in Woodrow Wilson's words, "the political leader of the nation" and "the vital place of action in the system."

Nevertheless, despite the fact that the modern Congress often operates in the shadow of the presidency, it remains the most independent and powerful legislative body among Western democracies. While the American SEPARATION OF POWERS system, as opposed to parliamentary government, creates the possibility of conflict, and even deadlock, between the legislative and executive branches, it has also ensured that the legislature remains free to exercise its independent will, even against the wishes of the executive branch.

Bibliography

Bacon, Donald C., Roger H. Davidson, and Morton Keller. *The Encyclopedia of the United States Congress.* New York: Simon & Schuster, 1995.

Evans, C. Lawrence, and Walter J. Oleszek. *Congress Under Fire: Reform Politics and the Republican Majority.* Boston: Houghton Mifflin, 1997.

Greenberg, Ellen. *The House and Senate Explained: The People's Guide to Congress.* New York: W. W. Norton, 1996.

Kravitz, Walter. *Congressional Quarterly's American Congressional Dictionary.* 2d ed. Washington, D.C.: Congressional Quarterly, 1997.

Ornstein, Norman J., Thomas E. Mann, and Michael J. Malbin. *Vital Statistics on Congress, 1991-1992.* Washington, D.C.: Congressional Quarterly, 1992.

Joseph M. Bessette

Conscientious Objection

Refusal to participate in a war or military training on the grounds of moral objection, conscientious objection involves moral rejection of military service.

Conscientious objection (often called "CO") traces its roots to pacifism, the complete rejection of war on moral grounds. As early as the third century, leaders of the Roman Catholic Church denounced war as the antithesis of Christ's teachings. Later, splinter groups in the Protestant Reformation expanded their notions of pacifism to encompass rejection of governments generally.

Immigrant Conscientious Objectors. The first instances of conscientious objection in the United States came from immigrant religious groups such as the Quakers and Mennonites, who had embraced pacifism in Europe. Members of these and other groups refused to serve in colonial militias. Because members of these religious groups were regarded as moral, hardworking, and otherwise law-abiding citizens, their refusal to serve was generally tolerated by fellow citizens. Responding to the surge of conscientious objection claims by Civil War draftees, Abraham Lincoln stated that the Union needed good farmers as well as good soldiers.

As the nation grew, so did the number of groups claiming conscientious objector status. Jehovah's Witnesses, for example, allowed that their individual status as ministers exempted them from any draft. In times of military conscription, COs were usually allowed to perform alternative duties to fulfill their service obligations. Absolute objectors, those who refused to perform alternative service or register for the draft, faced possible prison sentences.

With the Korean War of the early 1950's the nature of conscientious objection began to change from objection on the basis of religious beliefs to objection on the grounds of personal philosophy. The two new variants on conscientious objection were nonreligious, or secular, objection and selective objections.

Nonreligious and Selective Objection. Nonreligious, or secular, objectors do not have the same protection against mandated service as that granted to established pacifist religions. Secular objectors resist war and military service on the grounds of personal beliefs independent of organized religion. Such dissidence has been supported by the U.S. Supreme Court's liberal interpretation of what can constitute an individual's personal credo (religion).

Selective conscientious objectors (SCOs) are neither religious nor philosophical pacifists. They may view some wars (and the need for obligatory service) as just and others as unjust. Their underlying philosophy is that the right to determine the rectitude of any war belongs to the individual: A person who decides that a particular war is wrong has no obligation to further its purpose. The primacy of individual independence in SCO philosophy challenges the sovereignty of government and, taken to the extreme, threatens anarchy.

One of the first selective conscientious objectors was Henry David Thoreau. He regarded the Mexican-American War (1846-1848) as U.S. imperialism at its worst and refused to pay the portion of his tax earmarked to finance the war. Thoreau subsequently popularized the phrase "CIVIL DISOBEDIENCE" by affixing it to an essay which celebrated his night in jail as the result of not paying the war tax. On the other hand, Thoreau was a fervent abolitionist and saw the Civil War as a holy war.

The Vietnam War. As the conflict in Southeast Asia deepened and American casualties worsened in the 1960's, U.S. authorities moved to make the burden of the draft more equal by limiting exemptions. Consequently, levels of protest rose, and draft evasion and draft avoidance increased. At the same time the Supreme Court redefined conscientious objector status in a broader, more inclusive

While many conscientious objectors are opposed to all wars, conscientious objection typically increases greatly during unpopular conflicts, such as the Vietnam War. (Library of Congress)

manner, allowing exemptions for "beliefs that are purely ethical or moral in source."

In 1968 newly elected President Richard Nixon convened a commission to study the feasibility of an all-volunteer service. The commission found the military draft to be an unfair and costly burden on selected young men and recommended it be replaced. In 1973 MILITARY CONSCRIPTION was abandoned. Since then, young men have still been required to register for the draft at age eighteen, but no draft calls have occurred since the end of the Vietnam War. Conscientious objection and its ramifications for society have consequently faded as a public issue.

Bibliography

Goossen, Rachel W. *Women Against the Good War: Conscientious Objection and Gender on the American Home Front, 1941-1947.* Chapel Hill: University of North Carolina Press, 1997.

Moskos, Charles C., and John W. Chambers. *The New Conscientious Objection: From Sacred to Secular Resistance.* New York: Oxford University Press, 1993.

Schlissel, Lillian, comp. *Conscience in America.* New York: E. P. Dutton, 1968.

John A. Sondey

Conservatism

Modern American conservatism is concerned with limiting the authority of the state to regulate the economy and supports the traditional institutions of society. As an ideology and state of mind, conservatism challenged and sought to replace—with some success during the 1980's and 1990's—the liberal ideology that had dominated American political life through the previous half-century.

After the 1960's, the United States witnessed a resurgence of conservatism as a social and political movement. Modern American conservatism is primarily a reaction to the pro-government public philosophy and welfare LIBERALISM that had dominated the country's political life since the New Deal era in the 1930's.

Historically, the American political tradition, which is antistatist and antimonarchical, is liberal. It had few conservative authors and leaders. In its political culture and tradition, its government roots and ideals—as enshrined in patriotic emblems such as the DECLARATION OF INDEPENDENCE, the Pledge of Allegiance, and the Gettysburg Address—the United States reflects deeply established liberal and progressive values. In the late 1960's, however, overt conservative views began to be expressed by southern Democrats and (especially) the Barry Goldwater wing of the REPUBLICAN PARTY, which later supported Ronald Reagan in the 1970's and 1980's.

The rise of conservatism has been closely associated with the general perception of the cause of economic and social malaise in the country. In the economic sphere, conservatives identified the problem of a stagnant economy coupled with inflation—"stagflation"—with the "big government" of "tax-and-spend" Democrats, who had been taking away taxpayers' hard-earned money and spending it on questionable social welfare programs for the undeserving poor.

Several events, such as New York City's fiscal crisis in the mid-1970's and the California tax revolt embodied in Proposition 13 in 1978, helped conservatives make a popular antigovernment case that big government is responsible for the country's economic woes. In the cultural and social domain, conservatives have criticized liberals on issues such as race, family, "permissiveness," and CRIME. They argue in favor of supporting the traditional institutions of society, such as family, church, and neighborhood schools.

Varieties of Conservatism. The meaning and substance of conservatism in the United

States differ from those in Europe, where conservatism originated to defend the alliance between monarchy, church, and aristocracy. European conservatives, following the basic principles of traditional conservatism as outlined by Edmund Burke in the eighteenth century, believe in tradition, custom, a hierarchical manorial society, a strong state, mercantilism, and natural leaders. Since they are pessimistic about people's ability to improve their lot through the use of reason, they resist change.

American conservatism, on the other hand, is individualistic in conception and antistatist in orientation. Taking inspiration from the Constitution and European philosophers such as Burke, American conservatives essentially believe in a limited government. The WELFARE state is their main target of attack, and they ask for the dismantling of much of the New Deal legislation. Conservatives differ, however, on the specifics of economic and social policy.

Neoconservatism and the New Right. Two distinct traditions, neoconservatism and the NEW RIGHT, can be identified in modern American conservatism. The dominant theme of neoconservatism—as articulated by political leaders such as Ronald Reagan—is the economic ideology of free market CAPITALISM, first articulated by Adam Smith in *The Wealth of Nations* (1776), and of antistatism, which has been summed up as "private, good; public, bad." In particular, neoconservatives advocate de-

regulating the economy, eliminating some national programs and decentralizing others, privatizing public functions, pursuing a nationalist foreign policy, and supporting so-called traditional institutions in society.

The Radical, or New, Right is closely associated with the New Christian Right movement and is the extreme right group within the Republican Party. It emphasizes social and cultural issues. Leaders of the New Right movement, such as Jerry Falwell and Pat Robertson,

President Ronald Reagan was an icon of conservatism through the 1980's, when he advocated sweeping tax cuts and a hardline stance against the Soviet Union. (Library of Congress)

Georgia Republican Newt Gingrich became a leading spokesperson for conservatism after he became speaker of the House of Representatives in 1994. (AP/Wide World Photos)

are mainly concerned with the decline in traditional values. They particularly oppose abortion, sex in television and films, and forced BUSING to integrate public schools. The New Right leaders advocate a return to morality—defined in terms of the moral code of Christian Fundamentalism—in government and society. In the 1980's and 1990's they launched a national debate on moral issues central to the movement. They failed, however, to become the voice of the Republican Party.

The Future of Conservatism. The conservative majority has dominated presidential politics since 1968 and taken control of the Republican Party. Reagan's election in 1980, followed by George Bush's in 1988, symbolized the end of the liberal era in modern American politics. In 1992 the DEMOCRATIC PARTY plat-

form and Bill Clinton accepted a number of conservative ideas in order to win the presidential election.

The "Republican Revolution" in the 1994 elections—the party's greatest sweep since 1946—led to a conservative majority in both houses of the Congress. The Republicans thereupon launched a full-scale attack on the notion that the federal government should play a central role in the life of a nation. Under the leadership of Newt Gingrich, the new Speaker of the House, the Republican Party promised in its "Contract with America" to dismantle the welfare state and the "welfare-state bureaucracy" brick by brick. The conservatives succeeded in putting liberals on the defensive regardless of the outcome of specific conservative policy initiatives.

Bibliography

Carter, Dan T. *From George Wallace to Newt Gingrich: Race in the Conservative Counterrevolution, 1963-1994.* Baton Rouge: Louisana State University Press, 1996.

Hodgson, Godfrey. *The World Turned Right Side Up: A History of the Conservative Ascendancy in America.* Boston: Houghton Mifflin, 1996.

Lind, Michael. *Up from Conservatism: Why the Right Is Wrong for America.* New York: Free Press, 1996.

Will, George F. *The Woven Figure: Conservatism and America's Fabric, 1994-1997.* New York: Charles Scribner's Sons, 1997.

Sunil K. Sahu

Constitution

The U.S. Constitution codified several unique governmental concepts. It divided power among three branches, with checks and balances to prevent any one branch from seizing control. It assigned specific powers to the federal government, and others to the states. Its "elastic clauses" have enabled it to respond to changing conditions for more than two centuries.

The most fundamental law of the United States, the Constitution designed the framework of the federal system of government. It established the three branches of government, granted them authority to perform the activities of government, and limited that authority. It stipulated the qualifications persons must meet to serve in CONGRESS and the PRESIDENCY and the general jurisdiction of the federal courts.

Historical Background. When the United States declared independence from Great Britain in 1776, the question of who properly exercised the powers of American government arose. The Continental Congress assumed governing responsibility simply because there was no other institution capable of supporting the war effort and exercising the authority of government at that time. The process of transforming that body into a legitimate government began with the approval of the Articles of Confederation in 1777. The Articles of Confederation became the first governing document of the new nation after it was ratified by all thirteen original states in 1781. It remained in effect until the adoption of the Constitution in 1789.

The Articles of Confederation stressed limited national government and states' rights. Each state received one vote in a unicameral Congress. Congress received authorization to maintain a volunteer army, conduct foreign relations, dispose of western lands ceded to it by the states, regulate trade with Native Americans, borrow money, request funds from the states, issue paper money, create executive offices, and exercise a limited judicial power in admiralty cases and disputes arising among the states. All other important powers, including the power to levy and collect taxes and to regulate foreign and interstate commerce, were reserved to the states.

Demands for revision of the Articles of Confederation began soon after its adoption, increasing after 1784 for several reasons. Some people realized that Congress was too weak to alleviate the severe economic depression that began in 1784, caused by interstate trade barriers and British and Spanish limitations on American trade with their empires. Some worried about the potential problems of concentrating too much power in Congress without effective checks on that power. Others worried that the government could not repay its loan obligations without a dependable source of revenue. Still others realized that the Articles' requirement for unanimous consent from all thirteen states for amendment limited its ability to grow with the country. Finally, some people were concerned with an occurrence of civil disobedience in western Massachusetts known as Shays's Rebellion. Farmers in that

The Pennsylvania Packet, *and Daily Advertiser.*

[Price Four-Pence.] WEDNESDAY, SEPTEMBER 19, 1787. [No. 2690.]

WE, the People of the United States, in order to form a more perfect Union, establish Justice, insure domestic Tranquility, provide for the common Defence, promote the General Welfare, and secure the Blessings of Liberty to Ourselves and our Posterity, do ordain and establish this Constitution for the United States of America.

ARTICLE I.

Sect. 1. ALL legislative powers herein granted shall be vested in a Congress of the United States, which shall consist of a Senate and House of Representatives.

Sect. 2. The House of Representatives shall be composed of members chosen every second year by the people of the several states, and the electors in each state shall have the qualifications requisite for electors of the most numerous branch of the state legislature.

No person shall be a representative who shall not have attained to the age of twenty-five years, and been seven years a citizen of the United States, and who shall not, when elected, be an inhabitant of that state in which he shall be chosen.

Representatives and direct taxes shall be apportioned among the several states which may be included within this Union, according to their respective numbers, which shall be determined by adding to the whole number of free persons, including those bound to service for a term of years, and excluding Indians not taxed, three-fifths of all other persons. The actual enumeration shall be made within three years after the first meeting of the Congress of the United States, and within every subsequent term of ten years, in such manner as they shall by law direct. The number of representatives shall not exceed one for every thirty thousand, but each state shall have at least one representative; and until such enumeration shall be made, the state of New-Hampshire shall be entitled to chuse three, Massachusetts eight, Rhode-Island and Providence Plantations one, Connecticut five, New-York six, New-Jersey four, Pennsylvania eight, Delaware one, Maryland six, Virginia ten, North-Carolina five, South-Carolina five, and Georgia three.

When vacancies happen in the representation from any state, the Executive authority thereof shall issue writs of election to fill such vacancies.

The House of Representatives shall chuse their Speaker and other officers; and shall have the sole power of impeachment.

Sect. 3. The Senate of the United States shall be composed of two senators from each state, chosen by the legislature thereof, for six years; and each senator shall have one vote.

Immediately after they shall be assembled in consequence of the first election, they shall be divided as equally as may be into three classes. The seats of the senators of the first class shall be vacated at the expiration of the second year, of the second class at the expiration of the fourth year, and of the third class at the expiration of the sixth year, so that one-third may be chosen every second year; and if vacancies happen by resignation, or otherwise, during the recess of the Legislature of any state, the Executive thereof may make temporary appointments until the next meeting of the Legislature, which shall then fill such vacancies.

No person shall be a senator who shall not have attained to the age of thirty years, and been nine years a citizen of the United States, and who shall not, when elected, be an inhabitant of that state for which he shall be chosen.

The Vice-President of the United States shall be President of the senate, but shall have no vote, unless they be equally divided.

The Senate shall chuse their other officers, and also a President pro tempore, in the absence of the Vice-President, or when he shall exercise the office of President of the United States.

The Senate shall have the sole power to try all impeachments. When sitting for that purpose, they shall be on oath or affirmation. When the President of the United States is tried, the Chief Justice shall preside: And no person shall be convicted without the concurrence of two-thirds of the members present.

Judgment in cases of impeachment shall not extend further than to removal from office, and disqualification to hold and enjoy any office of honor, trust or profit under the United States; but the party convicted shall nevertheless be liable and subject to indictment, trial, judgment and punishment, according to law.

Sect. 4. The times, places and manner of holding elections for senators and representatives, shall be prescribed in each state by the legislature thereof; but the Congress may at any time by law make or alter such regulations, except as to the places of chusing Senators.

The Congress shall assemble at least once in every year, and such meeting shall be on the first Monday in December, unless they shall by law appoint a different day.

Sect. 5. Each house shall be the judge of the elections, returns and qualifications of its own members, and a majority of each shall constitute a quorum to do business; but a smaller number may adjourn from day to day, and may be authorised to compel the attendance of absent members, in such manner, and under such penalties as each house may provide.

Each house may determine the rules of its proceedings, punish its members for disorderly behaviour, and, with the concurrence of two-thirds, expel a member.

Each house shall keep a journal of its proceedings, and from time to time publish the same, excepting such parts as may in their judgment require secrecy; and the yeas and nays of the members of either house on any question shall, at the desire of one-fifth of those present, be entered on the journal.

Neither house, during the session of Congress, shall, without the consent of the other, adjourn for more than three days, nor to any other place than that in which the two houses shall be sitting.

Sect. 6. The senators and representatives shall receive a compensation for their services, to be ascertained by law, and paid out of the treasury of the United States. They shall in all cases, except treason, felony and breach of the peace, be privileged from arrest during their attendance at the session of their respective houses, and in going to and returning from the same; and for any speech or debate in either house, they shall not be questioned in any other place.

No senator or representative shall, during the time for which he was elected, be appointed to any civil office under the authority of the United States, which shall have been created, or the emoluments whereof shall have been encreased during such time; and no person holding any office under the United States, shall be a member of either house during his continuance in office.

Sect. 7. All bills for raising revenue shall originate in the house of representatives; but the senate may propose or concur with amendments as on other bills.

Every bill which shall have passed the house of representatives and the senate, shall, before it become a law, be presented to the president of the United States; if he approve he shall sign it, but if not he shall return it, with his objections to that house in which it shall have originated, who shall enter the objections at large on their journal, and proceed to reconsider it. If after such reconsideration two-thirds of that house shall agree to pass the bill, it shall be sent, together with the objections, to the other house, by which it shall likewise be reconsidered, and if approved by two-thirds of that house, it shall become a law. But in all such cases the votes of both houses shall

Immediately after the members of the Constitutional Convention finished their work in 1787, the Pennsylvania Packet *published the text of the new Constitution.* (Library of Congress)

area stopped foreclosure proceedings on their farms by seizing control of county courthouses, and the national government had no authority under the Articles to halt that breakdown of orderly legal procedures.

Congress called the Philadelphia Convention in 1787 to revise the Articles in order to address the concerns that had developed about that system of government. Delegates to the convention decided, however, that the Articles of Confederation were too flawed and that they should devise a wholly new document of government. The result was the Constitution.

Articles of the U.S. Constitution. The first of the Constitution's seven articles created Congress, designated its bicameral form, set forth qualifications for its membership. It also defined Congress's powers. Article 2 created the executive branch, defined qualifications for the presidency, and outlined presidential power. Article 3 created the judicial branch of government and defined the act of TREASON. Article 4 provided the guidelines state governments must follow in their relationship with citizens and one another, outlined procedures for admitting new states to the union, and guaranteed every state a republican form of government. Article 5 set out procedures for amending the Constitution. Article 6 ordained that the Constitution, the laws of the

Republican Party leaders gathered at the Capitol building steps in early 1997 to declare their support for a balanced budget amendment to the Constitution. (Reuters/Rick Wilking/Archive Photos)

United States, and treaties approved by the U.S. government were to be recognized by the states as superior to their own laws. Article 7 stipulated ratification requirements for the Constitution.

Amendments to the Constitution. There are several categories of constitutional amendments. Some provide guarantees of citizen rights by limiting the power of government on either the national or state level. Others extend specific rights not included in the original text of the Constitution. Still others grant additional authority to government not provided by the original text, or modify procedures provided for in the original Constitution.

In addition to its specific grants of authority to government, the Constitution also grants general authority that has allowed Congress to exercise its legislative power in ways not envisioned by the Framers who wrote the document. These so-called elastic clauses are found primarily in Article 1, section 8. The first paragraph of that section allows Congress, among other powers, to legislate for the "general Welfare of the United States." Its last paragraph allows Congress "to make all Laws which shall be necessary and proper for carrying into Execution" the powers specifically enumerated.

The "general welfare clause" and the "necessary and proper clause" give Congress great latitude in its power to legislate because of the imprecision of their language. Providing for the general welfare can be interpreted to include many acts that the Constitution did not specifically authorize Congress to accomplish. Government leaders have debated the precise meaning of the "necessary and proper clause" since President George Washington's administration, when Secretary of State Thomas Jefferson and Secretary of the Treasury Alexander Hamilton argued over the necessity and propriety of creating a national bank.

Disagreement over the proper interpretation of the elastic clauses generated two competing theories of constitutional interpretation. Loose construction, advocated by Hamilton, stressed the "proper" portion of "necessary and proper," and allowed generous interpretation of Constitutional provisions. Strict construction, advocated by Jefferson, stressed the "necessary" portion, and limited government actions to those authorized explicitly in the document or those absolutely necessary for carrying out a designated responsibility. Congressional practice and deci-

Amending the U.S. Constitution

Amendments allow the U.S. Constitution to change as the United States changes. They can be proposed in either of two ways: by a two-thirds vote of both houses of the U.S. Congress or by a special convention called by Congress upon the request of two-thirds of the state legislatures. To date, however, only the first method has been used to propose amendments. After an amendment is proposed, it must be ratified by three-fourths of the states, either by their legislatures or at specially called ratifying conventions. Only then is an amendment added to the Constitution.

These requirements for amendments ensure deliberate, often slow, consideration of changes but also allow needed and popular changes to be accomplished. Amendments to the earlier Articles of Confederation, which the Constitution replaced in 1789, required unanimous consent of the states. That unrealistically strict requirement prevented needed changes. For example, two amendments proposed for the Articles would have addressed the pressing need for improving government finances. Both failed to achieve the required unanimous consent of the states. Indeed, it might be said that the inadequacy of the amendment process under the Articles of Confederation played an important role in the move to create a new constitution for the United States.

sions rendered by the United States Supreme Court have favored Hamilton's loose construction and the general legislative authority it implies. The necessary and proper clause is generally understood to give Congress great latitude in determining the means by which it will carry out its delegated responsibilities.

Compromises. Disagreement over constitutional provisions is a long-standing tradition in the United States. The Constitution, in fact, is the product of debate and compromise. Delegates to the Philadelphia Convention that wrote the document in 1787 nearly deadlocked on several issues that threatened to end their work. However, they agreed to several compromises that saved the Constitution. These included the method of state representation in Congress, division of government power in the national government, and division of government power between the national government and the states.

The first issue provoked intense debate over two plans of representation. Delegates from New Jersey introduced a plan favored by small states that would continue to give each state equal voice in a unicameral Congress. Virginia delegates proposed a plan favored by large states that would apportion state representation in proportion to the size of their populations. Connecticut delegates formulated a plan known as the Connecticut Compromise, or Great Compromise, to divide Congress into two branches: a House of Representatives and a Senate. It also provided that representation in the House would be apportioned by population, while all states would be equally represented in the Senate.

Even that compromise, however, did not address all questions about representation. Southern state delegates contended that slave states should be allowed to count their entire slave populations for apportionment of their shares of House seats. Free-state delegates did not want slaves to be counted. A compromise allowed southern states to count three-fifths of their slave population for apportionment. This resulted in approximately equal representation of slave and free states in the House of Representatives when the new government began.

Discussion about the division of power within the national government centered on whether to make Congress the sole authority, with power to create executive and judicial branches, or to separate the latter two branches from Congress. Delegates decided that each branch would be independent.

Each branch was also limited by interaction with the other two, creating a system of CHECKS AND BALANCES that the delegates envisioned as a safeguard to keep one branch from becoming powerful enough to abuse the fundamental rights of the people. Congressional acts, for example, can be vetoed by the president, but Congress can override vetoes by a two-thirds majority vote. The delegates enhanced this safeguard by giving each branch a different source of authority. The president is elected by the ELECTORAL COLLEGE, while federal judges are appointed by the president and confirmed by the Senate. Originally, members of the House of Representatives were elected by voters whose eligibility to vote was determined by their state, while senators were elected by state legislatures. The Seventeenth Amendment, in 1913, changed the method of electing senators to election by popular vote.

Federalism. Discussion about the division of power between national and state governments surfaced because some delegates wanted to consolidate power in the national government, while others favored preserving the preeminence of state power. Delegates agreed to create a federal system, in which the two levels shared power. The national government received new, substantial powers, including the power to levy and collect taxes and to regulate foreign and interstate commerce. States retained significant authority, including the power to levy and collect taxes on their

The Constitution makes the vice president first in line to succeed to the presidency on the death of the president, as occurred when Lyndon B. Johnson succeeded John F. Kennedy on the latter's assassination in 1963. Johnson took the oath of office on the plane carrying Kennedy's body out of Dallas, Texas, as his wife, Lady Bird Johnson (behind him in white), and Kennedy's widow, Jacqueline Kennedy (right), looked on. (Lyndon Baines Johnson Library)

own and to regulate their own internal commerce. However, they were denied the power to tax foreign or interstate commerce, issue paper money, or pass laws impairing the obligations of private contracts. They were also required to acknowledge the supremacy of national laws, the Constitution, and treaty provisions.

The spirit of compromise exemplified by these agreements enabled the delegates to produce a new plan of government and helped in the ratification process. Some oppo-

nents of the Constitution maintained that it should not be ratified because it did not provide enough specific guarantees of personal rights. Supporters of ratification agreed to add those protections in a series of amendments, now known as the BILL OF RIGHTS, after ratification. The Constitution was ratified in 1789, and the BILL OF RIGHTS was added in 1791.

Although the United States has changed dramatically, its constitution has endured as its basic document of government for more than two centuries. There are three primary reasons for its longevity: It is a general framework of government and not a detailed outline which could have become outmoded; it can be amended to address new problems as they arise; and it became subject to judicial interpretation, which allowed for expansion of government authority as circumstances required.

Members of George Washington's first administration established many governmental practices consistent with the document, while succeeding administrations filled in more details as circumstances forced consideration of constitutional issues. The elastic clauses, couched in general language, allowed later expansion of authority to encompass activities unimagined in the 1780's.

Judicial Review. The process by which acts of legislatures, including Congress, are subjected to scrutiny by the federal court system is known as JUDICIAL REVIEW. This concept was not explicitly included in the Constitution. It evolved in later years and eventually became a central feature of constitutional change.

Bibliography
Center for Civic Education. *We the People: The Citizen and the Constitution.* Calabasas, Calif.: Author, 1995.

Kyvig, David E. *Explicit and Authentic Acts: Amending the U.S. Constitution, 1776-1995.* Lawrence: University Press of Kansas, 1996.

Lamm, Barbara. *The American Constitution in Context.* Commack, N.Y.: Nova Science Publishers, 1996.

Rakove, Jack N. *Original Meanings: Politics and Ideas in the Making of the Constitution.* New York: Alfred A. Knopf, 1996.

Stevens, Richard G. *The American Constitution and Its Provenance.* Lanham, Md.: Rowman & Littlefield, 1997.

Vile, John R. *A Companion to the United States Constitution and Its Amendments.* 2d ed. Westport, Conn.: Praeger, 1997.

Jerry Purvis Sanson

Constitutional Law

Constitutional law is the area of jurisprudence in which laws, governmental actions, and judicial decisions are examined to determine whether they have violated principles in the U.S. Constitution.

Constitutions of most nations enumerate the powers of government and individual rights. The degree to which constitutional law safeguards individual rights and limits abuse by governmental officials depends on a nation's history and traditions. In the United States, constitutional law centers on interpreting the U.S. CONSTITUTION, which is derived from the people and overrides laws passed by Congress and the states. The primary function of constitutional law is to ensure that governmental officials do not abuse their powers or violate individual rights.

Centrality of the U.S. Constitution. The U.S. Constitution, including its amendments, is the fundamental law that defines the powers of the executive, legislative, and judicial branches of the national government. It offers guidelines to the distribution of powers between the national government and the states. It also specifies the rights of its citizens that government may not abridge, such as the rights to freedom of speech, religion, and the press in the First Amendment and rights against unreasonable searches and seizures in the Fourth Amendment.

Most changes to the Constitution have not occurred through the use of the formal amendment process, but through federal court interpretations. The courts have defined fundamental rights that are merely implied by the Constitution's words, articulating basic principles of great importance to the development of constitutional law. Some of the most controversial implied fundamental rights are those derived from the "due process clauses" of the Fifth Amendment, as applied to the national government, and the Fourteenth

Amendment with respect to the states. These amendments state that public officials must not deprive any person of life, liberty, or property without DUE PROCESS OF LAW.

Judicial interpretation of the due process clauses has gone beyond requiring that government use correct procedures to deprive a person of life, liberty, or property. The clauses have been interpreted substantively to include rights to privacy, to use contraceptives, and to choose abortion, which are among the most controversial of all Supreme Court decisions.

The EQUAL PROTECTION clause of the Fourteenth Amendment also has been interpreted to include implied fundamental rights, including the rights of citizens to procreate, vote, travel interstate, and gain access to courts, although the Fourteenth Amendment was drafted to ensure equal protection before the law for African Americans.

Judicial Review. Some of the most important and controversial questions of constitutional law are decided when the Supreme Court uses the power of JUDICIAL REVIEW to declare statutes in violation of the Constitution. This means that they are unconstitutional and, therefore, null and void. Individuals or advocacy groups start the process of judicial review in state or lower federal courts by arguing that the government has abused its powers or violated the rights of citizens and thus has violated the Constitution.

A party that loses a case in a lower court can appeal to the Supreme Court. The Court receives thousands of appeals each year to overturn lower court decisions, interpret laws, and invalidate government actions. However, it hears and fully considers fewer than 175 cases each year. The Court uses two major constitutional principles to decide questions of constitutional law: those based on the powers of government institutions, which may be termed institutional principles, and principles based on individual rights in the Con-

The Second Lesson for Congress!

1. Pass them Regardless! (Constitutional or not!)
2. Pack the Court! (make them Constitutional!)

During the late 1930's President Franklin D. Roosevelt felt frustrated by the tendency of the conservative majority of justices on the Supreme Court to rule his New Deal legislation unconstitutional. To give the Court a liberal majority, he threatened to "pack" it with additional justices of his own choosing. (FDR Library)

stitution, which may be termed rights principles.

Institutional principles involve the legality, fairness, and legitimacy of the powers exercised and procedures used by public officials, including national, state, and local legislators, bureaucrats, chief executives, and judges. In deciding constitutional law cases, justices apply deeply held views on institutional principles, particularly with regard to whether constitutional questions should be decided in federal courts by nonelected judges or by institutions subject to ACCOUNTABILTY to citizens through elections. Judicial decisions are least controversial when they are grounded structurally in the powers that are enumerated in the Constitution, such as the powers of Congress and the president, or are directly implied by these principles of governance, such as the principle of SEPARATION OF POWERS. In many cases involving the application of institutional principles, however, courts must interpret the language of the Constitution, consider the history of government in operations, and formulate a theory of governance.

When John Tyler became the first vice president to succeed to the presidency on the death of William Henry Harrison in 1841, many people thought that "His Accidency" should be regarded only as a caretaker until the next election produced a real president. Tyler's insistence on assuming the full powers of the presidency set a constitutional precedent for all later presidents who rose to office the same way. (Library of Congress)

Rights principles are the legally enforceable claims by individuals and groups to be free from government constraints on their liberties, including the basic freedoms in the BILL OF RIGHTS. Rights principles also may be based on affirmative responsibilities that courts have placed on government to ensure that citizens' rights are protected. For exam-

ple, the Supreme Court has ruled that when states provide welfare benefits to their citizens, they may not deny these benefits to new arrivals. To do so would deny citizens the right to interstate travel, a right the Court has stated is implicit in various parts of the Constitution.

Most landmark cases require that justices consider both institutional and rights principles, determining what principles are at issue, whether they are in conflict, and, if so, how they are to be resolved.

Interpreting the Constitution. The two major approaches to interpreting the Constitution are originalism and nonoriginalism. Originalists advocate that justices and judges must rely on the institutional and individual rights principles of the Framers and ratifiers of the Constitution and values that are directly implied by these principles. Nonoriginalists believe that constitutional law must not be based on the institutional and rights principles that were specifically adopted by the Framers or that can be directly implied from those principles. They argue that the Framers' views on present constitutional questions cannot be known because of the subjectivity of those who analyze their views and because of inadequate records of the Constitutional Convention and the ratifying conventions. Nonoriginalists also argue that what words and doctrines in the Constitution mean in modern society can be determined only by reconsidering their meanings in the light of Court precedents, theories of constitutional interpretation, and ever-changing moral values, national problems, and expectations of government. Most justices have been nonoriginalists.

Topics central to the study of constitutional law include the powers of the courts; the distribution of power between the president and Congress and between the federal and state governments; equal protection before the law and discrimination based on such factors as race, gender, and country of origin; implied fundamental rights under the due process and equal protection clauses; freedom of expression, religion, and the press; the rights of citizens against the government's arbitrarily taking property; and the rights of criminal defendants.

Roots of Constitutional Law. American constitutional law has its roots in institutional and rights principles formulated in the late eigh-

teenth century. The relationship between institutional principles and the protection of individual rights was of central concern to both the Antifederalists and the Federalists, the two major factions of the Founders. The central issue was the distribution of power between state and national political institutions. The Founders perceived questions of governmental power as an issue of how the allocation of governmental power influences the protection of individual rights and securing the public interest.

Of central concern to both Federalists and Antifederalists was whether state or federal government would better protect individual rights and the public interest. The Antifederalists believed that states, being smaller and more homogeneous, would be better forums for the deliberation of public issues, protection of minority rights, and educating citizens and linking them to government. They questioned the Federalist assumption that federal supremacy over the states would protect citizen rights, maintain the confidence of citizens in the Constitution and the new governmental institutions, and protect citizens against tyranny by either the majority or a governmental elite. Federalists and Antifederalists also differed over whether rights could best be protected by securing institutional principles in the Constitution, the Federalist position, or by stating specific individual rights in a Bill of Rights.

The Federalist theory of government won out over Antifederalist arguments, in part because some Antifederalists feared that minority factions in the states would retard economic development and the military security of the nation. Although the Antifederalists lost most of the battles over institutional principles, they secured passage of the Bill of Rights. Both Federalists and Antifederalists supported the power of judicial review. Since the founding, but especially since the 1950's, the Supreme Court as a decision-making body has had to balance increasingly complex institutional and individual rights principles, requiring it to be more innovative in its decision making and raising controversies, in part because of conflicts between the originalist and nonoriginalist philosophies.

Bibliography

Epstein, Lee, and Thomas G. Walker. *Constitutional Law for a Changing America: A Short Course.* Washington, D.C.: Congressional Quarterly Press, 1996.

Galloway, Russell, and Rose E. Bird. *A Student's Guide to Basic Constitutional Analysis.* New York: Matthew Bender/Irwin, 1996.

Griffin, Stephen M. *American Constitutionalism: From Theory to Politics.* Princeton, N.J.: Princeton University Press, 1996.

Gunther, Gerald, and Kathleen Sullivan. *Constitutional Law.* 13th ed. Westbury, N.Y.: Foundation Press, 1997.

Renstrom, Peter G. *Constitutional Law and Young Adults.* Santa Barbara, Calif.: ABC-Clio, 1992.

Ronald C. Kahn

Consumerism

Consumer protection movements have historically advocated the interests of buyers of goods and services, using education, lobbying, legal actions, and boycotts to further their goals.

The terms "consumerism," "consumer protection," and "the consumer movement" have all been applied to the twentieth century phenomenon of intervention of buyers to protect themselves from dangerous or inferior goods and services and fraudulent or unfair sales tactics.

Historical Background. The first major period of consumerism began in the late nineteenth century. As food and textiles were be-

ginning to be mass produced, and businesses were concentrating their power, mass production created imbalance in buyer-seller relationships by breaking the links between producers and consumers. This period coincided with the Progressive movement, which not only worked for political and business reforms, but also began the move toward consumer issues with its attempts to control the sale of food and drugs.

Laws regulating food and drugs were not passed until after publication of one of the earliest muckraking books, Upton Sinclair's *The Jungle* (1906). This novel's vivid descriptions of the filthy and exploitative conditions in the meat industry so enraged the public that Congress quickly passed the Meat Inspection

Books That Changed American Consumerism

The power of the pen has been especially evident in the consumer movement. Public reactions to books by Upton Sinclair, Frank Norris, and others in the early twentieth century led directly to federal legislation protecting consumers. During the late 1950's, a new era of consumer awareness was spurred by books such as Vance Packard's *The Hidden Persuaders* (1957), which exposed the manipulative effects of political and product advertising. The following year, John Kenneth Galbraith's *The Affluent Society* stirred public awareness by asserting that advertising promoted the pursuit of private goods to the detriment of public good.

One of the most influential books of all was Rachel Carson's *Silent Spring* (1962), which exposed the dangers of pesticides and added environmental concerns to the widening focus of consumerism. In 1965 Ralph Nader published *Unsafe at Any Speed*, indicting automobile safety in general and General Motors in particular. That book helped make Nader the best-known and most durable consumer advocate in the United States.

and Pure Food and Drug Acts. The onset of World War I, however, put an end to this first cycle of the consumer movement.

Consumerism During the 1920's and 1930's. The second period of intense consumerism began in the mid-1920's. By this time the Industrial Revolution had further affected consumers in their homes, in large part because of the greater availability of electricity. In 1907 only 8 percent of American homes had electricity. By 1925 this number had risen to 53 percent. These newly electrified homes provided a ready market for such innovations as electric toasters, vacuum cleaners, and sewing machines. Such technological marvels, however, seemed so mechanically complicated that consumers did not have the knowledge to understand and evaluate their purchases. Having greater disposable income than before, and being presented with mysterious new technologies, consumers began to feel the need for impartial information to make sense of their many choices.

Two books ignited the second phase of consumerism in the United States. The first, *Your Money's Worth* (1927), by Frederick J. Schlink and Stuart Chase, advocated setting product standards and establishing impartial testing laboratories. Public interest was so great that Schlink started Consumers' Research, to test products and provide information. The *Consumers' Research Bulletin* disseminated their results.

At the federal level, the nature of New Deal programs of the 1930's helped to increase consumer representation in government. The New Deal widened the parameters for government control of the economy, and representatives from business, labor, and consumers were invited to participate in the process. Con-

Major Federal Consumer Protection Laws

Date	Legislation	Issue
1906	Pure Food and Drug Act	Adulterated food and drugs
1914	Federal Trade Commission Act	Deceptive food, drug, and cosmetic advertising
1938	Food, Drug and Cosmetics Act	Safety of drugs
1958	Food, Drug and Cosmetics Act amendments	Safety of food additives; banning of carcinogenic additives
1962	Food, Drug and Cosmetics Act amendments	Effectiveness of drugs
1966	Fair Packaging and Labeling Act	Deceptive packaging and labeling
1966	National Traffic and Motor Vehicle Safety Act	Safety standards for tires and motor vehicles
1968	Truth in Lending Act	Informing consumers of total loan costs
1970	Highway Safety Act	Creation of National Highway Traffic Safety Administration
1972	Consumer Product Safety Act	Creation of Consumer Product Safety Commission

sumers were consistently less successful than business and labor in making their needs and concerns felt, however, because they are an amorphous group and lacked a focused agenda. It was not until approximately a hundred people died from a new sulfa drug containing a toxic additive that consumer concerns again became a priority at the federal level. The Food, Drug, and Cosmetic Act of 1938 provided several new protections to consumers, regulating cosmetics and therapeutic devices for the first time. Proof of fraud was no longer required to stop false advertising claims. Drug manufacturers had to prove their products were safe

This second major period of consumerism was ended by World War II. After years of rationing and shortages, postwar consumer demand and a growing economy provided many Americans with extra time and money. New luxuries, such as television and more glamorous automobiles, took precedence in the public consciousness over regulation of products.

Consumerism After the 1950's. A third period of consumerism began in the late 1950's, spurred by books by Vance Packard, and others. Their influence and President Lyndon B. Johnson's Great Society programs of the 1960's helped create a new climate favorable to more government intervention. It took tragedy and scandal, however, before consumer protection legislation

Popular dislike of lawyers gave rise to three voter initiatives in California's 1996 election designed to limit lawyer fees and reduce litigation. Among those supporting these initiatives were members of a consumer activist organization called Voter Revolt. (AP/Wide World Photos)

again became a federal priority. Reports came from Europe of a rash of children born with gross physical defects that were linked to use of the drug thalidomide by pregnant women.

After publishing Unsafe at Any Speed *(1965) Ralph Nader became the leading spokesperson for consumers in the United States. He later founded a watchdog organization called Public Citizen to monitor government policy making generally.* (AP/Wide World Photos)

This tragedy gave impetus to the Kefauver-Harris Amendment to the federal Food, Drug, and Cosmetic Act, which required more stringent testing of new drugs.

The scandal involved General Motors' use of a private detective to investigate Ralph Nader, author of *Unsafe at Any Speed* (1962), a book challenging the safety of American automobiles, who was invited to testify before a Senate subcommittee on automobile safety. When the giant company's investigation was discovered and exposed, Nader's invasion-of-

privacy suit resulted in a settlement of more than $400,000, with which Nader funded several consumer organizations.

Antiregulatory Trends Since 1980. Federal interest in consumer protection declined under the antiregulatory Reagan administration of the 1980's. Nevertheless, public pressure for consumer protection has resulted in the passage of legislation, formation of agencies, funding of research, and other government responses on the federal, state, and local levels. At the federal level, many resources are directed toward consumer protection, but by the mid-1990's no independent agency existed that had a clear mandate for consumer welfare, regulatory power, and a budget sufficient to give it clout.

As national economies have become more globalized, the consumer protection movement has spread beyond its United States roots. Consumerism in industrialized countries generally focuses on eliminating unsafe products through the institution of government regulations and standards. Consumerism usually depends in great part on private organizations that test products and disseminate information to consumers and often is aligned with other social movements, such as labor or environmental groups.

The consumer protection movement has been an important force in enabling buyers to evaluate products, pressuring corporate interests to improve product safety and quality, and prodding governments to take responsibility for setting standards. In most countries, the movement derives its strength from the concerns of general citizens and tends to be less effective when public attention is not focused on a specific use.

Bibliography

Baca, Polly. *Consumer's Resource Handbook 1994.* Washington, D.C.: U.S. Office of Consumer Affairs, Pueblo, Colo., 1994.

Brobeck, Stephen, Robert N. Mayer, and Robert O. Herrmann. *Encyclopedia of the Consumer Movement.* Santa Barbara, Calif.: ABC-CLIO, 1997.

Krohn, Lauren. *Consumer Protection and the Law: A Dictionary.* Santa Barbara, Calif.: ABC-CLIO, 1995.

Maney, Ardith, and Loree G. Bykerk. *Consumer Politics: Protecting Public Interests on Capitol Hill.* Westport, Conn.: Greenwood Press, 1994.

Irene Struthers

County Government

Counties are the largest political subdivisions of U.S. states. Their governments perform state-mandated functions, such as local law enforcement and voting administration, and provide such local services as water supply and street maintenance.

In the late 1990's more than three thousand county governments operated throughout the United States. They are in every state except Connecticut and Rhode Island—in both of which town governments perform county functions. Counties are called "boroughs" in Alaska and "parishes" in Louisiana.

Historical Background. American county government was created as an administrative

---

Key Terms

DILLON'S RULE: principle that local government can perform only such functions as are expressly granted by its state government

GENERAL LAW COUNTY: a county that does not have home rule powers because it was created by a state general law and not by a special charter

HOME RULE: freedom of local governments to run their own affairs without state interference

MUNICIPAL CORPORATION: legal description of a city, town, or village that is formally incorporated as a municipality through a state charter

PROFESSIONALIZATION OF COUNTY GOVERNMENT: process wherein counties adopt the administrator or elected executive form of government, or adopt a merit system of employment

QUASI-MUNICIPAL CORPORATION: term used to describe the legal status of a county

UNINCORPORATED AREA: section of a county that is not incorporated into a municipality and is thus subject to direct county government control

agent of the state, patterned after English counties, originally called "shires." In the nineteenth and early twentieth centuries, most counties, administered by a board of commissioners or supervisors, provided only a few state-mandated services. This was particularly true in New England states, where towns were the most important local governmental units. Many county governments at that time were inefficient, corrupt, incompetent, and even chaotic.

As counties became more urbanized and their populations increased in the late twentieth century, their governments became more active in meeting new demands from their residents. As a result, county expenditures and functions increased significantly. Of all local governments—except special districts—counties grew the fastest during the 1980's. "Megacounties," such as Los Angeles in California, Cook in Illinois, Harris in Texas, and Dade in Florida, provide services to residents in unincorporated areas, in incorporated cities and towns, and occasionally even outside county lines.

Legal Basis of Counties. Because the U.S. CONSTITUTION does not mention counties, their governments are purely creations of their states. They are formed to administer state laws, unlike other local governments, which are established voluntarily by the local inhabitants to provide local services. Because county governments are subdivisions of states, they wield different powers and perform different functions from CITY GOVERNMENT. For this reason they are called "quasi-municipal corporations."

Like municipal corporations, such as cities and towns, county governments have corporate, governmental, and proprietary powers. Their corporate powers include the right to perpetuate their existence, ability to sue and be sued, and ability to buy and sell property. Their governmental powers include such compulsory activities as policing and taxation,

which they perform as agents for their states. Their proprietary powers include such enterprises as maintaining public utilities and garbage collection, which may compete with private businesses. County governments act more often as agents of the state than cities and towns do, are thus more subject to state legislative control.

County Functions. The concepts of governmental and proprietary powers provide a legal basis for the distinction between mandatory and optional functions of county government. Mandatory functions are those that county governments are required to perform by state laws. Property tax assessment, law enforcement, voting administration, public health, recording of deeds, and public welfare are examples of state-mandated functions.

Optional functions are those that county governments are permitted by state law to perform for the benefit of their residents. These functions include maintaining parks, utilities, water supply and sewage, garbage collection, transportation, parking, and housing. In the early years of the nation county governments served primarily as rural governments and performed mostly state-mandated functions. As populations increased and became more urbanized, many urban and suburban county governments provided more optional services.

County governments generate various types of revenues. They collect property and other taxes, including real property, personal property, sales, machinery and tools, cigarette, and transient occupancy taxes. They charge users fees for services such as swimming pools, park admissions, golf courses, and adult education. They also receive a significant amount of state aid and some federal aid. Finally, they can issue tax anticipation notes to cover short-term cash needs, and long-term bonds to finance capital projects, such as sport stadiums and bridges, that require large amounts of capital.

County Officials. County governments elect officials such as sheriffs, treasurers, coro-

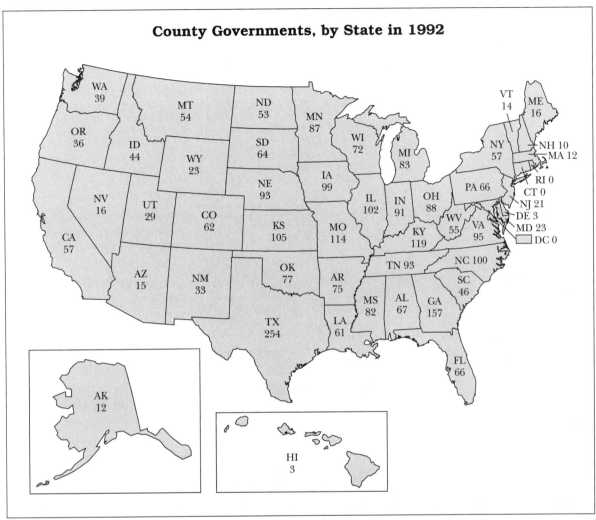

County Governments, by State in 1992

Source: U.S. Bureau of the Census, *Statistical Abstract of the United States: 1997.* 117th ed. Washington, D.C.: U.S. Government Printing Office, 1997.

ners, and commissioners or supervisors, and appoint many department directors and employees. Who elects or appoints these officials, what they do, and how they work together is determined primarily by the organizational structure of individual governments. Such governments usually have one of three organizational structures: commission form, administrator form, or elected executive form. These forms are imposed on counties by their states, except in home-rule counties.

Under the commission form, usually three or five commissioners or supervisors are elected by districts, or at-large by voters, and exercise both legislative and administrative powers. They can hold hearings, enact ordinances, set tax rates, appoint advisory board and commission members, and oversee their appointees. In addition to the commissioners, the voters elect other officers including sheriffs, clerks, tax assessors, coroners, attorneys, and recorders of deeds.

Under the administrator form, county administrators appointed by boards of commissioners have supervisory and budgetary powers over individual departments. They may be

Gloria Molina became the first Hispanic elected to the Los Angeles County board of supervisors in 1991. (AP/Wide World Photos)

ets and supervise staff services, and coordinate county programs, but usually do not directly supervise executive departments and do not appoint department chiefs. Administrative assistants perform mostly ADMINISTRATIVE PROCEDURES without any formal powers.

Under the executive form, county executives and several commissioners are directly elected by the voters. The executives have the power to oversee the operations of county departments, appoint and remove department directors, and veto acts of commissioners; the commissioners have the power to hold hearings on policy matters, pass ordinances, adopt budgets, and override the county executive's veto. Since the executives wield power over the operations of entire county administrations, they can represent the whole county administration, provide strong leadership, and be subject to ACCOUNTABILITY to residents for county policies.

called county managers, chief administrative officers, or administrative assistants. County managers have the most extensive powers of these types, and administrative assistants the fewest. County managers appoint and supervise most department directors and staff officers, prepare budgets, make policy decisions, and review county programs.

Chief administrative officers prepare budg-

Traditionally, the commission form was the most common form, but the administrator and executive forms gained popularity in the last part of the twentieth century, particularly in urban and suburban areas. By 1990 about a fifth of all counties had the elected executive form. The rest were almost evenly split between the commission form and the administrator form.

State Controls. Strong state control of county government is one of the most conspicuous aspects of county government operations. County governments are subject to almost unlimited state control. This tight state control of county operations is well expressed in Dillon's rule, which holds that all powers not explicitly granted to local governments belong to the state. An exception to the iron-fist control is found in home-rule counties, which can run their local affairs with little state intervention. Fewer than a tenth of all counties, however, exercise home-rule privileges. This lack of home-rule among county governments limits their ability to begin new initiatives without state approval.

General law counties (non-home-rule counties) and home-rule counties have significantly different powers in the four major areas: political structure, functional responsibility, fiscal administration, and personnel administration. General law counties must receive state approval to change their own organizational structures, to decide what additional services to provide, to determine what additional revenues to generate, or to change employee salary levels.

More counties adopted professional forms of government and the merit system of employment to meet the growing service challenges they faced and to eliminate the criticisms directed at their operations. While county governments have become more competent service providers, the need for their services has been increasing. Federal and state governments continuously shift their service responsibilities to local governments, or mandate additional services, sometimes without providing the means to fulfill them. Regional problems, such as air and water pollution, traffic congestion, and lack of environmental preservation, have forced small local governments to ally themselves with other local governments to deal with these problems. Since county governments are the largest political subdivisions of the state, they have an advantage in solving these types of regional problems.

Bibliography

Berman, David, ed. *County Governments in an Era of Change.* Westport, Conn.: Greenwood Press, 1993.

Jeffery, Blake R., Tanis J. Salant, and Alan L. Boroshok. *County Government Structure: A State by State Report.* Washington, D.C.: National Association of Counties, 1989.

Menzel, Donald C. *The American County: Frontiers of Knowledge.* Tuscaloosa: University of Alabama Press, 1996.

Keeok Park

Courts: Federal

Operating independently of state judicial systems, federal courts are responsible for hearing cases and administering justice respecting federal law. The courts are organized in three levels that include district courts, courts of appeals, and the Supreme Court.

The United States has established a national system of courts as its major means of administering justice at the federal level. Federal courts have the power to pronounce judgments, to punish, to rule on the constitutionality of legislative acts, and to interpret laws passed by Congress. In carrying out their work, courts strive to protect citizens from unwarranted interference of government in their lives. The courts were established to be impartial forums for the resolution of controversies between parties. Federal courts exist side-by-side with the fifty states' courts. Thus, the United States has two distinct court systems: state and federal.

Article 3, section 1, of the U.S. CONSTITUTION states that "judicial Power of the United States, shall be vested in one supreme Court and in such inferior Courts as the Congress may from time to time ordain and establish." In 1789 Congress set up the federal JUDICIAL

In 1992 William H. Rehnquist addressed an American Bar Association meeting in Dallas, Texas, where he asked the help of the legal profession in resisting what he called Congress's efforts to increase the workloads of federal judges. (AP/Wide World Photos)

SYSTEM with trial courts in each state. In 1891 Congress established a set of intermediate courts with appellate jurisdiction. This three-part judicial structure—trial courts, appellate courts, and the SUPREME COURT—has remained basically unchanged.

District Courts. The first level of courts in the federal system consists of district courts. The country and its territories have been divided into ninety-four districts. There is at least one district in every state, and in large and heavily populated states there are several. Almost all district courts have more than one judge available to try cases. District court judges, like other federal court judges, are appointed by the president of the United States. They hold office for life, so long as they are not guilty of judicial misconduct.

As the general trial-level courts in the federal system, district courts have jurisdiction over such matters as a CRIME against the United States, civil actions arising under federal law, and cases involving citizens of different states or citizens and aliens. They also review and enforce actions of certain federal administrative agencies, such as some rules of the Interstate Commerce Commission. Most federal cases begin and end in district courts, but many decisions are appealed to the next level of courts.

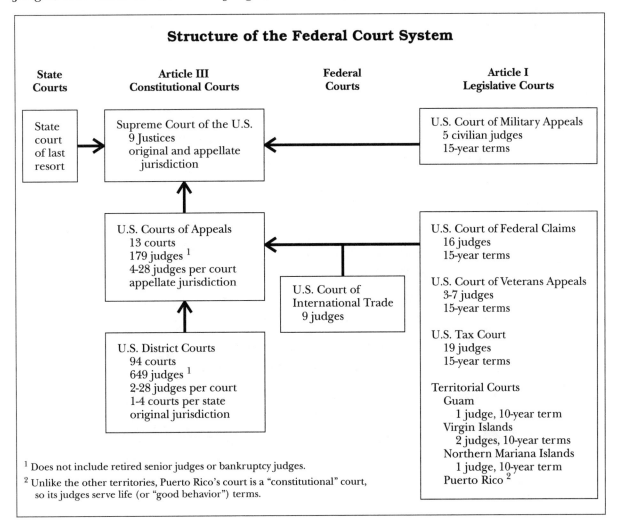

Structure of the Federal Court System

State Courts	Article III Constitutional Courts	Federal Courts	Article I Legislative Courts
State court of last resort	Supreme Court of the U.S. 9 Justices original and appellate jurisdiction		U.S. Court of Military Appeals 5 civilian judges 15-year terms
	U.S. Courts of Appeals 13 courts 179 judges [1] 4-28 judges per court appellate jurisdiction	U.S. Court of International Trade 9 judges	U.S. Court of Federal Claims 16 judges 15-year terms
			U.S. Court of Veterans Appeals 3-7 judges 15-year terms
	U.S. District Courts 94 courts 649 judges [1] 2-28 judges per court 1-4 courts per state original jurisdiction		U.S. Tax Court 19 judges 15-year terms
			Territorial Courts Guam 1 judge, 10-year term Virgin Islands 2 judges, 10-year terms Northern Mariana Islands 1 judge, 10-year term Puerto Rico [2]

[1] Does not include retired senior judges or bankruptcy judges.

[2] Unlike the other territories, Puerto Rico's court is a "constitutional" court, so its judges serve life (or "good behavior") terms.

Courts of Appeals. Courts of Appeals are the second level of courts in the federal system. Judgments made in district courts are reviewable by the courts of appeals in the judicial circuits in which the district courts are located. Congress has established thirteen federal judicial circuits, twelve of which are organized on a geographic basis. For example, the First Circuit includes Maine, Massachusetts, New Hampshire, Rhode Island, and Puerto Rico. The one circuit court that is not geographically organized, the Court of Appeals for the Federal Circuit, was established in 1982 to handle cases involving subjects such as public contracts, customs issues, and patent appeals.

Circuit courts have jurisdiction to review decisions of their district courts and orders of major administrative agencies. The judges of the circuit courts have the same tenure and salary benefits as district court judges. The number of judges on each of the thirteen appellate courts varies depending on the amount of work in the circuit, but most circuits have between ten and fifteen. In theory, decisions at the appellate level are made on the basis of the records, and no new evidence may be presented to the court.

U.S. Supreme Court. The third level of courts in the federal system is the Supreme Court. It has nine judges or justices, but Congress can increase or decrease that number. One justice is designated Chief Justice of the United States; the others are associate justices. Like other federal judges, justices hold office for life, so long as they are not guilty of judicial misconduct. When vacancies occur, the president of the United States nominates new justices, subject to confirmation by the Senate. The Court sits in Washington, D.C., and its annual term stretches from October to June.

The Supreme Court has jurisdiction over all federal appellate courts and also over decisions of the highest state courts when those courts decide questions of federal law. In

Most efforts to impeach federal office holders in U.S. history have been directed against judges; however, all but a few such efforts have failed. (AP/Wide World Photos)

terms of the Constitution's list of disputes over which the Supreme Court has original jurisdiction, the Court's major work has been with controversies between two or more states, such as the conflict between Arizona and California over water rights. The Court's primary work, however, is appellate, and in that work it is the final arbiter of the meaning of the Constitution.

There are several ways that a case that has been decided by a lower court could reach the Supreme Court, but by far the most important is the Court's granting of a writ of *certiorari*. A disappointed litigant can petition the Court to consider an adverse ruling from a lower court. In its discretion, the Court can then decide whether to hear the case. If four justices agree that the case merits consideration, *certiorari* is granted. When the Court does not take up cases, the lower court decisions stand as the final word.

Special Legislative Courts. In addition to the three levels of constitutional courts in the federal system, Congress has established a number of special legislative courts under its power to constitute tribunals inferior to the Supreme Court. Among these are the U.S. Court of International Trade, the U.S. Claims Court, the Court of Military Appeals, the Court of Veterans Appeals, the Tax Court, the Claims Court, and bankruptcy courts. Each has a specific jurisdiction in its area.

The U.S. Court System. The American judicial system is the most complicated in the world. The major reason for this is the simultaneous existence of state and federal systems of courts. With two major legal systems, there is a multiplicity of laws and overlapping jurisdictions. Every citizen of the United States is at all times subject to laws of the federal government and the laws of a particular state.

The U.S. Supreme Court has been careful to acknowledge that a state's highest court is the authority on state law so long as no federal question is involved. It also has affirmed con-sistently that governmental powers beyond those given to the federal government are reserved for the states. This dual court system takes account of the need for a strong central government while respecting the values and strengths of states' rights, personal freedom, and self-determination that were so important in Revolutionary War days. The name given to such a system of government is FEDERALISM.

Bibliography
Barrow, Deborah J., Gary Zuk, and Gerard S. Gryski. *The Federal Judiciary and Institutional Change.* Ann Arbor: University of Michigan Press, 1996.
Carp, Robert A., and Ronald Stidham. *The Federal Courts.* 2d ed. Washington, D.C.: Congressional Quarterly Press, 1991.
Meador, Daniel J. *American Courts.* St. Paul, Minn.: West, 1991.
Wheeler, Russell R., and Cynthia E. Harrison. *Creating the Federal Judicial System.* 2d ed. Washington, D.C.: Federal Judicial Center, 1994.

Roger G. Gaddis

Courts: State and Local

State and local court systems handle most civil and criminal cases in the United States. As the judicial branches of state governments, they issue decisions that control the acts of local authorities, state officials, and all citizens within their jurisdictions.

While no two court systems of local and STATE GOVERNMENTS are identical, most share many common features, such as separation into three distinct levels. These similarities are critical to any understanding of how the courts function. Each system normally has courts of limited jurisdiction, courts of general jurisdiction, and courts of appellate jurisdiction. Courts at each level provide services important to the functioning of the JUDICIAL SYSTEM as a whole within each state. The nature and type of each case determines which court will have jurisdiction.

Courts that hear and decide only certain limited legal issues are known as courts of limited jurisdiction. These courts hear matters such as certain types of minor civil or criminal cases. For example, they handle traffic tickets, set bail for criminal defendants, resolve small claims matters, and issue rulings on lawsuits dealing with contracts, personal injuries, or other matters where the amounts of money involved are small.

In the United States, there are approximately thirteen thousand local courts. These include county, magistrate, justice, and municipal courts. Judges may be either appointed or elected to these courts. The fact that these courts handle minor civil and criminal matters does not mean their duties are not important. The only direct contact most citizens have with the judicial system occurs in such courts.

General Jurisdiction Courts. Courts of limited jurisdiction also may hear certain specialized matters such as probate of wills and estates, divorces, child custody matters, and juvenile hearings. In some states, these matters are heard in local courts. In others, there are courts of general jurisdiction that are designated by statute to hear and decide specific types of cases. For example, California "superior courts" are courts of general jurisdiction. However, certain of them hear only juvenile matters; they thus become courts of limited jurisdiction when they sit as JUVENILE courts.

Courts of general jurisdiction are granted authority to hear and decide all issues that are brought before them. They are known by a variety of names, such as superior courts, circuit courts, district courts, or courts of common pleas. These courts normally hear major civil or criminal cases. They have authority to decide issues that occur anywhere within the state. Typically, these courts hear civil cases

involving the same types of issues that courts of limited jurisdiction hear, but the amounts of damages are higher and may reach millions of dollars. These courts also hear the most serious criminal matters, including CAPITAL PUNISHMENT cases.

Courts of general jurisdiction traditionally have the power to issue injunctions prohibiting certain acts or requiring individuals or entities to perform certain functions or duties. This authority is derived from the equity power that resides in courts of general jurisdiction. Equity is the concept that JUSTICE is administered according to fairness, as contrasted with the strict rules of LAW.

Appellate Courts. Appellate jurisdiction is reserved for courts that hear appeals from both limited and general jurisdiction courts. These courts do not hold trials or hear evidence. They decide matters of law and issue formal written decisions or opinions. The two classes of appellate courts are intermediate and final.

Intermediate appellate courts are known as courts of appeals. Approximately half the states have designated intermediate appellate courts. These courts may be divided into judicial districts and hear all appeals within their district. They hear and decide all issues of law that are raised on appeal in both civil and criminal cases. These courts accept the facts as determined by the trial courts. Since they deal strictly with legal or equitable issues, they do not use juries to decide factual disputes. Intermediate appellate courts have the authority to reverse decisions of lower courts and send the matters back with instructions to retry the cases in accordance with their opinion. Parties who lose appeals at this level may file appeals with the next higher appellate court.

Final appellate courts are the highest state appellate courts. They may be known as supreme courts or courts of last resort. Five, seven, or nine justices generally sit on these courts, depending on the state. Such courts have jurisdiction to hear and decide issues dealing with all matters decided by lower courts, including ruling on state constitutional or statutory issues. Their decisions are binding on all other courts within the state. Once such a court decides an issue, the only appeal left is to file in the federal court system.

Judges. Since local and state court judges are usually elected to their positions, they can and do claim that they answer only to the general public. Many state court systems have a presiding judge who is elected or appointed by the other judges. This judge may act as a supervisor and regulate the type and amount of cases assigned to all other judges, but cannot censure or remove another judge for incompetence or wrongdoing. That function is normally left in the hands of the state supreme court, a state judicial panel, or the state legislature. Therefore, no one person or agency is responsible for the effective administration of the state's court system.

Dividing courts into courts of limited and general jurisdiction results in specialization and fragmentation of duties. Within each state court system, courts may be further divided into areas of specialization, with one judge hearing all probate matters, another hearing all FAMILY matters, and another hearing all juvenile matters. While this system may allow judges to develop expertise in their special areas, it can result in uneven workloads.

Geographical organization

is a third common characteristic of state and local courts. Courts have established boundaries that have implications for the citizens that reside within their jurisdictions. These courts reflect the different social values and attitudes of their citizens. For example, courts in rural jurisdictions may view certain types of CRIME—such as harming farm animals—as more seri-

In November, 1997, Pennsylvania judge Seamus P. McCaffery presided over a makeshift courtroom inside Philadelphia's Veterans Stadium to dispense speedy trials to fans arrested for disorderly behavior during an Eagles football game. (AP/Wide World Photos)

ous offenses than would courts in urban areas.

In many ways state court judicial systems mirror the federal government, which also has three distinct branches of government. State courts interpret state constitutions, statutes, and other issues of concern to state citizens. Their decisions normally have a more direct impact on the lives of Americans than decisions issued by federal courts other than the U.S. SUPREME COURT.

Most state court time goes to criminal cases. Not only are more crimes committed than civil wrongs, but other factors cause state court systems to give criminal cases priority over civil cases. The Sixth Amendment to the U.S. CONSTITUTION requires that criminal defendants receive speedy trials, mandating that criminal cases take precedence over civil matters. As a result, it is not unusual for a civil case to languish for five years before it is tried.

Courts and judicial administrators have responded to this predicament by trying a variety of nonjudicial methods to handle civil cases. Some courts limit the amount of discovery (search for evidence) or pretrial investigation that can occur. Other systems have instituted printed forms that all parties must use. Many court systems have encouraged, or even mandated, that certain civil matters be decided by arbitration or other alternative dispute resolution mechanisms. Alternative methods of resolving civil disputes are usually less costly than court trials. More important, they proceed faster than courts. Despite attempts at modernization and use of alternative dispute mechanisms such as arbitration or mediation, local and state court systems are overcrowded and respond very slowly to most issues.

Bibliography

Fino, Susan P. *The Role of State Supreme Courts in the New Judicial Federalism.* New York: Greenwood, 1987.

Glick, Henry Robert. *State Court Systems.* Englewood Cliffs, N.J.: Prentice-Hall, 1973.

Meador, Daniel J. *American Courts.* St. Paul, Minn.: West, 1991.

Rottman, David B., Carol R. Flango, and R. Shedine Lockley. *State Court Organization, 1993.* Washington, D.C.: U.S. Dept. of Justice, 1995.

Tarr, G. Alan. *State Supreme Courts in State and Nation.* New Haven, Conn.: Yale University Press, 1988.

Harvey Wallace
Shanda Wedlock

Crime

Crime is any behavior that violates the law and makes the offender subject to punishment. Definitions of criminal behavior are at the core of the American justice system and have much to do with how members of the society categorize certain individuals and classes of people as outlaws.

The term "crime" is popularly associated with violent or patently unacceptable adult behavior, such as murder, rape, TREASON, theft, or housebreaking. In strict legal terms, a crime is any behavior that contravenes laws. However, this narrow definition does not match broader social definitions of crime, which are shaped by customs, cultural value systems, and other factors. For example, jaywalking and double-parking are technically crimes in many communities; however, community members seldom regard people who break such laws as "criminals." Conversely, some members of society regard certain behaviors—such as extramarital sex or swearing—as morally criminal, although such behaviors are legal.

Traditional Concepts of Crime. The essence of criminal behavior is misconduct that threatens the security, welfare, or sense of propriety of the community as a whole. Acts such as murder, arson, theft, rape, assault, and treason are thus almost universally regarded as

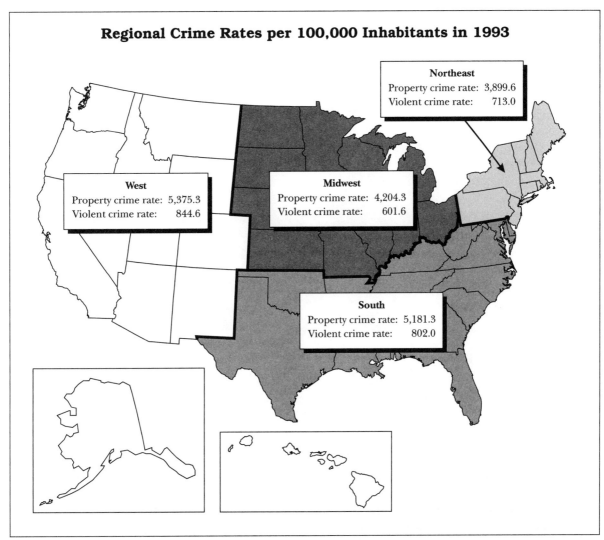

Regional Crime Rates per 100,000 Inhabitants in 1993

Northeast
Property crime rate: 3,899.6
Violent crime rate: 713.0

West
Property crime rate: 5,375.3
Violent crime rate: 844.6

Midwest
Property crime rate: 4,204.3
Violent crime rate: 601.6

South
Property crime rate: 5,181.3
Violent crime rate: 802.0

Source: U.S. Department of Justice, Federal Bureau of Investigation, *Crime in the United States* (Uniform Crime Reports). Washington, D.C.: U.S. Government Printing Office, 1994.

criminal and virtually all societies have laws against them. Such actions are regarded as more than wrongs against individuals: They are wrongs so outrageous that all members of the society must collectively act to prevent them and to punish their perpetrators.

While certain behaviors are almost universally regarded as unacceptable, definitions of specific crimes vary widely among communities. The severity of punishments for criminal behavior has always tended to reflect the awfulness of the crime against the community as a whole. For example, before modern fire departments existed, many societies regarded arson as worse than murder because fires might destroy entire communities.

Categories of Crime. In modern societies, criminal acts fall into three fundamental categories: crimes against the government, crimes against "common morality," and crimes against persons. Tax fraud, sabotage, and treason are examples of crimes against government. Certain sex behaviors—such as homosexuality or adultery—may be considered

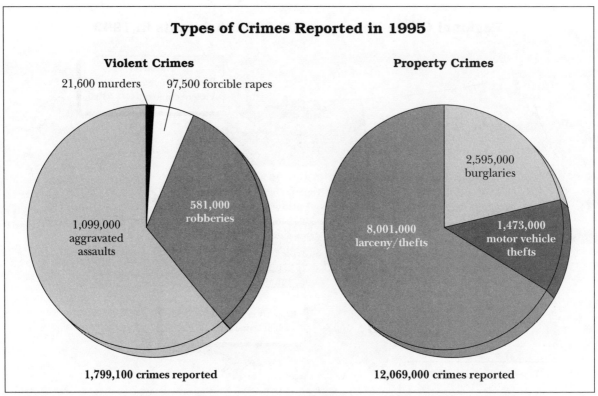

Types of Crimes Reported in 1995

Violent Crimes

21,600 murders   97,500 forcible rapes

581,000 robberies

1,099,000 aggravated assaults

1,799,100 crimes reported

Property Crimes

2,595,000 burglaries

1,473,000 motor vehicle thefts

8,001,000 larceny/thefts

12,069,000 crimes reported

Source: U.S. Bureau of the Census, *Statistical Abstract of the United States: 1997.* 117th ed. Washington, D.C.: U.S. Government Printing Office, 1997.

examples of crimes against common morality. Murder, assault, and theft are examples of crimes against persons.

Crimes Against Persons. Although crimes such as assault, theft, and murder are committed against individual persons, governments regard them as offenses against the community as a whole. When such crimes occur, government reacts as if the offense were against it. Criminal wrongs are distinguished from civil wrongs, another type of wrong done to a person. A common example of a civil wrong is the failure of a person or corporate body to fulfill a legal contract.

In modern society, determination that an act constitutes criminal behavior requires the *intent* to commit the crime. Acts such as arson and murder that are normally regarded as crimes may not be considered criminal if they are committed by persons found to be men-

tally ill, who therefore cannot form criminal intent. Exempting the mentally ill and incompetent from criminal prosecution is a long-standing modern commitment, but it has had challenges within the fields of psychology and psychiatry.

Violent and Nonviolent Crimes. Distinctions between violent and nonviolent crime are widespread in Western societies. Violent crimes involve physically harming, or threatening to harm, human beings. Such crimes, which include murder, rape, assault, and armed robbery, attract the most serious attention by law enforcement agencies, as well as the most severe punishments.

Nonviolent crimes include drug dealing, gambling, theft, housebreaking, vandalism, computer fraud, and many other activities. A broad category of nonviolent criminal behaviors has become popularly known as "white-collar" crimes because they are associated with executive and management-level job holders. Such crimes include fraud and embezzlement—both of which can be difficult to detect and even more difficult to prosecute and punish.

Distinctions between violent and nonviolent crimes are not always sharp, as some nonviolent crimes can generate unexpected violence. Burglary, for example, is normally considered a nonviolent crime; however, if burglars unexpectedly encounter someone, their nonviolent crimes can quickly turn into violent assaults.

Felonies and Misdemeanors. Another basic distinction used to separate crimes is their seriousness. For example, petty shoplifting and grand theft are both considered crimes, but the latter is regarded as much more serious. Most legal codes in the United States use the terms "felonies" and "misdemeanors" to separate crimes, with felonies being the more serious and misdemeanors the less serious.

Criminal statutes generally classify as felonies crimes for which punishments may include jail or prison terms longer than one year. Felony convictions may also carry such additional penalties as loss of professional licenses and loss of the right to vote or hold public office.

Misdemeanors are typically lesser offenses for which maximum periods of incarceration are less than a year. This distinction is not exact, however, as persons convicted of felonies sometimes serve less prison time than persons convicted of misdemeanor offenses. Misdemeanors

Total Estimated Arrests in the United States in 1993	
Total	**14,036,310**
Arrests for FBI "Index Crimes"	
Murder and nonnegligent manslaughter	23,400
Forcible rape	38,420
Robbery	173,620
Aggravated assault	518,670
Burglary	402,700
Larceny-theft	1,476,300
Motor vehicle theft	195,900
Arson	19,400
Arrests for Other Crimes	
Other assaults	1,144,900
Forgery and counterfeiting	106,900
Fraud	410,700
Embezzlement	12,900
Stolen property; buying, receiving, possessing	158,100
Vandalism	313,000
Weapons; carrying, possessing, etc.	262,300
Prostitution and commercialized vice	97,800
Sex offenses (except forcible rape and prostitution)	104,100
Drug abuse violations	1,126,300
Gambling	17,300
Offenses against family and children	109,100
Driving under the influence	1,524,800
Liquor laws	518,500
Drunkenness	726,600
Disorderly conduct	727,000
Vagrancy	28,200
All other offenses	3,518,700
Suspicion (not included in totals)	14,100
Curfew and loitering law violations	100,200
Runaways	180,500

Source: U.S. Department of Justice, Federal Bureau of Investigation, *Crime in the United States* (Uniform Crime Reports). Washington, D.C.: U.S. Government Printing Office, 1994.

Note: Arrest totals are based on data from all agencies reporting to the Uniform Crime Reporting Program and estimates for unreported areas. Because of rounding, figures may not add to total.

are typically nonviolent crimes, but such nonviolent activities as usury, gambling, and drug dealing are often classified as felony offenses. In contrast, minor cases of violent assault may in certain circumstances be treated as misdemeanors.

Certain crimes, such as murder, rape, and armed robbery, are always treated as felonies. Other crimes, such as petty theft, parking offenses, and smoking in elevators, are virtually always regarded as misdemeanors. For many crimes, however, distinctions between misdemeanor and felony offenses are matters of degree. For example, distinctions between misdemeanor and felony theft are typically defined by amounts of money or values of the stolen goods. Likewise, distinctions between misdemeanor and felony drug possession may be defined by the quantities of illegal drugs that offenders possess. Many criminal codes leave distinctions between misdemeanor and felony criminal behavior flexible to allow DISTRICT ATTORNEYS to choose between misdemeanor and felony charges against suspects.

Individual vs. Organized Crime. A further classification of crimes is between acts committed by individual persons and those committed by organized groups. Such distinctions do not necessarily have anything to do with the seriousness of the crimes. The distinction is of importance primarily to law enforcement agencies, which regard individual crimes as generally simpler to control than those committed by organized groups. Once an individual criminal is apprehended and incarcerated, that person's criminal behavior can usually be stopped, at least for a time. By contrast, criminal activities of groups do not necessarily end when their members are arrested and convicted.

Organized crime presents special challenges to law enforcement when criminal networks are too large for individual law enforcement agencies to monitor and control. Organized crime networks often extend beyond the jurisdictions of individual municipalities or even states, presenting local law enforcement agencies with the additional problems of being restrained by their jurisdictional boundaries. The rapid mobility made possible by modern society allows agents of organized crime to commit offenses in one jurisdiction and quickly flee to another. Historically, this fact has helped promote the development of police forces on the federal and state levels.

Organized crime most typically involves nonviolent crimes, which generally elicit less vigorous law enforcement responses than violent crimes. Organized criminal activity often mimics legitimate enterprises by building elaborate organizations and responding to market forces, such as changing demand for drugs. Many organized criminal groups buy and sell commodities and services—such as drugs, stolen goods, and prostitution—which require procuring, reselling, distribution, and delivery. Like legitimate business, organized

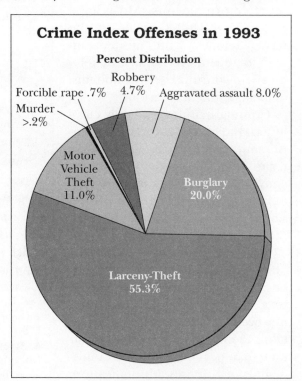

Crime Index Offenses in 1993

Percent Distribution

Forcible rape .7%
Murder >.2%
Robbery 4.7%
Aggravated assault 8.0%
Motor Vehicle Theft 11.0%
Burglary 20.0%
Larceny-Theft 55.3%

crime can benefit from running large, efficient operations.

Victimless Crime and Decriminalization. "Victimless" crimes are illegal activities in which all parties participate willingly. These crimes typically involve exchanging contraband goods (such as drugs) or services (such as gambling or prostitution). Distinguishing between victimless crimes and crimes with victims can be difficult. For example, persons who voluntarily buy illegal narcotics for their own use are not victims in the usual sense, but they may be regarded by society as victims of a larger evil. Further, willing participants in so-called victimless crimes who repent their initial decisions and elect to withdraw from the illegal activity may provoke violent responses from the persons with whom they are dealing.

As fears of violent crime have grown in the United States, there has been a growing public acceptance of the idea of decriminalizing victimless crimes. A primary motivation behind this trend has been the desire to see the nation's limited law enforcement resources respond more effectively to violent crimes. However, many Americans have such strong moral objections to such activities as prostitution and drug use that they regard them as inherently criminal. Further, many critics of decriminalization have argued that activities such as drug use, gambling, and prostitution foster other types of criminal behavior even if they themselves are legalized.

Crime Statistics. Every year the FEDERAL BUREAU OF INVESTIGATION (FBI) publishes the Uniform Crime Reports (UCR) under the title *Crime in the United States*. This annual publication provides the most objective available picture of the incidence of crime reported to law enforcement agencies. Voluntarily submitted by almost all American law enforcement agencies, the information in the UCR is divided into violent crimes against persons (such as murder, rape, robbery, and aggravated assault) and crimes against property (such as burglary,

---

"Victimless" Crimes

The best-known example of decriminalization of a victimless crime was the federal government's repeal of Prohibition in 1933. During the dozen years that the federal government banned the sale of alcoholic beverages under the Eighteenth Amendment (1919) to the U.S. Constitution, violations of the law were so widespread that a new amendment, the Twenty-first, was passed to end Prohibition. Since then, prohibitions on the manufacture, distribution, and sale of alcoholic beverages have been maintained by a small number of state and local governments.

Gambling is another pervasive form of criminal activity that is gradually being decriminalized. Legalized casino gambling was once limited to the state of Nevada, and betting on horse and dog races was limited to a small number of jurisdictions. By the 1990's, state-run lotteries for government revenue enhancement were commonplace, and other forms of gambling were increasingly being legalized.

---

larceny-theft, and motor vehicle theft).

UCR figures are based solely on reported crimes and can be distorted. Not all crimes are reported to the police. For example, violent crimes are more likely to be reported than property crimes. Further, murder and aggravated assault are more likely to be reported than rape, which many victims hesitate to report because of the stigma that attaches to victims. Automobile theft is far more likely to be reported than other kinds of theft, largely because automobile owners must report thefts to collect insurance. UCR data should be compared with that in the annual National Crime Victimization Survey, published annually by the U.S. Bureau of Justice Statistics; this survey collects crime data by polling households directly and therefore is able to measure crime that is never reported to police.

UCR figures are also distorted because

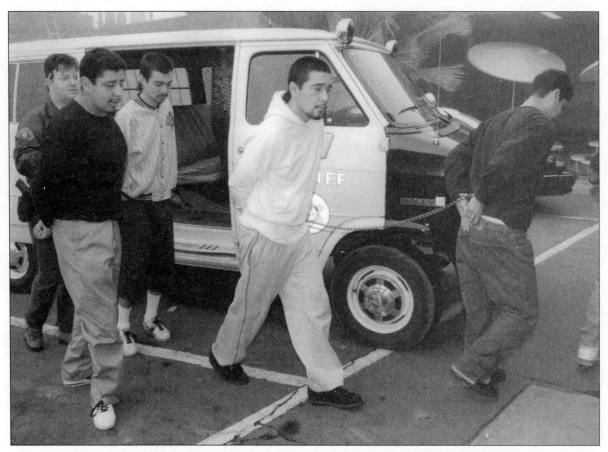

Carjacking suspects under arrest in Los Angeles County in 1993. (AP/Wide World Photos)

some jurisdictions underreport crimes, fearing that high crime rates reflect negatively on their communities. A well-known example of this was found by an audit showing that Washington, D.C., was downgrading almost a third of all grand larcenies to simple larceny to keep them out of the crime report. Finally, some categories of crimes, such as misdemeanor assaults and consumer fraud, are not included in the UCR.

Keeping the limitations of the UCR in mind, some generalizations can be made about crime in the modern United States. During the early 1970's, the nation's annual overall crime rate stood at about four criminal offenses per one thousand persons; by the mid-1990's, this figure had risen to about six offenses per one thousand persons. Among

property crimes, the incidence of burglary historically rose until the early 1980's, when it began to recede. However, other larcenies—particularly auto theft—began increasing substantially. Murder figures have fluctuated annually, but generally have ranged between 8.5 and 10 murders per 100,000 persons from the early 1970's through the mid-1990's. Meanwhile, robberies climbed substantially, while figures for rape nearly doubled.

Bibliography

Durham, Jennifer L. *Crime in America: A Reference Handbook.* Santa Barbara, Calif.: ABC-CLIO, 1996.

Friedman, Lawrence M. *Crime and Punishment in American History.* New York: Basic Books, 1993.

Kender, Suzanne E., ed. *Crime in America.* New York: H. W. Wilson, 1996.

Keve, Paul W. *Crime Control and Justice in America: Searching for Facts and Answers.* Chicago: American Library Association, 1995.

Schmalleger, Frank, and Gordon M. Armstrong, eds. *Crime and the Justice Systems in America: An Encyclopedia.* Westport, Conn.: Greenwood Press, 1997.

Winters, Paul A., ed. *Crime and Criminals: Opposing Viewpoints.* San Diego, Calif.: Greenhaven Press, 1995.

Richard L. Wilson

Criminal Justice System

The American criminal justice system is the total complex of local, state, and federal laws, policing forces, prosecuting offices, court systems, and correctional programs. It encompasses all the laws, procedures, and institutions that communities employ to apprehend, prosecute, and punish those who violate the property or person of others.

Criminal justice in the United States is primarily a state and local concern. More than nine-tenths of all CRIME is dealt with at the state and local levels. The crimes that most concern average citizens—property crimes such as burglary and violent crimes such as robbery and assault—are typically violations of state, not federal, laws. Outside the United States, most criminal offenses are defined by national laws; in most other countries, national, not local, institutions respond to violations of criminal codes.

The American system commonly designates the most serious crimes as felonies; in most jurisdictions, these are crimes that can be punished by prison sentences of at least a year. Lesser offenses are designated as misdemeanors—crimes for which punishments cannot exceed a year in jail. In some cases repeated commission of a misdemeanor can elevate the crime to a felony.

Police. County SHERIFFS and city and town POLICE bear the chief responsibility for responding to most property and violent crimes. During the 1990's such agencies employed more than half a million sworn officers and another 200,000 civilians throughout the United States. Nationally, more than two-fifths of all criminal justice expenditures go toward police protection. As many as three-fifths of crimes are never reported to the police. Unreported crimes range from many as three-quarters of all thefts to two-fifths of all aggravated assaults.

In 1992 more than fourteen million crimes of seven major types were reported to police; these included murder and non-negligent manslaughter, rape, robbery, aggravated assault, burglary, theft, and motor vehicle theft.

The sheer number of criminal acts limits most police activity to simply responding to crimes after they are committed. Police work thus consists mostly of tasks such as going to the scenes of crimes, interviewing witnesses, gathering physical evidence, searching for suspects, and preparing investigative reports.

In recent years, many Americans have called for the police to involve themselves more actively in the communities they serve by engaging in what is usually called "community policing": walking beats instead of cruising randomly in squad cars, establishing storefront offices to increase police visibility, meeting with community groups to identify problems, and other such proactive measures.

A major impediment to adopting community policing more widely is the enormous demand that merely responding to crimes places on police resources. In 1992 local police were able to make arrests in only a fifth of the major crimes reported.

Prosecutors and Courts. After arrests are made, cases are turned over to PUBLIC PROSECUTORS, public officials charged with representing the people in action against defendants. Most serious property and violent crimes are handled by offices of county prosecutors, usually called district, or state's, attorneys. In most jurisdictions DISTRICT ATTORNEYS are elected officials; they are often assisted by dozens or even hundreds of assistant district attorneys. Lesser offenses may be prosecuted by municipal attorneys. Specialized offenses—such as consumer fraud and commercial law violations—may be handled by prosecutors in the offices of state attorneys general.

Prosecutors perform several distinct functions: screening cases before charges are filed in court, interviewing victims and witnesses in preparing for trials, presenting evidence before GRAND JURIES, trying cases in court, and handling appeals. Although defendants cannot be convicted without proof "beyond a reasonable doubt," a lesser standard—"probable cause"—determines whether they should stand trial.

Either before a grand jury or in a preliminary hearing, the prosecutor must show that a crime probably occurred and that the defendant under arrest probably did it. Although most states allow either a preliminary hearing or grand jury in felony cases, some states require a grand jury proceeding before an accused felon can go to trial.

Millions of Americans closely followed former football star O. J. Simpson's criminal trial on murder charges, only to be left bewildered with the criminal justice system when a jury proclaimed him not guilty in October, 1995. (AP/Wide World Photos)

Courtroom Procedures. Trials are adversarial proceedings between prosecutors, who have the burden of proving guilt, and defendants, who are represented either by private attorneys or by PUBLIC DEFENDERS if they cannot afford private counsel. All trials are presided over by judges, who may be appointed or elected. Persons charged with serious crimes have the right to trial by jury. Juries weigh facts and determine whether defendants have committed the acts with which they are charged in violation of the criminal law. The judges are responsible for all legal rulings, particularly in applying the rules of evidence to the actual proceedings. When defendants choose not to exercise their right to trial by jury, the judges become the triers of fact.

Pleas. Although every defendant has the right to go to trial, most defendants plead guilty rather than contest their cases at trial. Nationally, about 90 percent of felony convictions result from guilty pleas; 6 percent result from jury trials and 4 percent from bench trials (in which judges determine guilt or innocence). Critics have charged that the high rate of guilty pleas indicates two dangerous flaws in the system. On one hand, it may imperil public safety when prosecutors reduce charges and potential punishments in exchange for guaranteed convictions. On the other hand, it may be unfair to innocent defendants who may be tempted to plead guilty in return for substantially reduced punishments rather than take chances on being convicted in a trial.

Sentencing. Sentencing systems throughout the United States are of two main types: determinate and indeterminate. In determinate sentencing systems, a judge who sentences a convicted felon to prison designates a specific number of years, and the offender must serve this time, minus credits for behaving well in prison ("good time") or for involvement in educational or job training programs. In indeterminate sentencing systems, the

judge designates a range of years, such as ten to twenty years in prison, and the actual time served is determined by a parole board once the inmate becomes eligible for release. Inmates of state prisons serve an average of only 35 percent of their maximum sentences.

Judges have traditionally had three basic options available when sentencing convicted felons: probation, several weeks or months in local jails, or a year or more in state prison. As expansion of the nation's prison population accelerated in the 1980's, a growing number of jurisdictions began experimenting with "intermediate sanctions." Punishments that are more severe than normal probation but less severe than incarceration, these include more intensive probation supervision, house arrest (sometimes monitored electronically with ankle bracelets), community service, and restitution to victims. Some proponents of such sanctions defend them as appropriate and less expensive alternatives to incarceration. Others support their use as alternatives to probation but regard them as insufficiently severe to use in place of incarceration.

Death Penalty. By the mid-1990's, the federal government and about three-fourths of the states had authorized the death penalty for certain specified offenses, principally murder. In 1990 there were 23,440 reported murders in the United States, about 11,000 murder convictions, 265 murderers sentenced to death, and 23 executions.

Correctional System Populations. By the end of 1993, 859,000 persons were inmates in state prisons; another 90,000 were in federal prisons, and 450,000 more were in local jails. About half of the latter were serving sentences; the rest were awaiting trial. These figures for state and federal prisoners are almost three times greater than those for 1980. Despite the amount that prison populations increased, nearly three-fourths of the 4.9 million offenders under correctional supervision in 1993 were not incarcerated, but were under super-

Convicted criminals sentenced to prison terms remain subject to the criminal justice system until they complete their sentences and terms of parole. (AP/Wide World Photos)

vision in the community. Of those under supervision, 2.8 million were on probation and 909,000 were on parole (a period of supervision after release from prison).

According to surveys of state prison inmate populations, typically about 11 percent are serving time for murder and non-negligent manslaughter, 9 percent for rape or other sexual assault, 15 percent for robbery, 8 percent for assault, 4 percent for other violent crimes, 12 percent for burglary, 13 percent for drug trafficking, and 28 percent for other crimes. Many state prison inmates have extensive prior records: Four-fifths have at least one prior conviction, three-fifths have at least two, more than half have at least three, and almost a fifth have at least six prior convictions. Sixty percent of those sent to state prisons are re-

turn prisoners; 25 percent are beginning at least their fourth term. Altogether, 93 percent of state prison inmates are either convicted violent offenders or convicted recidivists (repeat offenders).

Federal Criminal Justice System. Although the federal criminal justice system accounts for less than 5 percent of all felony convictions in the country and less than 10 percent of all prison inmates, the federal government enforces hundreds of criminal laws covering such offenses as counterfeiting, interstate drug trafficking, immigration violations, TERRORISM, assaults on federal officials, ESPIONAGE, and violations of federal regulations concerning such matters as environmental pollution and commercial transactions. There are more than fifty separate federal law en-

Steps in the Criminal Justice Process

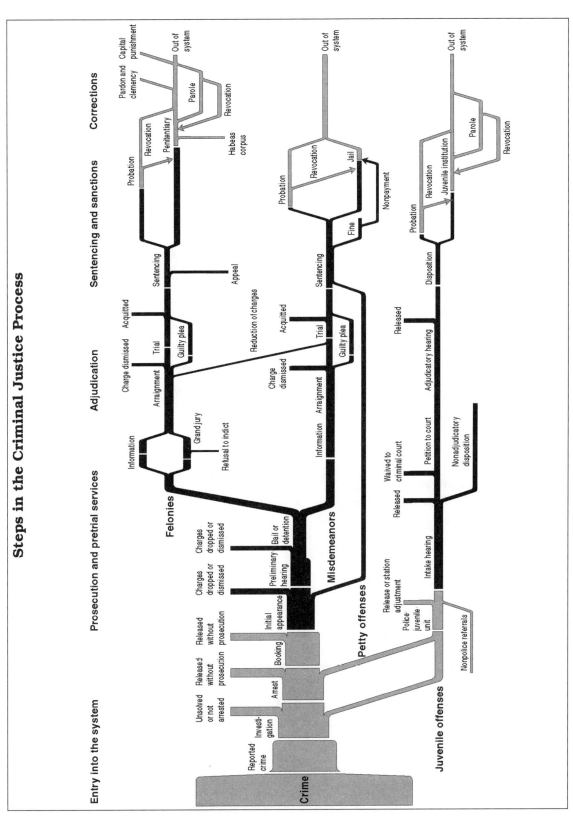

Graphic by Deborah Cowder; adapted from U.S. Bureau of Justice Statistics, *Drugs, Crime, and the Justice System*. Washington D.C.: U.S. Government Printing Office, 1992.

forcement agencies. The principal bodies include the FEDERAL BUREAU OF INVESTIGATION (FBI), which investigates a wide variety of federal offenses; the DRUG ENFORCEMENT ADMINISTRATION (DEA), which concentrates on drug law violations; the Bureau of Alcohol, Tobacco, and Firearms (ATF), which is especially important in monitoring weapons violations; the Secret Service, which investigates counterfeiting and threats to the safety of the president; and the Immigration and Naturalization Service (INS), which investigates IMMIGRATION law violations.

Responsibility for prosecution of federal offenses falls on the JUSTICE DEPARTMENT. It is headed by the ATTORNEY GENERAL, who is appointed by the president of the United States and confirmed by the U.S. Senate. Federal trials are conducted in federal district courts. Appeals of their decisions are made to federal appeals, or circuit, courts. The small fraction of such appeals that reach the SUPREME COURT usually raise basic constitutional questions or involve contradictory rulings from federal appeals courts in different parts of the country.

Resources Devoted to Criminal Justice. In 1990 federal, state, and local governments in the United States spent $74 billion for civil and criminal justice. This figure, which includes police protection, prosecution and courts, and corrections (prisons, jails, probation, and parole), accounted for 3.3 percent of all government spending in the nation that year. State and local governments devoted between 6 and 7 percent of their budgets to criminal justice, the federal government less than 1 percent. Nationally, criminal justice agencies employ about 1.6 million persons full-time. Nearly half work for police or investigative agencies; about a third work in corrections.

Bibliography

Cole, George F. *The American System of Criminal Justice.* 7th ed. Belmont, Calif.: Wadsworth, 1995.

Currie, Elliott. *Crime and Punishment in America.* New York: Henry Holt, 1998.

Free, Marvin D. *African Americans and the Criminal Justice System.* New York: Garland, 1996.

Schmalleger, Frank, and Gordon M. Armstrong. *Crime and the Justice Systems in America: An Encyclopedia.* Westport, Conn.: Greenwood Press, 1997.

U.S. Bureau of Justice Statistics. *Sourcebook of Criminal Justice Statistics.* Washington, D.C.: Author, annual.

Walker, Samuel. *Popular Justice: A History of American Criminal Justice.* 2d ed. New York: Oxford University Press, 1998.

Joseph M. Bessette